Application of Modern Production Theory: Efficiency and Productivity

Studies in Productivity Analysis

Ali Dogramaci, Editor
Rutgers University

Titles in the Series:

Adam, Dogramaci; *Productivity Analysis at the Organizational Level*

Dogramaci, Adam; *Aggregate and Industry-Level Productivity Analysis*

Dogramaci; *Productivity Analysis: A Range of Perspectives*

Dogramaci; *Developments in Econometric Analyses of Productivity: Measurement and Modelling Issues*

Sudit; *Productivity Based Management*

Färe, Grosskopf, Lovell; *The Measurement of Efficiency of Production*

Adam, Dogramaci; *Managerial Issues in Productivity Analysis*

Dogramaci; *Measurement Issues and Behavior of Productivity Variables*

Applications of Modern Production Theory: Efficiency and Productivity

edited by

Ali Dogramaci and Rolf Färe

Kluwer Academic Publishers
a member of the Kluwer Academic Publishers Group
Boston Dordrecht Lancaster

Distributors for the United States and Canada:
Kluwer Academic Publishers
101 Philip Drive
Assinippi Park
Norwell, MA 02061

Distributors for the UK and Ireland:
Kluwer Academic Publishers
MTP Press Limited
Falcon House
Queen Square
Lancaster LA1 1RN, UK

Distributors for all other countries:
Kluwer Academic Publishers Group
Distribution Centre
P.O. Box 322, 3300 AH Dordrecht
The Netherlands

Library of Congress Cataloging-in-Publication Data

Applications of modern production theory.

(Studies in productivity analysis)
"Dedicated in honor and appreciation of Ronald William Shephard"—P.
Includes bibliographies and index.
1. Production (Economic theory) 2. Agricultural productivity. 3. Industrial productivity. 4. Labor productivity. 5. Shephard, Ronald William.
I. Dogramaci, Ali. II. Färe, Rolf, 1942–
III. Shephard, Ronald William. IV. Series.
HB241.A67 1987 338.5 86-20816

ISBN-13: 978-94-010-7959-4 e-ISBN-13: 978-94-009-3253-1
DOI: 10.1007/978-94-009-3253-1

This book is dedicated in honor and appreciation of Ronald William Shephard. All royalties from the sale of this book will be presented to the library at Ronald Shephard's alma mater, the University of California at Berkeley.

Shephard's influence on the subject of production and cost theory is pervasive. The style of his work marked a new era in the field. The signs of the transition Shephard brought about are present in his early work, *Cost and Production Functions* (Princeton University Press, 1953). Only von Neumann, from which we have the "activity analysis" approach to production, and the linear programming approach of Dantzig, provide a comparable effect.

This is only a brief description of Ronald Shephard's broad effect on the world of production theory. We hope this dedication expresses the special personal regard that those of us who knew him have for Ronald William Shephard.

Sydney Afriat

Contents

Contributing Authors

Sydney N. Afriat, Department of Economics, University of Ottawa, Ottawa, Ont. K1N 6N5 CANADA

Rajiv D. Banker, School of Urban and Public Administration, Carnegie Mellon University, Pittsburgh, PA 15213

Julien van den Broeck, Rijks Universitair Centrum Antwerpen, Faculteit der Toegepaste Economische Wetenschappen, Middelheimlaan 1-2020, Antwerpen, BELGIUM

A. Charnes, School of Business Administration, University of Texas at Austin, Austin, TX 78712

Peter Chinloy, Department of Economics, University of Santa Clara, Santa Clara, CA 95053

W. W. Cooper, School of Business Administration, University of Texas at Austin, Austin, TX 78712

Michael Denny, Department of Economics, University of Toronto, Toronto, Ont. M5S 1A1 CANADA

Rolf Färe, Department of Economics, Southern Illinois University, Carbondale, IL 62901

Alain de Fontenay, Bell Communications Research, 290 West Mt. Pleasant Ave., LCC-1B120, Livingston, NJ 07039

S. Grosskopf, Department of Economics, Southern Illinois University, Carbondale, IL 62901

C. Knox Lovell, Department of Economics, University of North Carolina at Chapel Hill, Chapel Hill, NC 27514

A. Maindiratta, School of Business Administration, New York University, New York, NY 10003

King-Tim Mak, Information and Decision Sciences, University of Illinois at Chicago, Chicago, IL 60680

Catherine J. Morrison, Department of Economics, Tufts University, Medford, MA 02155

Vernon W. Ruttan, Department of Agriculture and Applied Economics, University of Minnesota, St. Paul, MN 55108

Peter Schmidt, Department of Economics, Michigan State University, East Lansing, MI 48824

Robin C. Sickles, Department of Economics, Rice University, Houston, TX 77005

Lung Fai Wong, Department of Agriculture and Applied Economics, University of Minnesota, St. Paul, MN 55108

Acknowledgment to Referees

Anonymous refereeing is a process that accompanies every paper that appears in the series Studies in Productivity Analysis. The list below includes the names of reviewers who contributed to the refereeing of at least one paper considered for this volume. To ensure anonymity, the list also includes names of some additional referees who evaluated papers for other volumes of Studies in Productivity Analysis. Furthermore, some of the referees of this volume are not listed here, but in other volumes of the series, again for the purpose of anonymity.

N. R. Adam	Rutgers The State University of New Jersey
I. Bernhardt	University of Waterloo
T. Boucher	Rutgers The State University of New Jersey
T. Cowing	State University of New York at Binghamton
N. M. Fraiman	International Paper Co. and Columbia University
W. H. Greene	New York University
J. Haltmeier	Board of Governors of the Federal Reserve System
L. Hjalmarsson	University of Gothenburg
L. F. Lee	University of Minnesota
R. R. Russell	New York University
V. K. Smith	Vanderbilt University
J. Stewart	University of North Carolina
W. Vickrey	Columbia University
E. Wolff	New York University

PART ONE

1 A COMPARISON OF ALTERNATIVE APPROACHES TO THE MEASUREMENT OF PRODUCTIVE EFFICIENCY

C. A. Knox Lovell and Peter Schmidt

1.1. Introduction

In standard microeconomic theory a transformation function provides a direct, or primal, description of production technology. It describes the maximum amount of one output that can be produced, for given levels of production of the remaining outputs and for given levels of input usage. Alternatively, it describes the minimum amount of one input required for the production of given outputs with given amounts of all other inputs. Corresponding to the primal transformation function are three value duals. The cost function describes the minimum cost of producing certain outputs with given input prices and technology. The revenue function describes the maximum revenue obtainable from certain inputs with given output prices and technology. The profit function describes the maximum profit that can be obtained with given output prices, input prices, and technology. Under certain regularity conditions the primal transformation function and the three value duals provide equivalent descriptions of the structure of production technology.[1]

A characteristic common to all four functions is that of optimality. Each specifies a maximum or a minimum value that can be achieved under the constraints imposed by technology and prices. That is, each describes a boundary, or a frontier. For a variety of reasons, interest frequently centers on the distance an observed production unit operates from a primal or dual frontier, since such a distance provides a measure of the primal or dual efficiency of the unit under observation. One example of such interest occurs in the measurement of the rate of growth of total factor productivity. The rate of growth of total factor productivity is typically calculated as the share-weighted sum of the rates of growth of outputs minus the share-weighted sum of the rates of growth of inputs (see Hulten 1973). This construction corresponds roughly to the distinction Solow (1957) drew between output growth attributable to movements along a production surface (input growth) and output growth attributable to shifts in the production surface (technical change). Indeed the concepts of total factor productivity growth and technical change are frequently used synonymously. However, the correspondence assumes that production is continuously technically efficient. If this assumption is relaxed, then the rate of total factor productivity growth can be decomposed into the rate of technical change and the rate of change of efficiency. If such a decomposition is possible, it enables one to enrich Solow's dichotomy by attributing observed output growth to movements along a path on or beneath the production surface (input growth), movement toward or away from the production surface (efficiency growth), and shifts in the production surface (technical change). The distinction between efficiency growth and technical change is important because they are fundamentally different phenomena with different sources, and so different policies may be required to address them.[2]

This chapter discusses and compares various methods for measuring and computing (or estimating) productive efficiency. We distinguish four approaches to the problem. These approaches differ in many ways, but for our purposes the two most significant differences occur in the method used to determine the shape and placement of the relevant frontier, and in the interpretation given to deviations from the frontier. Our purpose in this chapter is to review the four approaches, to explore the strengths and weaknesses of each, and to cite interesting applications of each.

The chapter unfolds as follows. In section 1.2 we describe the structure of efficient technology. In section 1.3 we discuss the measurement of primal and dual efficiency. In sections 1.4–1.7 we examine the four approaches to specification and estimation that are currently being employed. Concluding remarks and suggestions for further research are contained in section 1.8.

1.2. The Structure of Efficient Technology[3]

We consider a production unit employing variable inputs $x \equiv (x_1, \ldots, x_n) \in R^n_+$ in the production of outputs $u \equiv (u_1, \ldots, u_m) \in R^m_+$. Technology is modeled by an input correspondence $u \to L(u) \subseteq R^n_+$ or inversely by an output correspondence $x \to P(x) \subseteq R^m_+$. Here $L(u)$ is the subset of all input vectors capable of producing at least output vector u, and $P(x)$ is the subset of all output vectors obtainable from input vector x. The inverse relationship between the input correspondence and the output correspondence is $L(u) = \{x \in R^n_+ : u \in P(x)\}$ and inversely $P(x) = \{u \in R^m_+ : x \in L(u)\}$. Technology is well behaved in the sense that the input correspondence is assumed to satisfy

L.1 $0 \notin L(u), \quad u \geqslant 0 \qquad \text{and} \qquad L(0) = R^n_+$

L.2 $\|u^l\| \to +\infty \quad \text{as} \quad l \to +\infty \Rightarrow \bigcap_{l=1}^{+\infty} L(u^l) \quad \text{is empty}$

L.3 $x \in L(u) \Rightarrow \lambda x \in L(u), \qquad \lambda \geqslant 1$

L.4 L is a closed correspondence

L.5 $L(\theta u) \subseteq L(u), \qquad \theta \geqslant 1$

and occasionally stronger versions of the weak input disposability property L.3 and the weak output disposability property L.5, namely

L.3.S $y \geqslant x \in L(u) \Rightarrow y \in L(u)$

L.5.S $v \geqslant u \Rightarrow L(v) \subseteq L(u)$

Two subsets of $L(u)$ are of interest, the isoquant and the efficient subset, and they are defined by

$$\text{Isoq}\, L(u) \equiv \{x : x \in L(u), \quad \lambda x \notin L(u), \lambda \in [0, 1)\}, \qquad u \geqslant 0 \tag{1.1}$$

$$\text{Eff}\, L(u) \equiv \{x : x \in L(u), \quad y \leqslant x \Rightarrow y \notin L(u)\}, \qquad u \geqslant 0 \tag{1.2}$$

Clearly $\text{Eff}\, L(u) \subseteq \text{Isoq}\, L(u)$, and so $x \in \text{Isoq}\, L(u) \nRightarrow x \in \text{Eff}\, L(u)$.[4]

This property is important for the measurement of primal efficiency because we call input vector x technically efficient in the production of output vector u if and only if $x \in \text{Eff } L(u)$.

If the input correspondence satisfies properties {L.1–L.5} or {L.1–L.5, L.3S, L.5S}, then the output correspondence satisfies a similar set of properties. Isoquants and efficient subsets can be defined on the output correspondence as

$$\text{Isoq } P(x) \equiv \{u\colon\ u \in P(x),\quad \lambda u \notin P(x), \lambda > 1\},\qquad x \geqslant 0 \tag{1.3}$$

$$\text{Eff } P(x) \equiv \{u\colon\ u \in P(x),\quad v \geqslant u \Rightarrow v \notin P(x)\},\qquad x \geqslant 0 \tag{1.4}$$

and as before $\text{Eff } P(x) \subseteq \text{Isoq } P(x)$ so that $u \in \text{Isoq } P(x) \not\Rightarrow u \in \text{Eff } P(x)$. This is significant because we call output vector u technically efficient for input vector x if and only if $u \in \text{Eff } P(x)$.

It often proves useful to work with the production possibilities set, or the graph of the technology, defined as

$$GR \equiv \{(x,u)\colon\ x \in L(u), u \in R^m_+\} = \{(x,u)\colon\ u \in P(x), x \in R^n_+\} \tag{1.5}$$

Properties of GR are inherited from those of $L(u)$ and $P(x)$, and graph isoquants and efficient subsets are defined as

$$\text{Isoq } GR \equiv \{(x,u)\colon\ (u,x) \in GR,\ (\lambda^{-1}u, \lambda x) \notin GR,\ \lambda \in (0,1)\} \tag{1.6}$$

$$\text{Eff } GR \equiv \{(x,u)\colon\ (u,x) \in GR,\ (v,y) \notin GR,\quad v \geqslant u,\ y \leqslant x\} \tag{1.7}$$

and once again $\text{Eff } GR \subseteq \text{Isoq } GR$ so that $(u,x) \in \text{Isoq } GR \not\Rightarrow (u,x) \in \text{Eff } GR$, which is significant because we call input-output vector (x,u) technically efficient if and only if $(x,u) \in \text{Eff } GR$.

Note that we have introduced three different notions of technical efficiency. The technical efficiency of input vector x in the production of given output vector u is based on the input correspondence. The technical efficiency of output vector u obtained from given input vector x is based on the output correspondence. The technical efficiency of input-output vector (x,u) is based on the graph of the technology. The usefulness of each of these notions depends on whether inputs, outputs, or both are choice variables for the production unit.

If the production unit faces fixed input prices $w \equiv (w_1, \ldots, w_n) \in R^n_{++}$ and fixed output prices $p \equiv (p_1, \ldots, p_m) \in R^m_{++}$, then we may define value duals. The production unit's cost, revenue, and profit functions are defined by

$$Q(u,w) \equiv \min \{w^T x: x \in L(u)\} \quad (1.8)$$

$$R(x,p) \equiv \max \{p^T u: u \in P(x)\} \quad (1.9)$$

$$\pi(p,w) \equiv \max \{p^T u - w^T x: (x,u) \in GR\} \quad (1.10)$$

from which various input demand and output supply correspondences can be derived. These value duals can be also be used to measure primal (technical) efficiency, but their main role lies in their use in measuring dual (cost, revenue, or profit) efficiency. Again, the choice of value dual depends on whether inputs, outputs, or both are choice variables for the production unit.

Finally, if the production unit produces a single output, then we may define a production function as

$$\phi(x) \equiv \max \{u \in R_+: x \in L(u)\} = \max \{u: u \in P(x)\} \quad (1.11)$$

with associated input set $L(u) = \{x: u \leqslant \phi(x)\}$ and output set $P(x) = [0,\phi(x)]$.

1.3. The Measurement of Productive Efficiency

Consider a production unit operating at feasible input-output configuration $(x,u) \in GR$. The input-output vector (x,u) is called *technically efficient* if and only if $(x,u) \in \text{Eff } GR$. Given that (x,u) is technically efficient, it is called *allocatively efficient for* (p,w) if and only if $(p^T u - w^T x) = \pi(p,w)$. A production unit that is both technically efficient and allocatively efficient for (p,w) earns the maximum possible profit, and is called *profit efficient for* (p,w). It produces its chosen outputs with the minimum possible inputs, and produces the maximum possible outputs with its chosen inputs; this is what technical efficiency requires. It also produces the correct mix of outputs, given output prices, uses the correct mix of inputs, given input prices, and adopts the correct scale, given input and output prices; this is what allocative efficiency requires.

Similar definitions are possible using the input correspondence $L(u)$. The input vector x is called *technically efficient for* u if and only if $x \in \text{Eff } L(u)$. A technically efficient input vector $x \in \text{Eff } L(u)$ is called *allocatively* efficient for (u,w) if and only if $w^T x = Q(u,w)$. Thus a production unit whose input vector is technically efficient for u and allocatively efficient for (u,w) minimizes the cost of producing its output, and is called *cost efficient for* (u,w). However, there is no guarantee that the correct output mix is being chosen, given output prices. As a result, efficiency measurement with respect to the input correspondence $L(u)$ is most reasonable in cases in which the output vector u is exogenous to the production unit.

Similarly, output vector u is called *technically efficient for* x if and only if $u \in \text{Eff}\, P(x)$, and a technically efficient output vector u is called *allocatively efficient for* (x,p) if and only if $p^T u = R(x,p)$. Thus a production unit whose output vector is technically efficient for x and allocatively efficient for (x,p) maximizes the revenue obtainable from its inputs, and is called *revenue efficient for* (x,p). However this does not guarantee that the correct mix of inputs is being chosen, given input prices. Consequently, efficiency measurement with respect to the output correspondence $P(x)$ is appropriate in cases in which the input vector x is exogenous to the production unit.

Relationships among the three notions of technical efficiency, among the three notions of allocative efficiency, and among profit, cost, and revenue efficiency, can be established, but they are not so simple as might be expected.[5] First, to establish that input-output vector (x,u) is technically efficient if and only if x is technically efficient for u and u is technically efficient for x, we need conditions slightly stronger than {L.1–L.5, L.3.S, L.5.S}. Second, x is allocatively efficient for (u,w) and u is allocatively efficient for (x,p) if but not only if (x,u) is allocatively efficient for (p,w); this is because the latter condition also entails the selection of a proper scale that neither of the two former conditions entail.[6] Third, (x,u) is profit efficient for (p,w) if and only if x is cost efficient for (u,w) and u is revenue efficient for (x,p).

Given these definitions of productive efficiency, the problem is to devise a framework for measuring each type of efficiency, a framework that is theoretically consistent and empirically tractable. Following Debreu (1951) and Koopmans (1951), Farrell (1957) has proposed a framework that comes close to meeting these requirements. Farrell focused on the case in which inputs are the choice variables for the production unit, and proposed measures of the technical efficiency of x for u, the cost efficiency of x for (u,w), and the allocative efficiency of x for (u,w). The Farrell measure of the technical efficiency of input vector $x \in L(u)$ is given by

$$F(x;u) \equiv \min\,\{\lambda:\ \lambda x \in L(u),\quad \lambda \geqslant 0\} \tag{1.12}$$

The cost efficiency of input vector $x \in L(u)$ is given by

$$C(x;u,w) \equiv Q(u,w)/w^T x \tag{1.13}$$

and the allocative efficiency of input vector $x \in L(u)$ is given by

$$A(x;u,w) \equiv C(x;u,w)/F(x;u) \tag{1.14}$$

Figure 1-1 illustrates. Point (x^1,u) is observed. Point $(\lambda x^1,u)$ is technically, but not allocatively, efficient, given input prices whose ratio is (minus) the slope of the parallel straight lines. Point (y,u) is technically and allocatively, and hence cost, efficient.

The Farrell framework has three important virtues. The first is that there exists a duality relationship between $F(x;u)$ and $L(u)$. Since $F(x;u)$ is the inverse of the distance function, $L(u) = \{x\colon\ 0 < F(x;u) \leqslant 1\}$, and $F(x;u)$

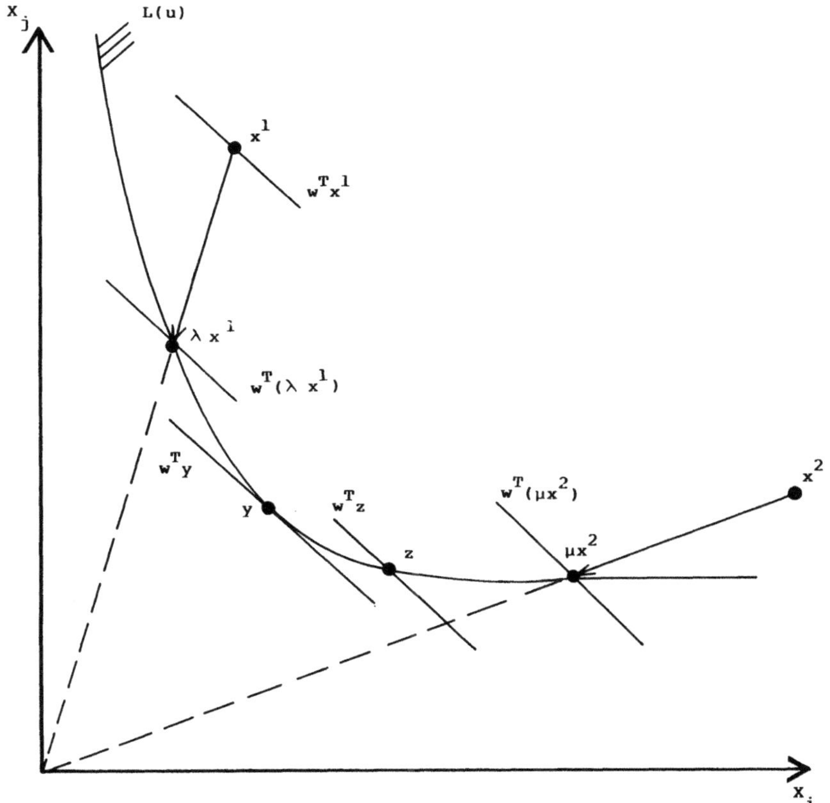

Figure 1-1 Farrell Efficiency Measurement Using the Input Correspondence

reveals everything about the structure of a well-behaved technology that is revealed by $L(u)$. The second virtue is that the Farrell decomposition enjoys a cost interpretation. As suggested by figure 1-1, $F(x;u) = \lambda = w^T(\lambda x)/w^Tx$, $A(x;u,w) = w^Ty/w^T(\lambda x)$, and $C(x;u,w) = w^Ty/w^Tx$. Finally, the Farrell measures are easy to calculate in empirical work.

In addition to these virtues, however, the Farrell framework has a drawback. The framework is constructed around a technical component that involves an equiproportionate reduction in all inputs, and there is unfortunately no guarantee that such a process must intersect the efficient subset. The Farrell measure of technical efficiency has the isoquant as its reference set, and although isoquants include efficient subsets, the converse is not necessarily true. This can lead to an overstatement of the true technical efficiency of an input vector—perhaps to the extent that it is labeled technically efficient when it is not—and so to an improper decomposition of cost efficiency into its technical and allocative components. Moreover, this is not merely a pathological possibility. It can occur in a wide variety of popular specifications of production technology, apparently including all flexible functional forms. Again, figure 1-1 illustrates. Suppose that point (x^2,u) is observed. Then $F(x^2;u) = \mu$ and $F(\mu x^2;u) = 1$. However, although $\mu x^2 \in \text{Isoq } L(u)$, $\mu x^2 \notin \text{Eff } L(u)$. Cost efficiency is properly calculated as $C(x^2;u,w) = w^Ty/w^Tx^2$, although it is not clear that the Farrell decomposition of this cost efficiency is sensible. What is desired is a framework that calculates the technical efficiency of (x^2,u) by comparing x^2 to some component of Eff $L(u)$, such as z, and the Farrell measure, because it is radial, does not always succeed. (Note that this problem does not occur with the point (x^1,u) because $\lambda x^1 \in \text{Eff } L(u)$.)

This difficulty with the Farrell framework can be resolved by resorting to nonradial measures of technical efficiency. The Russell measure, a nonradial generalization of the Farrell measure proposed by Färe and Lovell (1978), has the flexibility to select a vector from the efficient subset against which to compute the technical efficiency of an observed input vector. The Russell measure of the technical efficiency of input vector $x \in L(u) + R^n_+$ is given by

$$R(x;u) \equiv \min \Big\{ \Big[\sum_{i=1}^{n} \delta(x_i)\lambda_i \Big/ \sum_{i=1}^{n} \delta(x_i) \Big] : \\ (\lambda_1 x_1, \ldots, \lambda_n x_n) \in L(u),\ \lambda_i \in [0,1], \\ \delta(x_i) = 1 \quad \text{if } x_i > 0,\ \delta(x_i) = 0 \text{ otherwise} \\ \text{for } i = 1, \ldots, n \Big\} \tag{1.15}$$

Weighting different inputs differently gives $R(x;u)$ its nonradial character, and gives $R(x;u)$ the flexibility to call x technically efficient for u if and only if $x \in \text{Eff } L(u)$. Moreover, $R(x;u)$ contains $F(x;u)$ as a special case $(\lambda_1 = \cdots = \lambda_n)$.

The Russell measure produces a decomposition of cost efficiency that in general differs from the decomposition produced by the Farrell measure, and this difference is desirable since $R(x;u) = 1$ if and only if $x \in \text{Eff } L(u)$, a property not satisfied by $F(x;u)$. This is the great virtue of the nonradial Russell measure. However the Russell measure has its own drawbacks, noted by Kopp (1981a,b) among others. The duality property is weakened, and the cost interpretation is not so straightforward, relative to the radial Farrell measure.[7] Moreover, nonradial measures are somewhat less tractable in empirical work. Consequently, despite its shortcomings the Farrell framework is widely used in empirical work.[8]

Finally, the entire Farrell framework for efficiency measurement can be applied with obvious modifications to the problems of measuring revenue efficiency and its components, and of measuring profit efficiency and its components. The same virtues and drawbacks just discussed apply to these problems, and the same solutions (with their attendant difficulties) also apply. Details are given in Färe, Grosskopf, and Lovell (1985a).

Whether we are working in primal or dual space, and whether we are interested in cost, revenue, or profit efficiency, the problem remains the same. The goal is to measure efficiency, and to decompose efficiency into its technical and allocative components. In the next four sections we examine the abilities of four approaches to meet this goal. The designation of only four approaches is somewhat arbitrary, but it is convenient for expository purposes. It enables us to capture the essence of these different approaches, although we do not do justice to the rich variety of techniques that exists within each approach. For that the reader can consult the references cited in the text.[9]

1.4. The Pure Programming Approach

This approach utilizes a sequence of linear programs to construct a transformation frontier and to compute primal and dual efficiency relative to the frontier. The technique was proposed by Farrell (1957), and has been further developed by Charnes, Cooper, and their colleagues (who dub the technique "data envelopment analysis"),[10] and by Färe and his colleagues.[11]

Suppose we observe a sample of K production units, each of which uses inputs $x \in R^n_+$ available at prices $w \in R^n_{++}$ to produce outputs $u \in R^m_+$ for sale at prices $p \in R^m_{++}$. As a matter of notation, let x_i^k be the quantity of input i used by unit $k(k = 1, \ldots, K, \quad i = 1, \ldots, n)$, and let u_i^k be the quantity of output i produced by unit $k(k = 1, \ldots, K, \quad i = 1, \ldots, m)$. These data can be placed into the data matrixes **M**, a $K \times m$ matrix of output levels, whose k, ith element is u_i^k, and **N**, a $K \times n$ matrix of input levels, whose k, ith element is x_i^k.

The pure programming approach to efficiency measurement proceeds in the following sequence of steps. The first step is to construct the input set $L(u)$. For any $u \in R_+^m$, we define

$$L(u) = \left\{x\colon\ z \in R_+^K,\ \sum_{k=1}^{K} z_k = 1,\ \mu z^T\mathbf{M} = u,\ \delta x = z^T\mathbf{N}.\ \mu,\delta \in (0,1]\right\} \tag{1.16}$$

where **M** is the observed $K \times m$ output matrix, **N** is the observed $K \times n$ input matrix, and z is a $K \times 1$ intensity vector. The input set $L(u)$ so constructed satisfies properties {L.1–L.5}. In addition it satisfies L.3.S if ($\delta x = z^T\mathbf{N}, \delta \in (0,1]$) is replaced by ($x \geqslant z^T\mathbf{N}$). It satisfies L.5.S if ($\mu z^T\mathbf{M} = u$, $\mu \in (0,1]$) is replaced by ($z^T\mathbf{M} \geqslant u$). Finally, nonincreasing returns to scale can be imposed by changing ($\Sigma_{k=1}^K z_k = 1$) to ($\Sigma_{k=1}^K z_k \leqslant 1$), and constant returns to scale can be imposed by deleting ($\Sigma_{k=1}^K z_k = 1$).[12]

In the second step the Farrell technical efficiency measure is computed for each production unit in the sample by solving the programming problem

$$\begin{aligned} F(x^k;u^k) &= \min\left\{\lambda\colon\ z \in R_+^K,\ \sum_{k=1}^{K} z_k = 1,\ \mu z^T\mathbf{M} = u^k,\ \lambda\delta x^k = z^T\mathbf{N},\right. \\ &\qquad \left.\mu,\delta \in (0,1]\right\} \\ &= \min\{\lambda\colon\ \lambda x^k \in L(u^k)\} \end{aligned} \tag{1.17}$$

where the superscript k denotes a production unit.[13] The third step is to compute $Q(u^k,w^k)$, the minimum cost for each production unit in the sample, by solving the program

$$\begin{aligned} Q(u^k,w^k) &= \min\left\{w^{kT}x\colon\ z \in R_+^K,\ \sum_{k=1}^{K} z_k = 1,\quad \mu z^T\mathbf{M} = u^k,\ \delta x = z^T\mathbf{N},\right. \\ &\qquad \left.\mu,\delta \in (0,1]\right\} \\ &= \min\{w^{kT}x\colon\ x \in L(u^k)\} \end{aligned} \tag{1.18}$$

This generates measures of cost efficiency $C(x^k;u^k,w^k)$ and allocative efficiency $A(x^k;u^k,w^k)$ given by

$$C(x^k;u^k,w^k) = Q(u^k,w^k)/w^{kT}x^k, \tag{1.19}$$

$$A(x^k;u^k,w^k) = C(x^k;u^k,w^k)/F(x^k;u^k) \tag{1.20}$$

This three-step procedure can be easily modified if interest centers on revenue efficiency and its components or profit efficiency and its components.

The input set $L(u)$ constructed in equation (1.16) is nonparametric: in the construction of $L(u)$ no parameters are computed. The sample data are bounded, or "enveloped," by a convex weak-disposal hull consisting of a series of facets. Indeed the input set so constructed is the *smallest* set that includes all K observations in the sample, and which satisfies properties {L.1–L.5} required of any well-behaved input set. This is intuitively appealing. However, the smaller the input set is, the higher are the efficiency measures. Precisely because it constructs the smallest possible input set (consistent with certain regularity conditions), the pure programming approach generates *upper bounds* to the true but unknown efficiencies.

There is some guidance as to what one can hope to accomplish nonparametrically. The basic reference is Varian (1984a). He provides a set of conditions which are necessary and sufficient for the existence of an input set that "rationalizes" the data, in the sense that the data could be generated by cost-minimizing behavior, given that input set. The conditions are simple: if $u^j \geqslant u^i$ then $w^{iT}x^j \geqslant w^{it}x^i$, and if $u^j > u^i$ then $w^{iT}x^j > w^{iT}x^i$, $i, j = 1, \ldots, K$. Varian goes on to derive the tightest possible inner and outer bounds for any input set that rationalizes the data.[14] His inner bound is essentially identical to the input set constructed by the pure programming approach, in the sense that their efficient subsets coincide.

Banker and Maindiratta (1985b) extend Varian's work to the case in which the data do not satisfy Varian's rationalizability condition; that is, the data could not [all] have arisen from cost-minimizing behavior. They show how to identify the subset of observations that could have arisen from cost-minimizing behavior. They construct inner and outer bounds for all possible input sets that rationalize the rationalizable subset of observations. The inner bound is essentially the same as Varian's, while the outer bound is the same as Varian's except that it is computed only from the rationalizable subset of observations. Measuring technical efficiency relations to their inner bound provides an upper bound for possible efficiency values, while measuring technical efficiency relations to their outer bound provides a lower bound for possible efficiency values.

Perhaps the most appealing characteristic of the pure programming approach is that the input set it constructs is the smallest well-behaved set containing all the data. Such a set is piecewise linear, and the construction process achieves considerable flexibility because the breaks among the pieces are determined endogenously so as to fit the data as closely as possible.[15] Moreover, the construction process guarantees that the input set satisfies regularity conditions such as {L.1–L.5} globally.

However the construction process also causes a problem for the pure programming approach. Even if strong input disposability (L.3.S) is added to properties {L.1–L.5}, the programming technique guarantees that Eff $L(u) \subset$ Isoq $L(u)$ but that Eff $L(u) \neq$ Isoq $L(u)$. This being the case, it is possible that $F(x^k;u^k) = 1$ even though $x^k \notin$ Eff $L(u^k)$ for some k. This can happen if the minimum value of λ is one and there are nonzero slacks in the linear programming problem equivalent to (1.17). There seems to be no ideal solution to this problem, apart from replacing the radial Farrell measure of technical efficiency with some nonradial measure.[16]

The major problem with the pure programming approach results from the fact that the sample data are enveloped by a deterministic frontier. Consequently the entire deviation of an observation from the frontier is attributed to inefficiency. Since the frontier is nonstochastic, no accomodation is made for environmental heterogeneity, random external shocks, noise in the data, measurement error, omitted variables, and the like. All sorts of influences, favorable and unfavorable, beyond the control of the production unit are lumped together with inefficiency and called inefficiency. Obviously this can lead to under- or over-statement of the true extent of inefficiency. Furthermore, since the whole approach is nonstochastic, there is no way of making probability statements about the shape and placement of the frontier, or about the computed inefficiencies relative to the frontier.[17]

1.5. The Modified Programming Approach

This approach also uses a sequence of linear (or quadratic) programs to construct a transformation frontier and to compute primal and dual efficiency relative to the frontier. The only difference between the modified and pure programming approaches is that the frontier constructed by the modified programming approach is parametric. The modified programming approach was first suggested by Farrell (1957), and has been refined and extended by Aigner and Chu (1968), Försund and Jansen (1977), and Försund and Hjalmarsson (1979a,b) among others.

Suppose again that we observe a sample of K production units, but suppose now that each unit uses inputs $x \in R^n_+$ available at prices $w \in R^n_{++}$ to produce a single output $u \in R_+$ for sale at price $p \in R_{++}$. The reason for assuming a single output will become apparent shortly. The modified programming approach to efficiency measurement proceeds as follows. First, one posits the existence of a well-behaved production function $\phi(x)$, relative to which the input set is defined as

$$L(u) \equiv \{x\colon\ u \leqslant \phi(x)\} \tag{1.21}$$

The production function ϕ is given a specific functional form, say Cobb-Douglas for expository convenience, and so

$$L(u) = \left\{x\colon\ u \leqslant A \prod_{i=1}^{n} x_i^{\alpha_i},\quad A > 0, \alpha_i > 0, i = 1, \ldots, n\right\} \tag{1.22}$$

The set $L(u)$ satisfies {L.1–L.5} and whatever additional properties are associated with the parametric form selected for ϕ. In the Cobb-Douglas case this means invariant returns to scale (of magnitude $\Sigma_{i=1}^{n} \alpha_i$) and unitary partial elasticities of substitution among all input pairs.

Second, the parameters in ϕ (namely A and the α_i's) are computed by solving the linear program (a quadratic program is also possible)

$$\min\left\{\sum_{k=1}^{K}\left[\ln A + \sum_{i=1}^{n} \alpha_i \ln x_i^k - \ln u^k\right]\right\} \tag{1.23}$$

subject to

$$\left[\ln A + \sum_{i=1}^{n} \alpha_i \ln x_i^k - \ln u^k\right] \geqslant 0, \qquad k = 1, \ldots, K,$$

$$A > 0, \alpha_i > 0, i = 1, \ldots, n$$

The Farrell measure of technical efficiency is easily obtained from the functional constraints in the above program by defining

$$\varepsilon^k = \ln A + \sum_{i=1}^{n} \alpha_i \ln x_i^k - \ln u^k \tag{1.24}$$

the deviation of $\ln u^k$ from its fitted value. Then for each unit

$$F(x^k;u^k) = e^{-\varepsilon^k} \tag{1.25}$$

which for small ε is essentially the same as $(1 - \varepsilon^k)$.

The final step is to compute $Q(u^k,w^k)$ by solving the program

$$Q(u^k,w^k) = \min\left\{w^{kT}x: \left[\ln A + \sum_{i=1}^{n} \alpha_i \ln x_i - \ln u^k\right] \geqslant 0, \right.$$
$$\left. A > 0, \alpha_i > 0, i = 1,\ldots,n\right\} \qquad (1.26)$$

from which it follows that

$$C(x^k;u^k,w^k) = Q(u^k,w^k)/w^{kT}x^k \qquad (1.27)$$

$$A(x^k;u^k,w^k) = C(x^k;u^k,w^k)/F(x^k;u^k) \qquad (1.28)$$

The modified programming approach has two drawbacks that limit its appeal. The first drawback is that the approach, like the pure programming approach, is entirely deterministic, with no allowance made for noise, measurement error, and the like. Since the computed frontier is supported by a subset of the data, its shape and placement are highly sensitive to outliers. Timmer (1971), following a suggestion of Aigner and Chu (1968), attempted to deal with the problem of measurement error and other nonefficiency related deviations from the frontier by resorting to chance-constrained programming techniques. Essentially this modification involves discarding efficient observations until a certain percentage of the observations lie outside the recomputed input set, or until the computed parameter values stabilize.

The second drawback of the modified programming approach is its inability to deal easily with multiple outputs. It is possible, of course, to write a transformation frontier $t(u,x) \leqslant 0$, where $u \in R^m_+$, $x \in R^n_+$, in asymmetric form $u_j \leqslant \hat{t}(\hat{u},x)$, where $\hat{u} \in R^{m-1}_+$ and proceed as above. The problem with this remedy is that efficiency is measured with respect to $(m + n - 1)$ variables, and the resulting efficiency measures are sensitive to the selection of the dependent variable.[18] An alternative remedy draws on a proposal of Kopp and Diewert (1982) and Zieschang (1983a) to compute primal and dual efficiency relative to the dual cost frontier. In the first step a cost frontier, say Cobb-Douglas for simplicity, is specified. In the second step the parameters of the cost frontier are computed by solving the program

$$\min\left\{\sum_{k=1}^{K}\left[\ln(w^{kT}x^k) - B - \sum_{j=1}^{m} \gamma_j \ln u_j^k - \sum_{i=1}^{n} \beta_i \ln w_i^k\right]\right\} \qquad (1.29)$$

subject to

$$[\cdot] \geqslant 0, \qquad k = 1,\ldots,K,$$

$$\gamma_j > 0, \qquad j = 1, \ldots, m,$$

$$\beta_i > 0, \qquad i = 1, \ldots, n,$$

$$\sum_{i=1}^{n} \beta_i = 1$$

A measure of cost efficiency is obtained for each observation as $C(x^k;u^k,w^k) = \exp\ \{-[\cdot]\},\ k = 1, \ldots, K.$ The Kopp-Diewert-Zieschang algorithm then shows how to decompose cost efficiency into its technical and allocative components.

1.6. The Deterministic Statistical Frontier Approach

In contrast to the two programming approaches, this approach uses statistical techniques to estimate a transformation frontier and to estimate primal and dual efficiency relative to the estimated frontier. The technique was first proposed by Afriat (1972) and has been extended by Richmond (1974) and Greene (1980a,b), among others.

The first step in this approach is the same as in the modified programming approach. We suppose that each of K production units uses inputs $x \in R^n_+$ available at prices $w \in R^n_{++}$ to produce a single output $u \in R_+$ for sale at price $p \in R_{++}$, and define $L(u)$ as

$$L(u) = \left\{x\colon\ u \leqslant A \prod_{i=1}^{n} x_i^{\alpha_i}\right\} \tag{1.30}$$

where the Cobb-Douglas specification for ϕ is arbitrary. The second step is to convert the weak inequality in (1.30) to an equality by expressing the actual output obtained from input vector x as

$$u = A \prod_{i=1}^{n} x_i^{\alpha_i} \exp\{\varepsilon\} \tag{1.31}$$

where $\varepsilon \leqslant 0$ is a disturbance term having some specified one-sided distribution, such as truncated normal or exponential. Here ε represents technical inefficiency relative to the deterministic (or "full") production frontier $\phi(x)$. As in both programming approaches, the data are enveloped by a deterministic frontier. As in the modified programming approach, the deterministic frontier is parametric. In contrast to both programming approaches, the deterministic frontier is estimated rather than computed.

The third step is to estimate the parameters of $\phi(x)$ and $f(\varepsilon)$, the density of ε. The easiest way to estimate these parameters is by corrected ordinary least squares (COLS). Letting μ be the mean of ε, equation (1.31) can be written

$$\ln u^k = (\ln A + \mu) + \sum_{i=1}^{n} \alpha_i \ln x_i^k + (\varepsilon^k - \mu), \qquad k = 1, \ldots, K \quad (1.32)$$

where the new error term $(\varepsilon^k - \mu)$ has zero mean. This equation may be estimated by OLS to obtain best linear unbiased and consistent estimates of $(\ln A + \mu)$ and the α_i's. It remains to "correct" the constant term; that is, to obtain separate estimates of $\ln A$ and of μ. This can be done in either of two ways. First, μ is a function of the parameters of $f(\varepsilon)$, and can typically be estimated consistently from the second or higher moments of the OLS residuals. This estimate of μ is then subtracted from the estimated $(\ln A + \mu)$. A problem with this approach is that even after the constant term is corrected, some residuals may still have the wrong sign, so that these observations end up above, rather than on or beneath, the estimated production frontier. A second way to "correct" the constant term is to follow Gabrielson (1975) and simply increase it until the production frontier just envelops the data. This suggests defining $\hat{\mu}$ by

$$\hat{\mu} = -\min \left\{ |\mu| : \ \mu \leqslant 0, (\ln \hat{A} + \mu) - \mu + \sum_{i=1}^{n} \hat{\alpha}_i \ln x_i^k - \ln u^k \geqslant 0, \quad k = 1, \ldots, K \right\} \quad (1.33)$$

which guarantees that no observations lie above the estimated frontier. It provides a consistent estimate of μ (and hence also of $\ln A$) for any one-sided distribution of ε with positive density in a neighborhood of zero. A considerable advantage of this procedure is that there is no need to specify $f(\varepsilon)$ at all; one need only assume that the ε^k are independently and identically distributed from an unspecified one-sided distribution.

Another way of estimating the parameters of $\phi(x)$ and $f(\varepsilon)$ is by maximum likelihood. The advantage of MLE over COLS is that it allows direct estimation of the constant term, and should be more efficient since it uses all information on the density $f(\varepsilon)$. However MLE has two drawbacks. First, since the parameters of $\phi(x)$ and $f(\varepsilon)$ are estimated together, the estimated parameters of $\phi(x)$ depend on the particular distribution assumed for ε. (This is also true of COLS, if μ is estimated from moments of the residuals.)[19] Second, not just any one-sided distribution for ε will do. The range problem pointed out by Schmidt (1976) was partially solved by Greene (1980a), who found sufficient conditions on $f(\varepsilon)$ such that maximum likelihood is consistent and asymptotically efficient. A gamma distribution for ε satisfies these conditions, for example.

The final step is to compute $F(x^k;u^k)$, $C(x^k;u^k,w^k)$, and $A(x^k;u^k,w^k)$. This cannot be accomplished by COLS if any residuals are positive. It can be accomplished by MLE, or by COLS if the intercept-shift correction is used. $F(x^k;u^k)$ is calculated from the residuals, as in equation (1.25), while $C(x^k;u^k,w^k)$ and $A(x^k;u^k,w^k)$ are calculated from the derived cost frontier. The derived cost frontier is given (for the Cobb-Douglas case) by Schmidt and Lovell (1979, eqs. (9) and (10)), if their v in equation (9) is set to zero. The allocative efficiency measure depends on the deviations of the actual input proportions from the optimal input proportions, which are readily calculated (Schmidt and Lovell 1979, eq. (7)) given the input prices and the estimated α_i's; the cost efficiency measure depends on these and on the production frontier residuals.

For technologies more complicated than Cobb-Douglas, the explicit form of the cost frontier might not be known. In this case, allocative and cost efficiency measures could be calculated by simply computing minimum cost (given the estimated technology and input prices) for the observed outputs, and comparing it to actual cost. For complicated technologies, this could be a complicated set of calculations.

An alternative approach is to estimate a deterministic cost frontier directly. Any functional form, including a flexible functional form, can be specified. There is no need to worry about expressing the dual production frontier in closed form, since the Kopp-Diewert-Zieschang algorithm mentioned in connection with the modified programming approach is equally applicable to the deterministic frontier approach. The cost frontier residuals provide measures of cost efficiency, and these can be decomposed into measures of technical and allocative efficiency.[20]

The deterministic statistical frontier approach shares the weaknesses of the modified programming approach. It assumes a deterministic frontier, and all deviations from the frontier are attributed to technical inefficiency. No allowance is made for noise, measurement error, and the like. Also, like the modified programming approach, the extension to multiple outputs is difficult unless the dual cost frontier is estimated directly and the Kopp-Diewert-Zieschang decomposition algorithm is used. (In this event all deviations from the frontier are attributed to cost inefficiency.)

The important way in which the deterministic statistical frontier approach differs from the two programming approaches is that here the primal or dual frontier and related efficiencies are estimated by statistical techniques rather than computed by programming techniques. For statistical reasons, a large sample size is required, which is clearly a potential disadvantage. Furthermore, it is a disadvantage to have to specify a distribution for technical efficiency (a form for $f(\varepsilon)$) if a production frontier is estimated, or for cost efficiency if a cost frontier is estimated. Ideally the specification would be based on a knowledge of the forces, economic or otherwise, that generate the inefficiency. However such information is rarely available, and when it is available it might be preferable to enter it directly into the estimating equation. There being no a priori arguments for a particular distribution, choice is typically based on analytical tractability. Unfortunately, estimates of the parameters of $\phi(x)$ and of the magnitude of efficiency are not invariant with respect to the specification of a distribution for the efficiency term. On the other hand, the advantage of a statistical approach is the possibility of statistical inference based on the results, although such inference is of course conditional on the specified distribution being the true distribution. Specification tests to evaluate half-normal and truncated normal distributions have been developed by Lee (1983a) for stochastic frontier models, and these can be applied to deterministic frontier models as well.

1.7. The Stochastic Frontier Approach

Like the deterministic statistical frontier approach, the stochastic frontier approach uses statistical techniques to estimate a transformation frontier and to estimate efficiency relative to the estimated frontier. In contrast to the deterministic statistical frontier approach, but in accordance with the typical nonfrontier approach to the estimation of economic relationships, this approach allows the frontier to be stochastic. The technique was first proposed by Aigner, Lovell, and Schmidt (1977) and Meeusen and van den Broeck (1977b), and has been extended by Schmidt and Lovell (1979, 1980); Jondrow, Lovell, Materov, and Schmidt (1982); and Huang (1984), among others.[21]

The first step is to suppose that each of K production units uses inputs $x \in R^n_+$ available at prices $w \in R^n_{++}$ to produce a single output $u \in R_+$ at price $p \in R_{++}$, and define $L(u)$ as

$$L(u) \equiv \left\{x:\ u \leqslant A \prod_{i=1}^{n} x_i^{\alpha_i} \exp\{\varepsilon_1\}\right\} \tag{1.34}$$

where the Cobb-Douglas specification for ϕ is arbitrary. Here the symmetric disturbance term $\varepsilon_1 \gtrless 0$ permits random variation of the production frontier across observations, and captures the effects of noise, measurement error, and exogenous shocks beyond the control of the production unit. The production frontier is stochastic. The second step is to convert the weak inequality in (1.34) to an equality by expressing the actual output obtained from input vector x as

$$u = A \prod_{i=1}^{n} x_i^{\alpha_i} \exp\{\varepsilon_1 + \varepsilon_2\} \tag{1.35}$$

where $\varepsilon_2 \leqslant 0$ is a one-sided disturbance term that captures the effects of technical inefficiency relative to the stochastic production frontier. In contrast to all three previous approaches, in this approach the data are bounded by a stochastic frontier. Consequently the deviation of an observation from the deterministic kernel of the stochastic frontier comes from two sources: random variation of the deterministic kernel across observations captured by the component ε_1, and technical inefficiency captured by the component ε_2. Obviously the deterministic statistical frontier model is a special case of the stochastic frontier model, in which $\varepsilon_1 = 0$.

The third step is to estimate the parameters of $\phi(x)$, $f_1(\varepsilon_1)$ and $f_2(\varepsilon_2)$. Once a functional form for ϕ and probability distributions for f_1 and f_2 are specified, estimation can be carried out using either COLS or MLE techniques. The COLS estimates are easier to compute, although the MLE estimates are asymptotically more efficient. Note that the range problem that plagues the MLE technique in the deterministic statistical frontier approach does not appear in the stochastic frontier approach because of the presence of ε_1.

The fourth step is to estimate $F(x^k;u^k)$. The sample mean for the Farrell measure is simply $E(e^{\varepsilon_2})$, which is often approximated by $1 + E(\varepsilon_2)$. Jondrow, Lovell, Materov, and Schmidt (1982) have shown how to extract estimates of ε_1^k and ε_2^k from the composed error terms $(\varepsilon_1^k + \varepsilon_2^k)$ by calculating the distribution of ε_2 conditional on $(\varepsilon_1 + \varepsilon_2)$. Estimates of ε_2^k are then provided by either the mean or the mode of the distribution of $[\varepsilon_2^k \mid (\varepsilon_1^k + \varepsilon_2^k)]$. The drawback to these estimates is that they are not consistent; the variance of the conditional distribution remains no matter how large the sample.

The final step is to estimate allocative and cost efficiency. This can be accomplished in any of three ways. In one approach a set of first-order conditions for cost minimization is appended to the production frontier, and the system is estimated by MLE. Error terms on the first-order conditions represent allocative inefficiency. Certain assumptions on $\phi(x)$, $f_1(\varepsilon_1)$, $f_2(\varepsilon_2)$ and the error terms on the first-order conditions permit simultaneous estimation of $F(x^k;u^k)$, $A(x^k;u^k,w^k)$, and $C(x^k;u^k,w^k)$. The second approach is to simply do the same thing as was discussed in the previous section, for a deterministic statistical frontier; measure the deviations of the actual input proportions from the optimal input proportions, and calculate the efficiency measures from the analytically derived cost frontier. The third approach is to estimate the dual stochastic cost frontier directly. The Kopp-Diewert-Zieschang algorithm can be adapted to the stochastic frontier framework to generate estimates of cost, allocative, and technical efficiency. Or the stochastic cost frontier can be estimated jointly with the system of input demand or share equations, using Shephard's lemma. Schmidt (1984a) has shown how and why the disturbances in such a system might be related, so as to identify both technical and allocative inefficiency. Bauer (1985) has extended these ideas.

The stochastic frontier approach has some drawbacks, which it shares with certain other approaches. As in the deterministic statistical frontier approach, estimation requires a large sample size. As in the modified programming and the deterministic statistical frontier approaches, considerable structure is usually imposed on technology. Moreover, additional structure is imposed on the distribution of technical inefficiency, and sometimes on the distribution of allocative inefficiency as well. And finally, as in the modified programming and the deterministic statistical frontier approaches, the stochastic frontier approach has difficulty dealing with multiple outputs. However, each of these difficulties is, in principle if not yet in practice, potentially avoidable. For example, the Kopp-Diewert-Zieschang algorithm can be adapted to a stochastic cost frontier, and the use of a stochastic cost frontier solves the multiple output problem. Furthermore, as Schmidt (1984b) and Schmidt and Sickles (1984) have shown, the necessity to choose particular distributions for ε_1 and ε_2 can be avoided in the presence of panel data.

The biggest advantage of the stochastic frontier approach is that, unlike all three other approaches, it introduces a disturbance term representing noise, measurement error, and exogenous shocks beyond the control of the production unit. None of the other approaches makes any sort of accommodation for such phenomena, which affect every economic relationship. This in turn permits a decomposition of the deviation of an observation from the deterministic kernel of a frontier into two components, inefficiency and noise. Without such an accommodation statistical noise is bound to be counted as inefficiency.

1.8. Summary and Conclusion

If the measurement of efficiency in production is a useful exercise, and we believe that it is, then it deserves to be conducted properly, being both faithful to the underlying economic theory and respectful of the vagaries of the requisite economic data. In this paper we have sketched an outline of four different approaches to the measurement of productive efficiency. These approaches differ in the way they specify the relevant frontier (i.e., nonparametric or parametric), in the way the frontier is constructed (i.e., by programming or statistical techniques), and in the way deviations from the constructed frontier are interpreted (i.e., as inefficiency or as a mixture of inefficiency and noise). Although each approach has strengths and weaknesses, only the stochastic frontier approach has the ability to distinguish inefficiency from statistical noise, and we think this property is of great importance.

Much has been accomplished in the field of efficiency measurement, and much remains to be done. It is a field of research that has languished since 1977 but has exploded in the past decade. We conclude this essay by noting two accomplishments not mentioned above and by pointing to a valuable line of research that has just begun and that should be pursued further.

A line of research that has developed in parallel with that of efficiency measurement, and which uses the same techniques as the pure programming approach to efficiency measurement, is the development of a set of nonparametric tests of various regularity conditions in production analysis. Major contributions have been made by Afriat (1972), Hanoch and Rothschild (1972), Diewert and Parkan (1983), Varian (1984a,b), and Banker and Maindiratta (1985b).

A second line of research that has developed rapidly is the empirical application of the techniques of efficiency measurement to a wide variety of contexts. Among the applications are efficiency analysis in hospitals (Banker, Conrad, and Strauss 1986), airlines (Bauer 1985; Sickles 1985; Sickles, Good, and Johnson 1985); education (Bessent, Bessent, Charnes, Cooper, and Thorogood 1983; Bessent, Bessent, Kennington, and Regan 1982; Charnes, Cooper, and Rhodes 1981); mining (Byrnes, Färe, and Grosskopf 1984; Byrnes, Färe, Grosskopf, and Lovell 1985); postal services (Deprins, Simar, and Tulkens 1984); electric utilities (Färe, Grosskopf, Logan, and Lovell 1985; Kopp and Smith 1980; Seitz 1971); courts (Lewin, Morey, and Cook 1982); pharmacies (Morey, Capettini, and Dittman 1985); the armed services (Charnes, Clark, Cooper, and Golany 1986; Charnes, Cooper, Dieck-Assad, Golany, and Wiggins 1985; Charnes, Cooper, Divine, Klopp, and Stutz 1986; Lewin and Morey 1981); and water utilities (Byrnes, Grosskopf, and Hayes 1986). The techniques have also been applied to the study of efficiency in manufacturing industries around the world (Carlsson 1972; Lee and Tyler 1978; Levy 1982; Lovell and Sickles 1983; Meeusen and van den Broeck 1977b; Meller 1976; Toda

1976, 1977; Tyler and Lee 1979; van den Broeck 1983); and in agriculture around the world (Bagi and Huang 1983; Danilin, Materov, Rosefielde, and Lovell 1985; Färe, Grabowski, and Grosskopf 1985; Huang and Bagi 1984; Jamison and Lau 1982; and Seitz 1970).

A line of research that has been initiated but which, in our judgement, remains underdeveloped and in need of additional work, is a comparative evaluation of the strengths and weaknesses of the four alternative approaches to efficiency measurement. Many of the potentially significant advantages of each approach have been pointed out here, but a true comparison of the various approaches needs to be made on the basis of both artificial and real data. The comparisons that have been conducted to date have shed some light on the types of scenarios in which one approach may be preferred to another, but these comparisons have tended to be not comprehensive in their coverage and not carefully designed, the latter perhaps because most comparisons have been based on data that are less than ideal for the purpose. Among the more useful comparative analyses are those of Banker, Charnes, Cooper and Maindiratta (1987); Banker, Conrad, and Strauss (1985); Bowlin, Charnes, Cooper, and Sherman (1985); Corbo and De Melo (1983); and van den Broeck, Førsund, Hjalmarsson, and Meeusen (1980). The results of these studies vary widely, so much so as to provide scant guidance. The main message that emerges from these studies is that more work is called for.

Notes

1. An excellent exposition of duality theory is provided by Diewert (1982).

2. A model for separating efficiency growth from technical change has been developed and applied to Yugoslav data by Nishimizu and Page (1982).

3. The material in this section is drawn from Färe, Grosskopf, and Lovell (1985a, ch. 2). See also Teusch (1983) for a detailed analysis of production and efficiency.

4. To cite two simple examples, a Cobb-Douglas technology has Eff $L(u)$ = Isoq $L(u)$, while a Leontief technology has Eff $L(u) \subset$ Isoq $L(u)$.

5. See Färe, Grosskopf, and Lovell (1985a, ch. 6) for details. It is by no means necessary that all inputs and outputs be freely variable. On the treatment of categorical variables and fixed variables see Banker and Morey (1986a,b).

6. The important notion of optimal scale of operation is not addressed here, although it has been investigated using the tools of efficiency measurement. Among those who have investigated the notion of optimal scale, and the measurement of departures from it, are Banker (1984); Banker, Charnes, and Cooper (1984); Färe (1985); Färe and Grosskopf (1985); Färe, Grosskopf, and Lovell (1985b); and Försund and Hjalmarsson (1979a). It should be noted that there is a divergence of opinion over the appropriate definition of optimal scale.

7. The virtues of asymmetric and nonradial efficiency measures are discussed in Kopp

(1981a,b); Färe and Lovell (1981); and Färe, Lovell, and Zieschang (1983). Zieschang (1982, 1984) has proposed a Russell-extended Farrell measure of technical efficiency to deal with both of these shortcomings. This measure of the technical efficiency of input vector $x \in L(u) + R^n_+$ is given by

$$E(x;u) \equiv R(F(x;u) \cdot x;u) \cdot F(x;u)$$

where F and R are the Farrell and Russell measures of technical efficiency respectively. An exhaustive comparison of $F(x;u)$, $R(x;u)$, and $E(x;u)$ is provided by Russell (1985a,b,c).

8. A very different alternative to the Russell measure retains the Farrell framework and exploits the notion of *congestion* developed by Färe and Svensson (1980). This yields a three-way decomposition of inefficiency: purely technical, congestion, and allocative. See Färe and Grosskopf (1983a,b) or Färe, Grosskopf, and Lovell (1983, 1985c) for further details and computational techniques.

9. The relationship of efficiency measurement as we view it and Leibenstein's notion of X-efficiency is unclear to us, and we do not discuss it. For an introduction see Leibenstein (1976) and the ensuing exchange between Stigler (1978) and Leibenstein (1978).

10. See, for example, Charnes, Cooper, and Rhodes (1978, 1979, 1981) for early developments of DEA. An excellent substantive analysis of DEA is provided by Charnes and Cooper (1985).

11. See, for example, Färe, Grosskopf, and Lovell (1985a).

12. Banker, Charnes, and Cooper (1984) describe how increasing, constant, or decreasing returns to scale can be identified without resorting to additional computation by modifying the constraints on the intensity vector.

13. In equations (1.17)–(1.20) the Farrell measure of technical efficiency can be replaced by either the Russell measure or the Russell-extended Farrell measure, simply by modifying the linear programming problem (1.17).

14. Note the essential point that, without imposing a parametric form, only *bounds* on technology are possible.

15. Years ago Timmer (1971) and Afriat (1972) proposed a piecewise Cobb-Douglas alternative to the piecewise linear construction embodied in equation (1.16). This idea has recently been revivified by Banker, Charnes, Cooper, and Schinnar (1981); Banker and Maindiratta (1986); and Charnes, Cooper, Seiford, and Stutz (1982, 1983). These alternative constructions can be thought of as compromises between the nonparametric pure programming techniques and the globally parametric modified programming techniques. However, they would appear to sacrifice the desirable "tightest inner bound" property of the pure programming approach.

16. The solution proposed by Charnes, Cooper, and Rhodes (1979), to impose strict inequalities in place of nonnegativity restrictions on the dual variables, has been shown to be deficient by Boyd and Färe (1984), Färe and Hunsaker (1986), and Zieschang (1983b). For a defense of this solution see Charnes and Cooper (1984, 1985), and Charnes, Cooper, Golany, Seiford, and Stutz (1985).

17. Some preliminary steps toward a statistical treatment of DEA models can be found in Banker and Maindiratta (1985a), Sengupta (1982), and Varian (1984b).

18. There is another difficulty with this asymmetric approach. Some of the $(m + n - 1)$ elements of $(\hat{u},x)$, the inputs, must be contracted, while others, the outputs, must be expanded, in order to reach the frontier. This necessitates the use of a nonradial measure of technical efficiency and greatly complicates computation. See Färe, Grosskopf, and Lovell (1985a, ch. 5) for an introduction to so-called "hyperbolic" efficiency measures appropriate to this problem.

19. This point has been raised by Stevenson (1980), and further investigated by Cowing, Reifschneider, and Stevenson (1983), who examine the effect of alternative error term specifications on estimated cost frontiers. They find surprisingly little effect.

20. This approach has been used successfully by Lovell and Sickles (1985) in a flexible translog system of cost and input share equations.

21. The stochastic frontier approach is summarized in Schmidt (1985).

References

Afriat, S. N. 1972. "Efficiency Estimation of Production Functions." *International Economic Review* 13(3): 568–598.

Aigner, D. J., and S. F. Chu. 1968. "On Estimating the Industry Production Function." *American Economic Review* 58(4): 826–839.

Aigner, D. J., C. A. K. Lovell, and P. J. Schmidt. 1977. "Formulation and Estimation of Stochastic Frontier Production Function Models." *Journal of Econometrics* 6 (July): 21–37.

Bagi, F. S., and C. J. Huang. 1983. "Estimating Production Technical Efficiency for Individual Farms in Tennessee." *Canadian Journal of Agricultural Economics* 31:249–256.

Banker, R. D. 1984. "Returns to Scale, Scale Efficiency and Average Cost Minimization in Multi-Output Production," unpublished manuscript.

Banker, R., A. Charnes, and W. W. Cooper. 1984. "Models for the Estimation of Technical and Scale Inefficiencies in Data Envelopment Analysis." *Management Science* 30(9): 1078–1092.

Banker, R. D., A. Charnes, W. W. Cooper, and A. Maindiratta. 1987. "A Comparison of DEA and Translog Estimates of Production Frontiers Using Simulated Observations from a Known Technology," Chapter 2 of this volume.

Banker, R. D., A. Charnes, W. W. Cooper, and A. P. Schinnar. 1981. "A Bi-Extremal Principle for Frontier Estimation and Efficiency Evaluations." *Management Science* 27(12): 1370–1382.

Banker, R. D., R. F. Conrad, and R. P. Strauss. 1986. "A Comparative Application of DEA and Translog Methods: An Illustrative Study of Hospital Production." *Management Science,* 32(1): 30–44.

Banker, R. D., and A. Maindiratta. 1985a. "Maximum Likelihood Estimation of Monotonic and Concave Production Frontiers," unpublished manuscript.

Banker, R. D., and A. Maindiratta. 1985b. "Nonparametric Analysis of Technical and Allocative Efficiencies in Production," unpublished manuscript.

Banker, R. D., and A. Maindiratta. 1986. "Piecewise Loglinear Estimation of Efficient Production Surfaces." *Management Science,* 32, 126–135.

Banker, R. D., and R. C. Morey. 1986a. "Use of Categorical Variables in Data Envelopment Analysis." *Management Science,* forthcoming.

Banker, R. D. and R. C. Morey. 1986b. "Efficiency Analysis for Exogenously Fixed Inputs and Outputs." *Operations Research,* July–August, vol. 34.

Bauer, P. W. 1985. "An Approach for The Analysis of Multiproduct Technology and Efficiency Using Panel Data: An Application to the U.S. Airline Industry." Ph.D. Dissertation, University of North Carolina at Chapel Hill.

Bessent, A., W. Bessent, A. Charnes, W. W. Cooper, and N. Thorogood. 1983. "Evaluation of Educational Program Proposals by Means of DEA." *Educational Administration Quarterly* 19(2): 82–107.

Bessent, A., W. Bessent, J. Kennington, and B. Regan. 1982. "An Application of Mathematical Programming to Assess Productivity in the Houston Independent School District." *Management Science* 28(12): 1355–1367.

Bowlin, W. F., A. Charnes, W. W. Cooper, and H. D. Sherman. 1985. "Data Envelopment Analysis and Regression Approaches to Efficiency Estimation and Evaluation." *Annals of Operations Research,* 2: 113–138.

Boyd, G., and R. Färe. 1984. "Measuring the Efficiency of Decision Making Units: A Comment." *European Journal of Operational Research* 15(3): 331–332.

Byrnes, P., R. Färe, and S. Grosskopf. 1984. "Measuring Productive Efficiency: An Application to Illinois Strip Mines." *Management Science* 30(6): 671–681.

Byrnes, P., R. Färe, S. Grosskopf, and C. A. K. Lovell. 1985. "The Effect of Unions on Productivity: U.S. Surface Mining of Coal," unpublished manuscript.

Byrnes, P., S. Grosskopf, and K. Hayes. 1986. "Efficiency and Ownership: Further Evidence." *Review of Economics and Statistics,* 68(2), 337–341.

Carlsson, B. 1972. "The Measurement of Efficiency in Production: An Application to Swedish Manufacturing Industries, 1968." *Swedish Journal of Economics* 74(4): 468–485.

Charnes, A., C. T. Clark, W. W. Cooper, and B. Golany. 1985. "A Development Study of Data Envelopment Analysis in Measuring the Efficiency of Maintenance Units in the U.S. Air Forces." *Annals of Operations Research,* 2.

Charnes, A., and W. W. Cooper. 1984. "The Non-Archimedean CCR Ratio for Efficiency Analysis: A Rejoinder to Boyd and Färe." *European Journal of Operational Research* 15(3): 333–334.

Charnes, A., and W. W. Cooper. 1985. "Preface to Topics in Data Envelopment Analysis." *Annals of Operations Research,* 2: 59–94.

Charnes, A., W. W. Cooper, M. Dieck-Assad, B. Golany, and D. E. Wiggins. 1985. "Efficiency Analysis of Medical Care Resources in the U.S. Army Health Sciences Command," unpublished manuscript.

Charnes, A., W. W. Cooper, D. Divine, G. A. Klopp, and J. Stutz. 1985. "An Application of Data Envelopment Analysis to U.S. Army Recruitment Districts," in R. L. Schultz (ed.), *Applications of Management Science.* Greenwich, CN: JAI Press.

Charnes, A., W. W. Cooper, B. Golany, L. Seiford, and J. Stutz. 1985. "Foundations of Data Envelopment Analysis for Pareto-Koopmans Efficient Empirical Production Functions." *Journal of Econometrics,* 30, 91–107.

Charnes, A., W. W. Cooper, and E. Rhodes. 1978. "Measuring the Efficiency of Decision-Making Units." *European Journal of Operational Research* 2(6): 429–444.

Charnes, A., W. W. Cooper, and E. Rhodes. 1979. "Short Communication: Measuring Efficiency of Decision-Making Units." *European Journal of Operational Research* 3(4): 339.

Charnes, A., W. W. Cooper, and E. Rhodes. 1981. "Evaluating Program and Managerial Efficiency: An Application of Data Envelopment Analysis to Program Follow-Through." *Management Science* 27(6):668–697.

Charnes, A., W. W. Cooper, L. Seiford, and J. Stutz. 1982. "A Multiplicative Model for Efficiency Analysis." *Socio-Economic Planning Sciences* 16(5): 223–224.

Charnes, A., W. W. Cooper, L. Seiford, and J. Stutz. 1983. "Invariant Multiplicative Efficiency and Piecewise Cobb-Douglas Envelopments." *Operations Research Letters* 2(3): 101–103.

Corbo, V., and J. de Melo. 1983. "Measuring Technical Efficiency: A Comparison of Alternative Methodologies with Census Data," unpublished manuscript.

Cowing, T., D. Reifschneider, and R. Stevenson. 1983. "A Comparison of Alternative Frontier Cost Function Specifications," in A. Dogramaci (ed.), *Developments in Econometric Analyses of Productivity*. Boston: Kluwer-Nijhoff.

Danilin, S., I. Materov, S., Rosefielde, and C. A. K. Lovell. 1985. "Measuring Enterprise Efficiency in the Soviet Union: A Stochastic Frontier Analysis." *Economica* 52(206): 225–234.

Debreu, G. 1951. "The Coefficient of Resource Utilization." *Econometrica* 19(3): 273–292.

Deprins, D., L. Simar, and H. Tulkens. 1984. "Measuring Labor-Efficiency in Post Offices," in M. Marchand, P. Pestieau, and H. Tulkens (eds.), *The Performance of Public Enterprises: Concepts and Measurement*. Amsterdam: North-Holland.

Diewert, W. E. 1982. "Duality Approaches to Microeconomic Theory," in K. J. Arrow and M. D. Intriligator (eds.), *Handbook of Mathematical Economics Volume II*. Amsterdam: North-Holland.

Diewert, W. E., and C. Parkan. 1983. "Linear Programming Tests of Regularity Conditions for Production Functions," in W. Eichhorn, R. Henn, K. Neumann, and R. W. Shephard (eds.), *Quantitative Studies on Production and Prices*. Vienna: Physica-Verlag.

Färe, R. 1985. "A DEA Approach to Scale Efficiency," unpublished manuscript.

Färe, R., R. Grabowski, and S. Grosskopf. 1985. "Technical Efficiency of Philippine Agriculture." *Applied Economics* 17(2): 205–214.

Färe, R., and S. Grosskopf. 1983a. "Measuring Output Efficiency." *European Journal of Operational Research* 13:173–179.

Färe, R., and S. Grosskopf. 1983b. "Measuring Congestion in Production." *Zeitschrift fur Nationalökonomie* 43: 257–271.

Färe, R., and S. Grosskopf. 1985. "A Nonparametric Cost Approach to Scale Efficiency." *Scandinavian Journal of Economics,* 87(4), 594-604.

Färe, R., S. Grosskopf, J. Logan, and C. A. K. Lovell. 1985. "Measuring Efficiency in Production: With An Application to Electric Utilities," in A. Dogramaci and N. R. Adam (eds.), *Managerial Issues in Productivity Analysis*. Boston: Kluwer-Nijhoff.

Färe, R., S. Grosskopf, and C. A. K. Lovell. 1983. "The Structure of Technical Efficiency." *Scandinavian Journal of Economics* 85:181–190.

Färe, R., S. Grosskopf, and C. A. K. Lovell. 1985a. *The Measurement of Efficiency of Production*. Boston: Kluwer-Nijhoff.

Färe, R., S. Grosskopf, and C. A. K. Lovell. 1985b. "Scale Elasticity and Scale Efficiency," unpublished manuscript.

Färe, R., S. Grosskopf, and C. A. K. Lovell. 1985c. "Nonparametric Disposability Tests," unpublished manuscript.

Färe, R., and W. Hunsaker. 1986. "Notions of Efficiency and Their Reference Sets." *Management Science,* 32(2), 237–243.

Färe, R., and C. A. K. Lovell. 1978. "Measuring the Technical Efficiency of Production." *Journal of Economic Theory* 19 (October): 150–162.

Färe, R., and C. A. K. Lovell. 1981. "Measuring the Technical Efficiency of Production: Reply." *Journal of Economic Theory* 25 (December): 253–254.

Färe, R., C. A. K. Lovell, and K. D. Zieschang. 1983. "Measuring the Technical Efficiency of Multiple Output Production Technologies," in W. Eichhorn, R. Henn, K. Neumann, and R. Shephard (eds.), *Quantitative Studies on Production and Prices.* Vienna: Physica-Verlag.

Färe, R., and L. Svensson. 1980. "Congestion of Production Factors." *Econometrica* 48(7): 1745–1753.

Farrell, M. J. 1957. "The Measurement of Productive Efficiency." *Journal of the Royal Statistical Society,* ser. A, General, 120, pt. 3, 253–281.

Försund, F. R., and L. Hjalmarsson. 1979a. "Generalized Farrell Measures of Efficiency: An Application to Milk Processing in Swedish Diary Plants." *Economic Journal* 89 (June): 274–315.

Försund, F. R., and L. Hjalmarsson. 1979b. "Frontier Production Functions and Technical Progress: A Study of General Milk Processing in Swedish Dairy Plants." *Econometrica* 47(4): 893–900.

Försund, F. R., and E. S. Jansen. 1977. "On Estimating Average and Best Practice Homothetic Production Functions via Cost Functions." *International Economic Review* 18(2): 463–476.

Gabrielson, A. 1975. "On Estimating Efficient Production Functions." Working Paper No. A-85 (Chr. Michelsen Institute, Department of Humanities and Social Science, Bergen, Norway).

Greene, W. H. 1980a. "Maximum Likelihood Estimation of Econometric Frontier Functions." *Journal of Econometrics* 13 (May): 27–56.

Greene, W. H. 1980b. "On the Estimation of a Flexible Frontier Production Model." *Journal of Econometrics* 13 (May): 101–115.

Hanoch, G., and M. Rothschild. 1972. "Testing the Assumptions of Production Theory: A Nonparametric Approach." *Journal of Political Economy* 80(2): 256–275.

Huang, C. J. 1984. "Estimation of Stochastic Frontier Production Function and Technical Inefficiency via the EM Algorithm." *Southern Economic Journal* 50(3): 847–856.

Huang, C. J., and F. S. Bagi. 1984. "Technical Efficiency on Individual Farms in Northwest India." *Southern Economic Journal* 51(1): 108–115.

Hulten, C. R. 1973. "Divisia Index Numbers." *Econometrica* 41(6): 1017–1026.

Jamison, D. T., and L. J. Lau. 1982. *Farmer Education and Farm Efficiency.* Baltimore: Johns Hopkins University Press.

Jondrow, J., C. A. K. Lovell, I. S. Materov, and P. Schmidt. 1982. "On the Estimation of Technical Inefficiency in the Stochastic Frontier Production Function Model." *Journal of Econometrics* 19 (August): 233-238.

Koopmans, T. C. 1951. "An Analysis of Production as an Efficient Combination of Activities," in T. C. Koopmans (ed.), *Activity Analysis of Production and Allocation.* Cowles Commission for Research in Economics, Monograph No. 13. New York: Wiley.

Kopp, R. 1981a. "The Measurement of Productive Efficiency: A Reconsideration." *Quarterly Journal of Economics* 96(3): 477-503.

Kopp, R. 1981b. "Measuring the Technical Efficiency of Production: Comment." *Journal of Economic Theory* 25(3): 251-252.

Kopp, R., and W. E. Diewert. 1982. "The Decomposition of Frontier Cost Function Deviations into Measures of Technical and Allocative Efficiency." *Journal of Econometrics* 19 (August): 319-331.

Kopp, R., and V. K. Smith. 1980. "Frontier Production Function Estimates for Steam-Electric Generation: A Comparative Analysis." *Southern Economic Journal* 46(4): 1049-1059.

Lee, L. -F. 1983. "A Test for Distributional Assumption for the Stochastic Frontier Functions." *Journal of Econometrics* 22 (August): 245-267.

Lee, L. -F., and W. G. Tyler. 1978. "The Stochastic Frontier Production Function and Average Efficiency: An Empirical Analysis." *Journal of Econometrics* 7 (June): 385-389.

Leibenstein, H. 1976. *Beyond Economic Man.* Cambridge, MA: Harvard University Press.

Leibenstein, H. 1978. "X-Inefficiency Xists—Reply to an Xorcist." *American Economic Review* 68(1): 203-211.

Levy, V. 1981. "On Estimating Efficiency Differentials Between the Public and Private Sectors in a Developing Economy—Iraq." *Journal of Comparative Economics* 5(3): 235-250.

Lewin, A. Y., and R. C. Morey. 1981. "Measuring the Relative Efficiency and Output Potential of Public Sector Organizations: An Application of Data Envelopment Analysis." *Journal of Policy Analysis and Information Systems* 5(4): 267-285.

Lewin, A. Y., R. C. Morey, and T. J. Cook. 1982. "Evaluating the Administrative Efficiency of Courts." *Omega* 10(1): 401-411.

Lovell, C. A. K., and R. C. Sickles. 1983. "Testing Efficiency Hypotheses in Joint Production—A Parametric Approach." *Review of Economics and Statistics* 65(1): 51-58.

Lovell, C. A. K., and R. C. Sickles. 1985. "Testing for Aggregation Bias in Efficiency Measurement," unpublished manuscript.

Meeusen, W., and J. van den Broeck. 1977a. "Efficiency Estimation from Cobb-Douglas Production Functions with Composed Error." *International Economic Review* 18(2): 435-444.

Meeusen, W., and J. van den Broeck. 1977b. "Technical Efficiency and Dimension of the Firm: Some Results on the Use of Frontier Production Functions." *Empirical Economics* 2(2): 109-122.

Meller, P. 1976. "Efficiency Frontiers for Industrial Establishments of Different Sizes." *Explorations in Economic Research,* Occasional Papers of the National Bureau of Economic Research 3, 3 (Summer): 379–407.
Morey, R. C., R. Capettini, and D. A. Dittman. 1985. "Pareto Rate-Setting Strategies: An Application to Medicaid Drug Reimbursement." *Policy Sciences* 18: 169–200.
Nishimizu, M., and J. M. Page, Jr. 1982. "Total Factor Productivity Growth, Technological Progress and Technical Efficiency Change: Dimensions of Productivity Change in Yugoslavia, 1965–78." *Economic Journal* 92 (December): 920–936.
Richmond, J. 1974. "Estimating the Efficiency of Production." *International Economic Review* 15(2): 515–521.
Russell, R. R. 1985a. "Measures of Technical Efficiency." *Journal of Economic Theory* 35 (February): 109–126.
Russell, R. R. 1985b. "The Axiomatic Approach to the Measurement of Technical Efficiency," unpublished manuscript.
Russell, R. R. 1985c. "On the Continuity of Measures of Technical Efficiency," unpublished manuscript.
Schmidt, P. 1976. "On the Statistical Estimation of Parametric Frontier Production Functions." *Review of Economics and Statistics* 58(2): 238–239.
Schmidt, P. 1984a. "An Error Structure for Systems of Translog Cost and Share Equations," unpublished manuscript.
Schmidt, P. 1984b. "Estimation of a Fixed-Effect Cobb-Douglas System Using Panel Data," unpublished manuscript.
Schmidt, P. 1985. "Frontier Production Functions." *Econometric Reviews* 4(2):
Schmidt, P., and C. A. K. Lovell. 1979. "Estimating Technical and Allocative Inefficiency Relative to Stochastic Production and Cost Frontiers." *Journal of Econometrics* 9 (February): 343–366.
Schmidt, P., and C. A. K. Lovell. 1980. "Estimating Stochastic Production and Cost Frontiers when Technical and Allocative Inefficiency Are Correlated." *Journal of Econometrics* 13 1 (May): 83–100.
Schmidt, P., and R. Sickles. 1984. "Production Frontiers and Panel Data." *Journal of Business and Economic Statistics* 2(4): 367–374.
Seitz, W. D. 1970. "The Measurement of Efficiency Relative to a Frontier Production Function." *American Journal of Agricultural Economics* 52(4): 505–511.
Seitz, W. D. 1971. "Productive Efficiency in the Steam-Electric Generating Industry." *Journal of Political Economy* 79(4): 878–886.
Sengupta, J. K. 1982. "Efficiency Measurement in Stochastic Input-Output Systems." *International Journal of System Sciences* 13(3): 273–287.
Sickles, R. C. 1985. "Allocative Inefficiency in the Airline Industry: A Case for Deregulation." This volume, ch. 6.
Sickles, R. C., D. Good, and R. Johnson. 1985. "On Characterizing the Regulatory Transition of the U.S. Airline Industry," unpublished manuscript.
Solow, R. M. 1957. "Technical Change and the Aggregate Production Function." *Review of Economics and Statistics* 39(3): 312–320.

Stevenson, R. E. 1980. "Likelihood Functions for Generalized Stochastic Frontier Functions." *Journal of Econometrics* 13(1): 57–66.

Stigler, G. J. 1978. "The Xistence of X-Efficiency," *American Economic Review* 68(1): 213–216.

Teusch, W. 1983. *Aufbau and Bewinnung Shephardscher Produkfionsfunktionen unter Berücksichtigung empirischer Aspekte,* Mathematical Systems in Economics Vol. 78. Althenäum, Hain, Hanstein: Verlagsgruppe.

Timmer, C. P. 1971. "Using a Probabilistic Frontier Production Function to Measure Technical Efficiency." *Journal of Political Economy* 79(4): 776–794.

Toda, Y. 1976. "Estimation of a Cost Function When the Cost Is Not Minimum: The Case of Soviet Manufacturing Industries, 1958–71." *Review of Economics and Statistics* 58(3): 259–268.

Toda, Y. 1977. "Substitutability and Price Distortion in the Demand for Factors of Production: An Empirical Estimation." *Applied Economics* 9(2): 203–217.

Tyler, W. G., and L. -F. Lee. 1979. "On Estimating Stochastic Frontier Production Functions and Average Efficiency: An Empirical Analysis with Columbian Micro Data." *Review of Economics and Statistics* 61(3): 436–438.

van den Broeck, J. 1983. "Stochastic 'Frontier' Inefficiency and Firm Size for Selected Industries of the Belgian Manufacturing Sector: Some New Evidence," unpublished manuscript.

van den Broeck, J., F. R. Försund, L. Hjalmarsson, and W. Meeusen. 1980. "On the Estimation of Deterministic and Stochastic Frontier Production Functions: A Comparison." *Journal of Econometrics* 13 (May): 117–138.

Varian, H. R. 1984a. "The Nonparametric Approach to Production Analysis." *Econometrica* 52(3): 579–597.

Varian, H. R. 1984b. "Nonparametric Analysis of Optimizing Behavior with Measurement Error," unpublished manuscript.

Zieschang, K. D. 1982. "Recovering Indices of Technical Efficiency from the Cost Function," unpublished manuscript.

Zieschang, K. D. 1983a. "A Note on the Decomposition of Cost Efficiency into Technical and Allocative Components." *Journal of Econometrics* 23 (December): 401–405.

Zieschang, K. D. 1983b. "Measuring Technical Efficiency in DEA Models," unpublished manuscript.

Zieschang, K. D. 1984. "An Extended Farrell Technical Efficiency Measure." *Journal of Economic Theory* 33 (August): 387–396.

2 A COMPARISON OF DEA AND TRANSLOG ESTIMATES OF PRODUCTION FRONTIERS USING SIMULATED OBSERVATIONS FROM A KNOWN TECHNOLOGY

Rajiv D. Banker
Abraham Charnes
William W. Cooper
Ajay Maindiratta

2.1. Introduction

Data envelopment analysis (DEA), introduced in Charnes, Cooper, and Rhodes (1978), provides a new approach to the estimation of relative efficiencies of decision making units (DMUs). As described by Banker (1980b) and Banker, Charnes, and Cooper (1984), DEA also encompasses estimation of production frontiers making minimal assumptions—such as convexity—about the production possibility set. DEA may be employed to estimate technical and scale efficiencies as in Banker, Charnes, and Cooper, rates of substitution between inputs as in Banker, Charnes, and Cooper and Charnes, Cooper, and Rhodes (1978), and returns to scale and most productive scale sizes as in Banker (1984) and Banker, Charnes, and Cooper (1984). These estimates of different production characteristics pertain to the efficient production surface, unlike the commonly employed regression techniques which estimate the average production correspondence. In this chapter, we report on the results of a simulation study

This research was supported in part by ONR Contract 1-51123 at Carnegie-Mellon University's School of Urban and Public Affairs.

in which DEA was employed to estimate the production frontier from input and output data randomly generated from a known technology.

Some recent work in econometrics has also focused on the estimation of frontier production functions.[1] One branch of work pertains to stochastic frontier estimation. But here we encounter problems with lengthy algorithms for estimation and difficulty in isolating estimates for individual observations. The second branch of work pertains to full frontier estimation without a two-sided disturbance term. We report the results of such full-frontier estimation employing a translog "flexible" function and the same set of input-output data. We also compare the results of the two estimation methods with the "known" underlying technology from which the input and output observations were randomly generated.

We shall first describe the simulation model and the two estimation models. We shall then compare the estimates of technical efficiency, returns to scale, and rates of substitution obtained by employing the two methods, with the "true" values of these parameters obtained from the known technology. In our study we find that the nonparametric DEA performs better than the parametric translog estimation when an underlying piecewise loglinear technology is employed. A similar pattern of relative performance was also observed on repeating the study with an underlying translog technology.

2.2. The Simulation Model

The simulation data for our study were generated from a known technology with one output and two inputs.[2] The technology may be specified by means of its efficient production function $Q = f(K,L)$ where Q represents the maximum output that can be produced from levels K and L of the two inputs. The efficient production function employed in this study is represented by a piecewise loglinear function:

$$Q = \begin{cases} 0.631K^{0.65}L^{0.55} & \text{for } 5 \leqslant K \leqslant 10,\ 5 \leqslant L \leqslant 10 \\ 0.794K^{0.65}L^{0.45} & \text{for } 5 \leqslant K \leqslant 10,\ 10 \leqslant L \leqslant 15 \\ 1.259K^{0.35}L^{0.55} & \text{for } 10 \leqslant K \leqslant 15,\ 5 \leqslant L \leqslant 10 \\ 1.585K^{0.35}L^{0.45} & \text{for } 10 \leqslant K \leqslant 15,\ 10 \leqslant L \leqslant 15 \end{cases} \tag{2.1}$$

The actual output level Y can be derived from the expression $Y = eQ$, where e represents the output efficiency.[3]

We randomly generated 500 observations for the inputs K and L from the uniform probability distribution over the interval [5,15]. These values $K_j, L_j, j = 1, \ldots, 500$, were then substituted in the efficient production function specified in equation (2.1) to obtain the corresponding values $Q_j = f(K_j, L_j)$ for the efficient output quantity. Next we randomly generated the efficiency values e_j from the probability distribution defined by

$$\Pr\{e_j = 1\} = 0.3 \qquad \Pr\{0.65 \leqslant e_j < 1\} = 0.7 \tag{2.2}$$

with the specific values of e_j when $e_j < 1$ being obtained from the uniform distribution of the interval [0.65,1). These values of e_j and Q_j were then employed to generate the values for actual output quantities $Y_j, j = 1, \ldots, 500$.

The functional specification in equation (2.1) was also employed to compute production characteristics such as rate of substitution between inputs, returns to scale, and most productive scale size for each of the 500 observations. Because the production function is *piecewise* loglinear, the values of the exponent α for the input K and the exponent β for the input L depend on the specific values of K_j and L_j for each observation. The rate of substitution of L for K is given by $-(\beta/\alpha)\ (K_j/L_j)$ with the appropriate values being chosen for the exponents α and β. The returns to scale prevailing locally for each input mix corresponding to the 500 observations are determined by the sign of $\rho = \alpha + \beta - 1$. If $\rho > 0$ then we have local increasing returns to scale and if $\rho < 0$ then we have local decreasing returns to scale. It is therefore evident from the definition of production function in equation (2.1) that for $5 < K < 10$ we have increasing returns to scale and for $10 < K < 15$ we have decreasing returns to scale.

The concept of returns to scale is closely related to the concept of the most productive scale size (mpss). This relation is discussed and further developed by Banker (1984) for the case of multiple inputs and multiple outputs. Returns to scale and mpss are characteristics of the production function and are independent of input and output prices. Both concepts are defined for specific input and output mixes. In other words, for the case of multiple inputs and multiple outputs, we need to fix the input mix and the output mix in order to examine returns to scale and mpss for specific mixes. The mpss is defined by Banker (1984) as the scale size that maximizes the productivity for a given mix of inputs and outputs. More rigorously, for a specific input mix represented by a vector X_0 and output mix represented by a vector Y_0, we define the mpss as the scale size that maximizes the ratio of scalars y/x, where yY_0 are outputs that can be produced from the inputs xX_0 with the given technology.

In the regions 2 and 3 of figure 2-1, the input mixes are such that the relative proportion of K to L is between 2/3 and 2. For each such input mix,

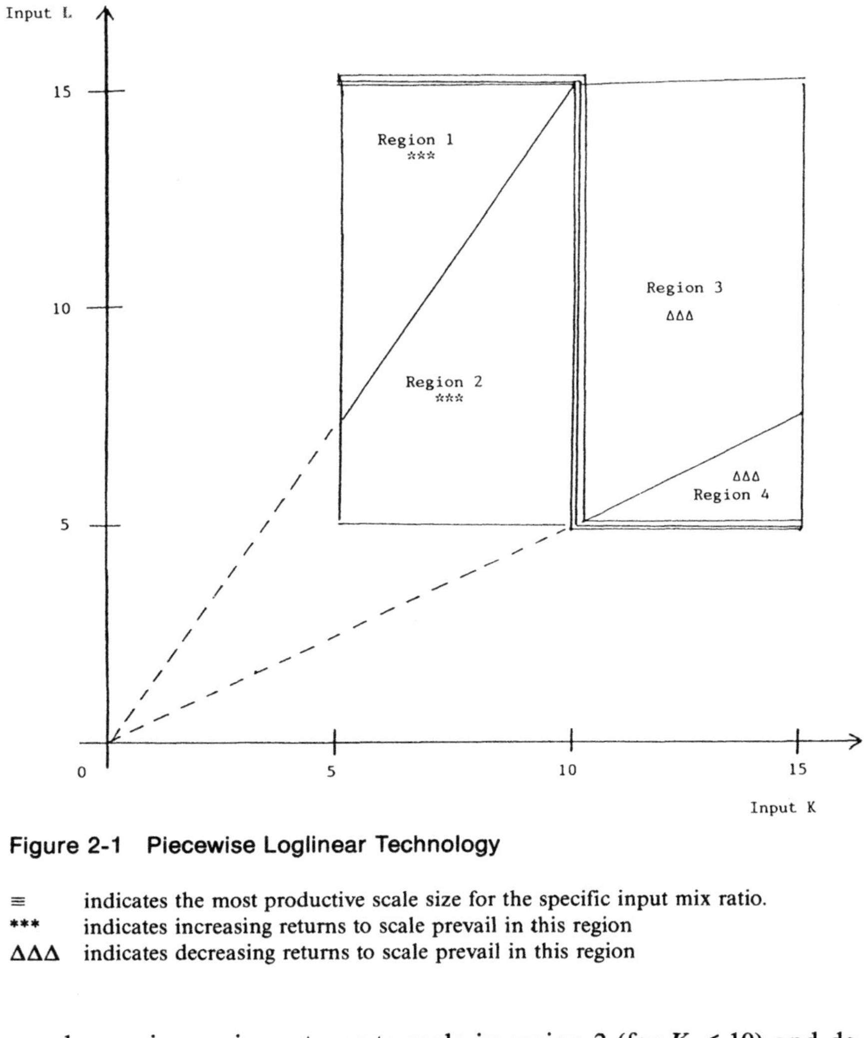

Figure 2-1 Piecewise Loglinear Technology

≡ indicates the most productive scale size for the specific input mix ratio.
*** indicates increasing returns to scale prevail in this region
ΔΔΔ indicates decreasing returns to scale prevail in this region

we observe increasing returns to scale in region 2 (for $K_j < 10$) and decreasing returns to scale in region 3 (for $K_j > 10$). Therefore, the mpss measured for the input K is equal to 10 when the relative proportion of K to L is between 2/3 and 2. Next, for input mixes with $K_j/L_j < 2/3$, we observe increasing returns to scale only in region 1 because the production possibility set is bounded above by $L = 15$. Therefore, in these cases the mpss measured for the input K is given by the expression 15 K_j/L_j. Similarly, when the input mixes are such that $K_j/L_j > 2$, the mpss measured for the input K is given by $5K_j/L_j$ because the production possibility set is bounded below by $L = 5$.

An observation is scale efficient if and only if it is operating at the most productive scale size for its input and output mix.[4] Since probability mass at any point in the domain of our uniform probability distributions for generating the values for inputs K and L is zero, we chose to specify a range around the theoretical mpss for categorizing an observation as scale efficient. In particular, an observation (K_j, L_j) in our simulation is considered scale efficient if and only if $0.975K^* \leqslant K_j \leqslant 1.025K^*$, where the mpss K^* measured for input K is defined by:

$$\begin{aligned} K^* &= 15K_j/L_j && \text{for } K_j/L_j < 2/3 \\ &= 10 && \text{for } 2/3 \leqslant K_j/L_j \leqslant 2 \\ &= 5K_j/L_j && \text{for } 2 < K_j/L_j \end{aligned}$$

2.3. The Estimation Models

An axiomatic development of the application of DEA to the estimation of production frontiers is presented in Banker (1980b) and Banker, Charnes, and Cooper (1984). The production possibility set $T = \{(X, Y) |$ the outputs Y can be produced from the inputs $X\}$ is postulated to have the following three properties:

Postulate 1: Convexity:

If $(X_j, Y_j) \in T, j = 1, \ldots, n$, and $\lambda_j \geqslant 0$ are nonnegative scalars such that

$$\sum_{j=1}^{n} \lambda_j = 1,$$

then

$$\left(\sum_{j=1}^{n} \lambda_j X_j, \sum_{j=1}^{n} \lambda_j Y_j\right) \in T$$

Postulate 2: Inefficiency Postulate:

(a) If $(X, Y) \in T$ and $\bar{X} \geqslant X$, then $(\bar{X}, Y) \in T$.
(b) If $(X, Y) \in T$ and $\bar{Y} \leqslant Y$, then $(X, \bar{Y}) \in T$.

Postulate 3: Minimum Extrapolation:

> T is the intersection set of all $\hat{T}$ satisfying the earlier postulates, and subject to the condition that each of the observed vectors $(X_j,Y_j) \in \hat{T}, j = 1,\ldots,n$.

If T satisfies the above three postulates, then T can be expressed as

$$T = \left\{(X,Y) \mid X \geqslant \sum_{j=1}^{n} \mu_j X_j,\ Y \leqslant \sum_{j=1}^{n} \mu_j Y_j,\ \ \sum_{j=1}^{n} \mu_j = 1,\ \mu_j \geqslant 0\right\}$$

The technical efficiency of an observation (X_0,Y_0) is a ratio measure reflecting the distance of this point from the production frontier measured along a ray from the origin.[5] This output efficiency measure $e_0^* = (f_0^*)^{-1}$ is evaluated by the following linear programming formulation:[6]

$$\min f_0 = VX_0 + v_0 \tag{2.3}$$

subject to

$$UY_0 = 1$$

$$UY_j - VX_j + v_0 \leqslant 0, \qquad j = 1,\ldots,n \qquad (v_0 \text{ is unconstrained in sign})$$

$$U \geqslant \varepsilon E^s,\ V \geqslant \varepsilon E^m$$

where $\varepsilon > 0$ is a small non-Archimedean number, $E^s \equiv (1,\ldots,1)$ and $Y_j \geqslant 0$ are s-dimensional vectors, and $E^m \equiv (1,\ldots,1)$ and $X_j \geqslant 0$ are m-dimensional vectors.

The maximum value of $e_0^* = (f_0^*)^{-1}$, obtained from the programming problem (2.3), measures the purely technical efficiency of (X_0,Y_0) at its present scale of operations. The following programming problem can be formulated to measure the combined effect of both technical and scale efficiencies:[7]

$$\max g_0 = z_0 + \varepsilon\left[\sum_{r=1}^{s} d_r + \sum_{i=1}^{m} s_i\right] \tag{2.4}$$

subject to

$$\sum_{j=1}^{n} \lambda_j x_{ij} + s_i = \quad x_{i0}, \qquad i = 1,\ldots,m$$

$$\sum_{j=1}^{n} \lambda_j y_{rj} - d_r = z_0 y_{r0}, \qquad r = 1, \ldots, s$$

$$z_0, \lambda_j, s_i, d_r \geqslant 0$$

and $\varepsilon > 0$ is a small non-Archimedean number.

The combined technical and scale efficiencies are measured by h_0^*, the inverse of the maximum value g_0^* obtained from the programming problem in (2.4). The purely scale efficiency can then be estimated as $\Psi_0^* = h_0^*/e_0^*$.

The two programming formulations in (2.3) and (2.4) permit multiple inputs and multiple outputs. For the purpose of our simulation study we have the number of inputs $m = 2$ and the number of outputs $s = 1$. In particular, we write the vector V in (2.3) as (v_K, v_L) where v_K is the coefficient for the consumption of input K and v_L is the coefficient for the consumption of input L. In Banker (1980b) and Banker, Charnes, and Cooper (1984) it is shown that $U^*Y - V^*X + v_0^* = 0$ (where U^*, v_0^* and V^* are the optimal values of U, v_0, and V in (2.3)) is the equation representing a supporting hyperplane tangential to the production possibility set at the technically efficient point corresponding to the observation (X_0, Y_0) evaluated in (2.3). Therefore, the rate of substitution of L for K can be estimated as $-v_K^*/v_L^*$.

The returns to scale can be identified as increasing or decreasing on the basis of the sign of $\rho_0^* = 1 - \Sigma_{j=1}^{n} \lambda_j^*$ where λ_j^* are the optimal values of λ_j in (2.4); or equivalently on the basis of the sign of v_0^* obtained from (2.3). A positive value for ρ_0^* and v_0^* indicates that there exist local increasing returns to scale and a negative sign indicates that there exist local decreasing returns to scale. If $\rho_0^* = v_0^* = 0$, then local constant returns to scale are indicated. The estimate of the mpss for a specific output and input mix is given by $(z_0^*/\Sigma_{j=1}^{n} \lambda_j^*)K_0$ when measured in terms of the input K in our simulation model.

The second estimation procedure employed in our simulation study is a direct adaptation of the COLS method suggested by Richmond (1974) and discussed by Försund, Lovell, and Schmidt (1980). We use a translog parametric function defined by:

$$\ln Y_j = \alpha_0 + \alpha_k \ln K_j + \alpha_L \ln L_j + \tfrac{1}{2}\beta_{KK}(\ln K_j)^2 + \beta_{KL}(\ln K_j)(\ln L_j) + \tfrac{1}{2}\beta_{LL}(\ln L_j)^2 - u_j \qquad (2.5)$$

The parameters of (2.5) are estimated first by ordinary least squares (OLS) method, and then the constant term α_0 is "corrected" by shifting it up until no residual u_j is positive and at least one is zero. The procedure provides a consistent estimate of all the parameters.

The technical efficiency is estimated as the ratio of the actual output value Y_j divided by the predicted output value obtained from the estimated parametric values for (2.5). The rate of substitution of L for K is measured by the expression

$$-\frac{K_j}{L_j}\frac{(\alpha_L^* + \beta_{KL}^* \ln K + \beta_{LL}^* \ln L)}{(\alpha_K^* + \beta_{KK}^* \ln K + \beta_{KL}^* \ln L)}$$

where

$$\alpha_K^*, \alpha_L^*, \beta_{KK}^*, \beta_{KL}^*, \quad \text{and} \quad \beta_{LL}^*$$

are the OLS estimates for the corresponding parameters. Finally, the returns to scale are estimated to be increasing if

$$\alpha_K^* + \alpha_L^* + (\beta_{KK}^* + \beta_{KL}^*) \ln K + (\beta_{KL}^* + \beta_{LL}^*) \ln L$$

is greater than one and the returns to scale are decreasing if this expression is less than one. However, these estimates are likely to be unreliable if there is a collinearity problem in estimating (2.5).

2.4. Efficiency Estimates

The technical efficiencies of individual observations were estimated by the DEA approach and also the parametric approach using a translog function; first for a sample of 500 randomly generated observations and then for the set consisting of the first 100 of these 500 observations. The absolute value of the difference between estimated and actual efficiencies was computed for each observation. The mean absolute deviations are reported in table 2-1.

Table 2-1. Mean Absolute Difference Between Estimated and Actual Technical Efficiencies

	$n = 0.500$	$n = 100$
DEA	0.0032	0.0100
Translog	0.0237	0.0444

The DEA technical efficiency estimates on the average differ by only 0.01 from the actual efficiencies in the case of the smaller sample size with 100 observations. For the larger sample size of 500 observations, DEA performs even better with the average absolute difference being only 0.003. This evidence is consistent with a consistency property for the DEA

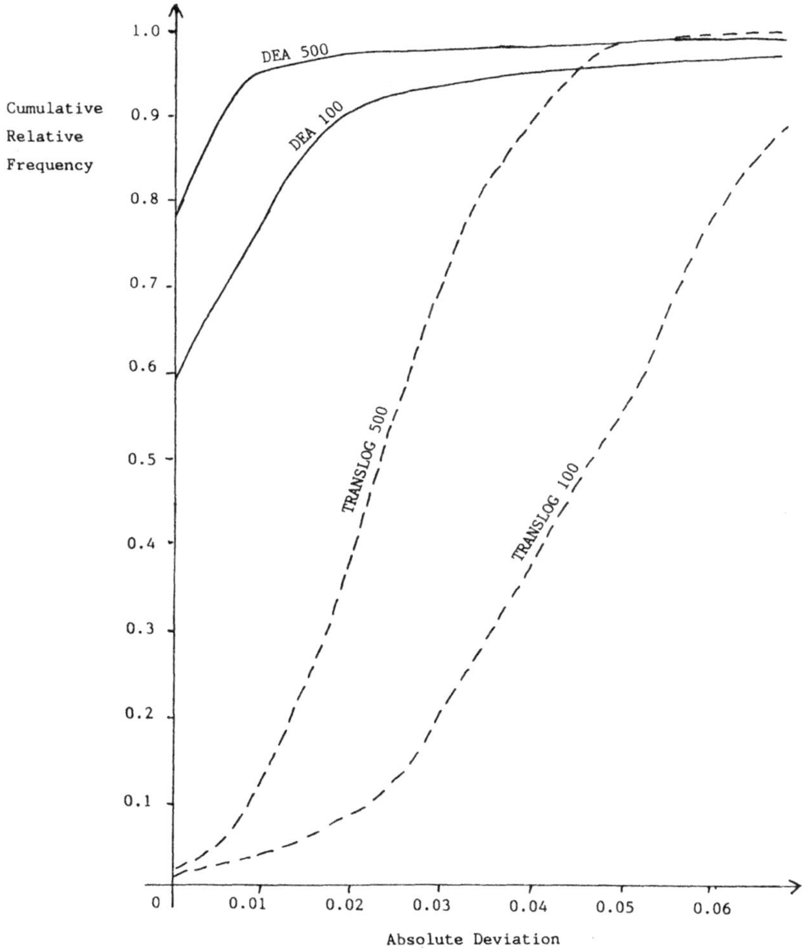

Figure 2-2 Cumulative Distributions for Absolute Differences Between Estimated and Actual Efficiencies
Piecewise Loglinear Technology

technical efficiency estimates. Furthermore, the DEA procedure also outperforms the parametric translog approach in both cases. Both these results are also strikingly apparent from figure 2-2 where we have plotted the cumulative distributions for the absolute deviations for the two procedures for both sample sizes.

DEA also enables us to estimate both technical and scale efficiencies. A value of one for the efficiency measure in the CCR formulation in (2.4) indicates that the observation is both technical and scale efficient. A value of one for the efficiency measuring the BCC formulation in (2.3) indicates that the observation is technically efficient. The data in table 2-2 and table 2-3 indicate that this criterion performs well in identifying observations that are both technical and scale efficient or only technically efficient.

The DEA procedure classified the efficient points correctly in almost all cases. The misclassifications occur for "corner" points—points for which one of the inputs or the outputs has a very small or very large value. For the purpose of our simulation model, we define a "corner" point as an observation with at least one of the inputs less than 5.5 or more than 14.5. The "corner" points tend to get erroneously classified as efficient by DEA because there are not an adequate number of referent points to compare with a "corner" point to establish its inefficiency. A similar result is proved in a corollary by Banker (1980a).

2.5. Estimates of Other Production Characteristics

The estimates of rates of substitutions obtained from the BCC formulation in (2.3) differ from the actual values by about 15% on the average for the smaller sample of 100 observations and by about 8% for the larger sample of 500 observations. This evidence is also consistent with the consistency property of these estimates. Furthermore, the DEA procedure outperforms the parametric translog method, as can be seen from the data in table 2-4. These results are also evident from the cumulative distributions of absolute percentage deviations plotted in figure 2-3.

The estimation results for returns to scale were generally favorable. A scrutiny of these data in table 2-5 reveals that the proportion of observations misclassified by DEA methods is considerably less than the proportion of observations misclassified by the parametric translog method. Furthermore, the proportion misclassified by DEA when $n = 500$ is also substantially less than the proportion misclassified when $n = 100$.

DEA also enables us to estimate the mpss for specific input and output mixes. The mean absolute percentage difference between the actual and

Table 2-2 DEA Efficiency Estimates: $n = 100$

		Technical and Scale Efficient	*Technically Efficient Only*	*Scale Efficient Only*	*Neither Technical Nor Scale Efficient*	
CCR	$h_0^* = 1$	4	4	0	1[b]	9
Estimates	$h_0^* < 1$	0	20	4	67	91
Total		4	24	4	68	100
BCC	$e_0^* = 1$	4	23	0	6[c]	33
Estimates	$e_0^* < 1$	0	1[a]	4	62	67

[a]Efficiency estimate $e_0^* > 0.99$.
[b]Actual technical efficiency > 0.99 and $L = 5.44$
[c]One point with actual technical efficiency > 0.998 and five other "corner" points.

Table 2-3 DEA Efficiency Estimates: (n = 500)

		Technical and Scale Efficient	*Technically Efficient Only*	*Scale Efficient Only*	*Neither Technical Nor Scale Efficient*	
CCR	$h_0^* = 1$	9	4	0	1[b]	14
Estimates	$h_0^* < 1$	5[a]	136	28	317	486
Total		14	140	28	318	500
BCC	$e_0^* = 1$	13	94	1[c]	5[c]	113
Estimates	$e_0^* < 1$	1[a]	46[a]	27	313	387

[a]All observations with efficiency estimate $e_0^* > 0.99$.
[b]Actual technical efficiency > 0.99 and $L = 5.44$
[c]All observations are "corner" points.

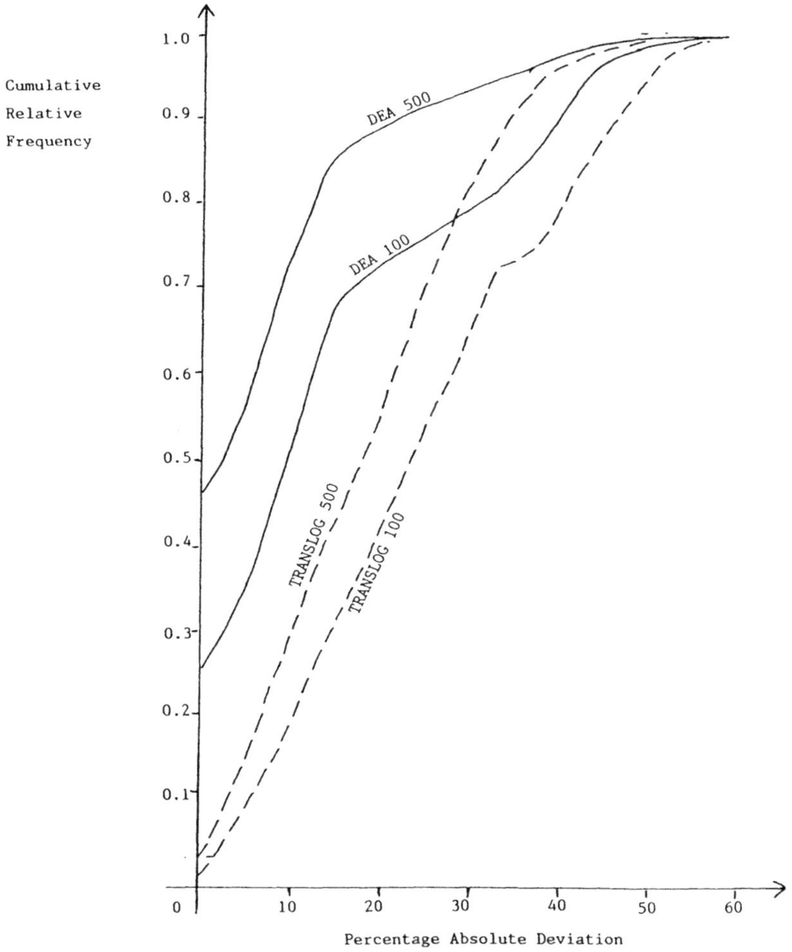

Figure 2-3 Cumulative Distributions for Percentage Absolute Deviations Between Estimated and Actual Marginal Rates of Substitution

estimated mpss was 4.46 for $n = 100$ and 3.68 for $n = 500$. Once again, therefore, DEA provided close estimates for a production characteristic, and the estimation accuracy improved with larger sample size.

We also note that the mpss measured for the input K is equal to 10 for both regions B and C indicated in figure 2-4. Because our production possibility set is bounded, the mpss measured for input K is less for region A

Table 2-4 Mean Absolute Percentage Difference Between Estimated and Actual Rates of Substitution

	$n = 500$	$n = 100$
DEA	8.47	15.19
Translog	18.07	24.27

than for regions B and C, while for region D it is greater than that for regions B and C. The estimation results reported in table 2-6 are consistent with this characteristic of the production possibility set.[8]

2.6. Simulation Study with a Translog Technology

In order to confirm that the relatively superior performance of DEA was not purely an artifact of our choice of technology, we repeated the study with a translog (i.e., log-quadratic) technology, which presumably would be the most favorable circumstances for estimation with a similar parametric translog specification. The underlying translog technology in this case was specified as follows:

$$\ln Q = 0.085 + 0.5 \ln K + 0.44 \ln L + 0.14(\ln K)^2 + 0.09(\ln L)^2 - 0.22(\ln K)(\ln L) \quad \text{for } 5 \leqslant K \leqslant 15,\ 5 \leqslant L \leqslant 15 \tag{2.6}$$

We used the same simulated input observations $K_j,L_j, j = 1,\ldots,500$, as in the piecewise loglinear case, to generate the "efficient" outputs $Q_j = f(K_j,L_j)$, where the efficient production function is now as in (2.6) above. We also used the same simulated output efficiency measures e_j, $j = 1,\ldots,500$, to obtain the "actual" outputs $Y_j, j = 1,\ldots,500$. As in the piecewise loglinear case, we estimated the characteristics of the production frontier for the entire sample of 500 observations and also for the set consisting of the first 100 of the 500 observations. We found that the general pattern of relatively superior performance of DEA continued to prevail in this instance when we used an underlying translog technology. We first report the results of the estimation of the technical efficiencies of individual observations in table 2-7 and figure 2-5. As in the case of an underlying loglinear technology, it is evident that DEA outperforms the parametric translog approach.

Table 2-5 Contingency Tables for Returns-to-Scale Estimates

Translog Estimates:

	Actual		
Estimated	*Increasing*	*Decreasing*	
Inc.	247	81	328
Dec.	0	172	172
	247	253	500

$\chi^2 = 255.98$

	Actual		
Estimated	*Increasing*	*Decreasing*	
Inc.	34	12	46
Dec.	8	46	54
	42	58	100

$\chi^2 = 35.61$

DEA Estimates:

	Actual		
	Increasing	*Decreasing*	
$\rho_0^* > 0$	229	11	240
$\rho_0^* = 0$	9	5	14
$\rho_0^* < 0$	9	237	246
	247	253	500

$\chi^2 = 410.46$

	Actual		
	Increasing	*Decreasing*	
$\rho_0^* > 0$	33	4	37
$\rho_0^* = 0$	5	4	9
$\rho_0^* < 0$	4	50	54
	42	58	100

$\chi^2 = 61.03$

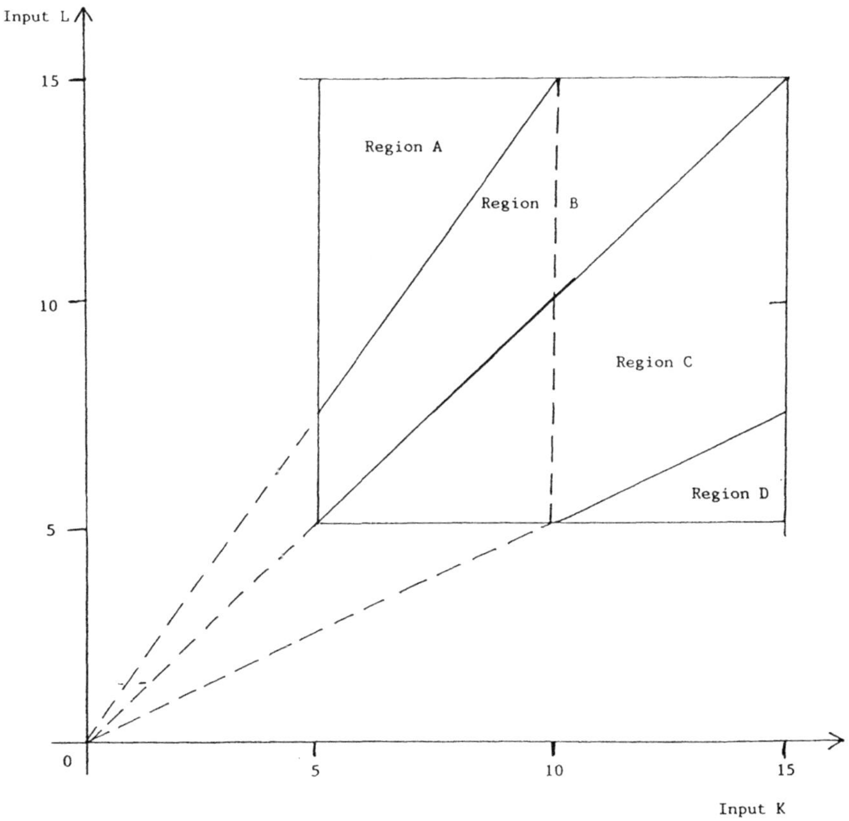

Figure 2-4 Piecewise Loglinear Technology

Region A: $\text{mpss}_K = 15K_j/L_j$
Region B: $\text{mpss}_K = 10$
Region C: $\text{mpss}_K = 10$
Region D: $\text{mpss}_K = 5K_j/L_j$

The results for the estimation of the rates of substitution are reported in table 2-8 and figure 2-6. We observe from table 2-8 that for the case of the 500-observation sample, the mean absolute percentage difference with DEA is greater than with translog estimation. This might indicate an overall poorer performance for DEA, but figure 2-6 reveals that the mean absolute percentage difference with DEA is high because of poor estimates for only a few points. For over 95% of the observations, the ab-

Table 2-6 Estimates of Most Productive Scale Size Measured for Input K

a. Sample of 100 Observations:

Region	*Number of Observations*	*Mean*	*Standard Deviation*	*Median*
A	6	7.76	1.04	7.91
B	38	9.83	0.20	9.83
C	49	9.71	0.59	9.36
D	7	11.96	1.56	11.05

Comparison of Regions	*Welch's Mean Test*		*Mann-Whitney Test*
	t	*P*	*P*
A and B	−4.841	0.0047	0.0001
A and C	−4.491	0.0065	0.0001
A and D	−5.784	<0.0001	0.0034
A and C	1.284	0.2041	0.1530
B and D	−3.625	0.0110	<0.0001
C and D	−3.789	0.0091	0.0001

b. Sample of 500 Observations:

Region	*Number of Observations*	*Mean*	*Standard Deviation*	*Median*
A	78	7.56	1.34	7.89
B	177	9.73	0.31	9.81
C	217	9.83	0.45	9.84
D	28	11.45	1.23	10.98

Comparison of Regions	*Welch's Mean Test*		*Mann-Whitney Test*
	t	*P*	*P*
A and B	−14.109	<0.0001	<0.0001
A and C	−14.646	<0.0001	<0.0001
A and D	−13.982	<0.0001	<0.0001
B and C	−2.646	0.0085	0.0500
B and D	−7.359	<0.0001	<0.0001
C and D	−6.902	<0.0001	<0.0001

Table 2-7 Mean Absolute Difference Between Estimated and Actual Technical Efficiencies

	n = 500	*n = 100*
DEA	0.0054	0.0064
Translog	0.0141	0.0493

solute percentage difference between the estimated and actual rates of substitution is less for DEA than for the parametric translog approach. In fact, DEA performs poorly for observations that fall in the region where the "true" production function is nonconcave and, correspondingly, the production possibility set is nonconvex, violating the convexity axiom in DEA.

A similar explanation applies also to the results of the estimation of returns to scale reported in table 2-9. Even though DEA performs better than the parametric translog estimation for the 500-observation sample, the proportion misclassified is somewhat higher with DEA for the smaller sample of 100 observations. In any case, we also note that the DEA results improve with a larger sample, whereas the translog estimation results are worse for the larger sample.

2.7. Conclusion

Data envelopment analysis fits pieces of hyperplanes to envelop the observed input–output data. This piecewise linear production function is more flexible in approximating the true production frontier than is the so-called flexible translog parametric functional form. The simulation results reported in this study also bear out this ability of DEA. Furthermore, the accuracy of DEA estimates improved for the larger sample size, suggesting that these estimates exhibit a consistency property.

The DEA models were also almost perfect in classifying observations that are both technically and scale efficient (CCR model) and observations that are technically efficient (BCC model). We are also able to state a priori that the observations that are likely to be misclassified as efficient by the DEA models are "corner" points with a very small or very large quantity for at least one of the inputs or the outputs, because of the inadequacy of referent points in the "corners" of a production possibility

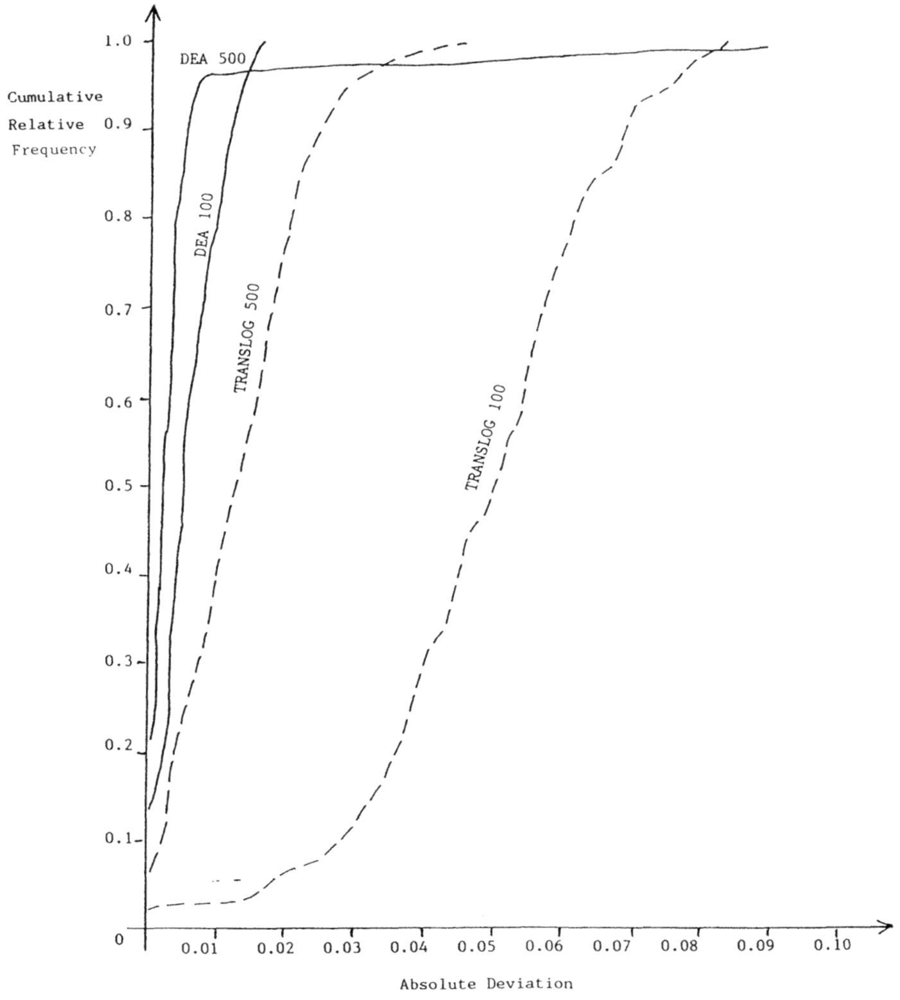

Figure 2-5 Cumulative Distributions for Absolute Differences Between Estimated and Actual Efficiencies Translog Technology

Table 2-8 Mean Absolute Percentage Difference Between Estimated and Actual Rates of Substitution

	n = 500	*n = 100*
DEA	19.82	12.49
Translog	12.48	24.33

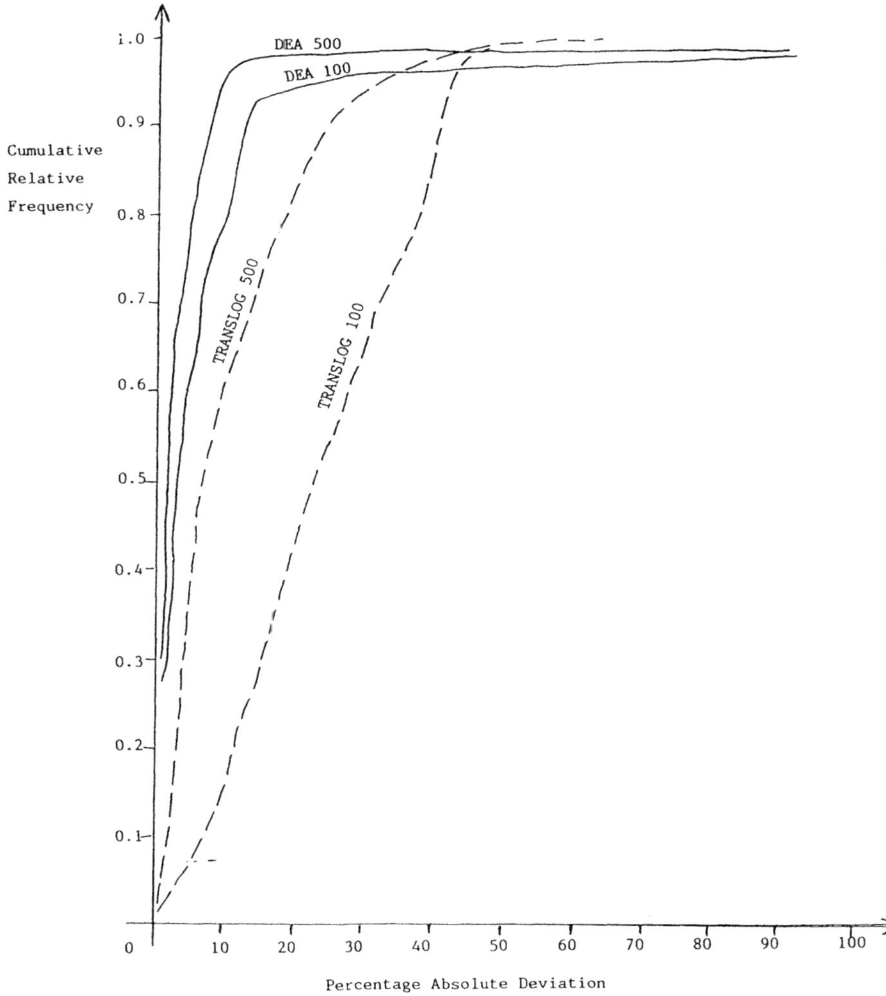

Figure 2-6 Cumulative Distributions for Absolute Differences Between Estimated and Actual Marginal Rates of Substitution Translog Technology

Table 2-9 Contingency Tables for Returns to Scale Estimates Translog Technology

a. Translog Estimates:

	Actual		
Estimated	*Inc.*	*Dec.*	
Inc.	34	14	48
Dec.	0	52	52
	34	66	100

	Actual		
Estimated	*Inc.*	*Dec.*	
Inc.	131	202	333
Dec.	0	167	167
	131	369	500

b. DEA Estimates:

	Actual		
Estimated	*Inc.*	*Dec.*	
Inc.	10	7	17
Con.	2	3	5
Dec.	22	56	78
	34	66	100

	Actual		
Estimated	*Inc.*	*Dec.*	
Inc.	29	16	45
Con.	3	5	8
Dec.	99	348	447
	131	369	500

set. Therefore, we not only know when DEA estimates are reliable, but also the few cases when they are not as reliable.

Notes

1. See Försund, Lovell, and Schmidt (1980) for a survey of this literature.
2. We report the results for only two different technologies. Our experience with other technologies with different parametric values for the production function and the distribution of technical efficiencies has been similar to the two cases reported here. However, to formally assess the robustness of these results a larger Monte Carlo study will be required.
3. See Färe and Lovell (1978) for a discussion of output and input efficiencies.
4. This definition is based purely on the production correspondence between the inputs and the outputs, and is independent of actual input and output prices, since prices tend to vary more than the purely technological parameters. This definition is in contrast to the usual definition in economics where the reference point is the profit-maximizing input-outuput configuration.

5. The relation of this measure with Shephard's (1953) distance function is discussed in Banker (1980b) and Banker, Charnes, and Cooper (1984).

6. We shall refer to the linear programming problem in equation (2.3) as the BCC formulation.

7. This formulation corresponds to the dual of the original efficiency evaluation measure suggested in Charnes, Cooper, and Rhodes (1978). We shall refer to the programming problem in (2.4) as the CCR formulation.

8. It should be noted, however, that the results of the Welch's Mean Test and the Mann-Whitney Test are reported in the spirit of descriptive statistics. They should not be interpreted in their usual inferential mode because the assumptions regarding the independence of the sample values will be violated.

References

Banker, R. D. 1980a. "A Game Theoretic Approach to Measuring Efficiency, *European Journal of Operational Research.* 5: 262–266.

Banker, R. D. 1980b. *Studies in Cost Allocation and Efficiency Evaluation.* Unpublished doctoral thesis, Harvard University, Graduate School of Business Administration.

Banker, R. D. 1985. "Productivity Measurement and Management Control." In P. Kleindorfer (ed.), *The Management of Productivity and Technology in Manufacturing.* New York: Plenum.

Banker, R. D. 1984. "Estimating Most Productive Scale Size Using Data Envelopment Analysis." *European Journal of Operational Research.* 17: 35–44.

Banker, R. D., A. Charnes, and W. W. Cooper. 1984. "Estimation of Technical and Scale Inefficiencies in Data Envelopment Analysis." *Management Science,* 30: 1078–1092.

Banker, R. D., A. Charnes, W. W. Cooper, and A. Schinnar. 1981. "A Bi-Extremal Principle for Frontier Estimation and Efficiency Evaluations." *Management Science* 27(12): 1370–1382.

Banker, R. D., R. F. Conrad, and R. P. Strauss. "A Comparative Application of Data Envelopment Analysis and Translog Methods." *Management Science,* 32(1): 30–43.

Banker, R. D., and A. Maindiratta. 1986. "Piece-wise Loglinear Estimation of Production Frontiers," *Management Science,* 32(1): 126–135.

Banker, R. D., and R. Morey. 1986. "Efficiency Analysis for Exogeneously Fixed Inputs and Outputs." *Operations Research,* July–August, 34.

Banker, R. D., and R. Morey. 1986. "Data Envelopment Analysis with Categorical Inputs and Outputs," *Management Science,* 32(12): 1613–1627.

Charnes, A., W. W. Cooper, and E. Rhodes. 1978. "Measuring the Efficiency of Decision-Making Units." *European Journal of Operational Research* 2(6): 429–444.

Charnes, A., W. W. Cooper, and E. Rhodes. 1979. "Short Communication: Measuring the Efficiency of Decision-Making Units." *European Journal of Operational Research* 3(4): 339.

Charnes, A., W. W. Cooper, and E. Rhodes. 1981. "Evaluating Program and Managerial Efficiency," *Management Science* 27(6): 668–697.

Färe, R., and C. A. K. Lovell. 1978. "Measuring the Technical Efficiency of Production," *Journal of Economic Theory* 19 (October): 150–162.

Farrell, M. J. 1957. "The Measurement of Productive Efficiency." *Journal of the Royal Statistical Society,* ser. A, 120: 253–290.

Farrell, M. J., and M. Fieldhouse. 1962. "Estimating Efficient Production Frontiers Under Increasing Returns to Scale." *Journal of the Royal Statistical Society,* ser. A, 125: 252–267.

Försund, F. R., C. A. K. Lovell, and P. Schmidt. 1980. "A Survey of Frontier Production Functions and of Their Relationship to Efficiency Measurement." *Journal of Econometrics* 13: 5–25.

Lancaster, K. 1968. *Mathematical Economics.* New York: MacMillan.

Mann, M. B., and D. R. Whitney. 1947. "On a Test of Whether One of Two Variables Is Stochastically Larger Than the Other." *Annals of Mathematical Statistics* 18: 50–60.

Menger, Karl. 1954. "The Laws of Return: A Study in Meta-Economics." In Oskar Morgenstern (ed.), *Economic Activity Analysis.* New York: Wiley. Part III.

Panzar, J. C., and R. D. Willig. 1977. "Economies of Scale in Multi-Output Production." *Quarterly Journal of Economics* 91(3): 481–493.

Richmond, J. 1974. "Estimating the Efficiency of Production," *International Economic Review* 15: 515–521.

Shephard, R. W. 1953. *Cost and Production Functions.* Princeton, NJ: Princeton University Press.

Shephard, R. W. 1970. *The Theory of Cost and Production Functions.* Princeton, NJ: Princeton University Press.

Welch, B. L. 1937. "The Significance of the Difference Between Two Means When the Population Variances are Unequal." *Biometrika* 29: 350–362.

Wilcoxon, F. 1947. "Individual Comparisons by Ranking Methods." *Biometrics Bulletin* 80–83.

This research was supported in part by ONR Contract 1-51123 at Carnegie Mellon University School of Urban and Public Affairs and by NSF Grant SES 8408134 with the Center for Cybernetic Studies at the University of Texas. It was also partly supported by the IC^2 Institute of the University of Texas at Austin. Reproduction in whole or in part is permitted for any purpose of the United States Government.

PART TWO

3 STOCHASTIC FRONTIER INEFFICIENCY AND FIRM SIZE FOR SELECTED INDUSTRIES OF THE BELGIAN MANUFACTURING SECTOR: SOME NEW EVIDENCE.*

Julien van den Broeck

3.1. Introduction

Since the seminal article of M. Farrell about relative production efficiency in 1957, several researchers have studied the possibilities of estimating the potential production (frontier) of a firm, given a certain amount of production factors and the state of technology. This interest in defining the production frontier had been inspired by a concern to know exactly the level of actual production in relation to the production frontier and from this how to reach this frontier by increasing the total productivity of the firm under consideration. It was Farrell's enormous contribution to develop a method that not only measured the production frontier but also abandoned the partial productivity approach by substituting for it a total productivity method. All the effects of production could now be taken into consideration. Once this step had been taken economists focused their efforts on measurement problems of the production frontier and the connected efficiency measure.

*We wish to thank Willem Buijink for providing the data and Wim Meeusen and Jan De Sitter for their valuable programming and computational assistance.

Two distinctive approaches to the relative production frontier can be considered: the deterministic and the stochastic. With the aid of programming techniques the deterministic method has been used to calculate the production frontier for a whole set of firms and—what is very important—the individual efficiency measure for each firm (e.g. Försund and Hjalmarsson 1979; Timmer 1971).

Highly efficient and inefficient firms can be immediately located. A serious disadvantage of this method, however, is the neglect of the statistical error, so that its results become debatable. It appears unreasonable to consider the total error as inefficiency because measurement errors, specification errors, and so on, are also a part of this error, which will impair the result of the measurements. The stochastic approach to the relative production frontier does take into consideration this statistical error and uses a production model with a composed error (Aigner, Lovell, and Schmidt 1977; Meeusen and van den Broeck 1977a). This method filters out the statistical error and calculates a less biased efficiency measure. However, the outlier problem still remains an important one. At this moment (as far as we know) outlier research is still in its experimental phase (cf. van den Broeck 1981) and further research is desirable.

In the first phase of its development a not unimportant disadvantage of the stochastic method seemed to be the impossibility of individualizing the efficiency measure. This difficulty overshadowed the progress made by the stochastic production model. The economists were obliged to choose this method which was mostly adapted to the problem they wanted to study (van den Broeck et al. 1980; Kopp 1981). A start on solving this problem of individual efficiency measurement was provided by the Materov article in 1981 about the full identification of a stochastic production model. A real breakthrough was only achieved with the publication of the article of Jondrow et al. (1982). These authors propose to individualize technical efficiency via a conditional distribution of the efficiency deviation given the total error for each firm. Calculating the mean of this conditional distribution and inserting the total error into it gives us the individual efficiency for each observation.

I think it is now about time to emphasize less the estimation problems (without however minimizing those problems which still have to be tackled such as, for instance, outliers and dynamic aspects of technical efficiency), and more the explanation of the efficiency differences themselves with the aim of increasing total productivity by reducing the inefficient use of the production factors.

The purpose of this article is to estimate individual efficiencies for each in a stochastic way in 14 selected three-digit sectors of Belgian industry in

1978. Linking up with previous investigations using stochastic models (e.g., Meeusen and van den Broeck 1977b; Pitt and Lee 1981) we also try in the first instance to find some relation between technical efficiency and firm size.

Using the assertions made by Leibenstein (1965) in his X-efficiency concept as a possible explanation of efficiency differences, it seems reasonable to us to analyze the relationship between efficiency and firm size as a first approach because we assume the latter to be an aggregate for the Leibenstein (1966) phenomena (such as human relations, bureaucracy, motivation) before introducing possible other variables in further work.

3.2. The Model

For the reasons explained earlier we employ a stochastic model that, next to a disturbance term due to inefficiency, contains a statistical disturbance due to randomness, specification, and measurement error. Based on our previous investigation of the Belgian manufacturing sector (van den Broeck 1978) we adopt the generalized Cobb-Douglas production function as a production model for describing the "frontier"

$$Y_i = e^{v_i} e^{-u_i} A \prod_j x_{ij}^{\alpha_j}, \qquad i \in N \tag{3.1}$$

where

- y_i represents actual output, x_{ij} are the inputs and N is the index-set of observations.
- e^{v_i} is a disturbance in the proper sense and is distributed in the $(0,\infty)$ interval.
- e^{-u_i} is a measure of technical efficiency and is distributed in the $(0,1)$ interval.
- v_i, u_i, and x_{ij} $(j = 1, \ldots, J)$ we assume to be mutually independent.

It is assumed that the v_i's are distributed normally with a zero mean and variance σ^2 and the u_i's are distributed exponentially with a λ mean. The economic justification for this choice can be found in our 1977 article introducing the composed error model (Meeusen and van den Broeck 1977a).

We obtain for the probability density function (pdf) of $w = v - u$

$$f(w) = \frac{1}{2\lambda}\,\mathrm{erf}\,c\left[\frac{\sigma}{\lambda\sqrt{2}} - \frac{w}{\sigma\sqrt{2}}\right] \exp\left[\frac{\sigma^2}{2\lambda^2} - \frac{w}{\lambda}\right] \tag{3.2}$$

where

$$\mathrm{erf}\,c(t) = 1 - \left(\frac{2}{\sqrt{\pi}}\right)\int_0^t e^{-\theta^2}\,d\theta$$

The application of the maximum likelihood method gives the estimates of the parameters and the standard errors. The average efficiency ($\bar{\varepsilon}$) of the set under consideration is

$$\bar{\varepsilon} = E(e^{-u}) = \frac{1}{1+\lambda} \tag{3.3}$$

However, the aim of the investigation is to find the individual technical efficiency level of each observation (firm). Following the suggestion of Jondrow et al. (1982) for calculating the conditional distribution where

$$\frac{f(u,w)}{f(w)} = f(u|w), \qquad w = v - u \tag{3.4}$$

we calculate the conditional distribution of u given w in order to find the mean of this distribution and from this the individual efficiency measure for each observation. Adopting the exponential distribution for u the mean of the conditional distribution becomes, in this case,

$$E(u|w) = \sigma\left[\frac{f\left(\frac{\sigma}{\lambda} - \frac{w}{\sigma}\right)}{\frac{1}{2}\,\mathrm{erf}\,c\left(\frac{\sigma}{\lambda\sqrt{2}} - \frac{w}{\sigma\sqrt{2}}\right)} - \left(\frac{\sigma}{\lambda} - \frac{w}{\sigma}\right)\right] \tag{3.5}$$

where f represents the standard normal density.

Substitution of w for its calculated value for each observation gives us the corresponding mean value of u and from this the individual technical efficiency for each firm under consideration ($\varepsilon_i = (1 + \lambda_i)^{-1}$). Once this measure has been defined, we can try to explain the phenomenon of inefficiency by relating the stochastically estimated efficiency measure to other variables. The adoption of nonvariable returns to scale for the production model—as in our case—could lead to some misspecification error and impair further efficiency analyses. However, it should be remembered that by using the composed error approach we assume that this misspecification is captured by the disturbance term in the proper sense, e^{v_i}, and that only this term will be affected, not the measure of technical efficiency. So we can consider the latter as unbiased and suitable for further research. Here we focus our attention on the impact of firm size on efficiency. In order to find a specific structure in this relation we employ different models that describe a particular structure. The models taken into consideration are of the following nature:

$$\text{linear} \qquad \varepsilon_i = a + bS_i \tag{3.6}$$

$$\text{power function} \qquad \varepsilon_i = aS_i^b \tag{3.7}$$

$$\text{exponential} \qquad \varepsilon_i = ae^{bS_i} \tag{3.8}$$

$$\text{parabolic} \qquad \varepsilon_i = a + bS_i + cS_i^2 \tag{3.9}$$

where

$$\varepsilon_i = \frac{1}{1 + \lambda_i}$$

It is quite obvious that the first three models describe an increasing or decreasing pattern, designating a positive or negative relation between efficiency and firm size. The parabolic model tries to find out whether a middle class of firms is more efficient or less efficient than the smaller or bigger firms. The U-shape or inversed U-shape of the parabolic model may provide some answer in this respect.

3.3. Data and Results

In order to calculate a reliable technical efficiency measure for each firm in Belgian industry we need qualitatively good firm data. Fortunately, since 1977 all Belgian firms with 50 employees or more, with sales (without value-added tax) greater than 50 million Belgian francs (BF), or total assets of at least 25 million BF and without any major financial activities (thus no banks or insurance companies) are obliged to deposit an annual standardized financial account with additional information at the Accounts Center of the National Bank of Belgium.[1] Using these detailed annual accounts it is possible to calculate very precisely the variables we need. With the aim of reducing the heterogeneity of the production variable we decided to work only with three-digit sectors according to the NACE-classification system.[2] Our great concern to analyze only sectors that are representative, that is, contain enough firms that must deposit their accounts, have caused us (in selecting the industries) to use some minimal criteria, namely the set must contain: (a) more than 50% of total sales of the sector under consideration; (b) at least 10% of the firms of the total three-digit sector; and (c) at least 30 firms.

It appears from an evaluation report concerning the quality of the information obtained via the annual accounts (Jegers and Buijink 1983) that the account information can be affected by human errors, such as incorrect filling out of documents, and so we decided that it would be useful to submit all firms to a series of tests (see appendix 3.A). On the basis of the results of these tests, we eliminated nonreliable firms and, where relevant, the whole sector that does not satisfy the minimal criteria. This procedure must guarantee the reliability and the representative character of the data (e.g., exclude firms without wages or very high capital intensity as a consequence of expressing capital items in single Belgian francs (BF) instead of thousands of BF). Careful screening of the data resulted in retaining only 14 reliable sectors out of 113 three-digit sectors in the NACE classification from 2 to 4. The small number of firms at the three-digit level is not alone responsible for this; the incorrectly filled out annual accounts also play a major role (Jegers and Buijink 1983).

Production has been measured in gross value added expressed in millions of BF by adding up a series of account items (see chapter appendixes). The capital stock variable is also an aggregate of the net book values of well-defined capital items such as machines, buildings, etc. in millions of BF (see chapter appendixes). Labor has been expressed in equivalent labor units, which are the result of total wages and salaries (without social benefits) divided by the average hourly wage of normal skilled labor (for the month of October, men and women (National Institute of Statistics (NIS) 1980). Highly qualified labor is now transformed into average skilled labor for better comparison within each sector. The use of wages as a labor variable has the advantage of taking into specific consideration the quality of labor. The error term will also be free of the quality bias introduced by unweighted labor.

In table 3-1 the selected sectors of the Belgian manufacturing sector have been presented, and the number of firms in each sector (absolute and relative) has been indicated.

It appears that the firms from the selected industries are strongly con-

Table 3-1 Selected Industries of the Belgian Manufacturing Sector in 1978: Total and Selected Firms and Sales

		Firms			*Sales*		
			Selected			*Selected*	
NACE Code	*Industry*	*Total (Units)*	*Units*	*% of Total*	*Total (10^6 BF)*	*10^6 BF*	*% of Total*
231	Building and refract. clays	303	42	13.9	13427	7587.2	56.5
241	Clay products	184	44	23.9	9869	5209.4	52.8
243	Concrete, cement, or plaster products	660	101	15.3	27620	26528.3	96.—
257	Pharmaceutical products	141	37	26.2	29314	28374.1	96.8
316	Tools and finished metal goods	1136	115	10.1	46834	30432.7	65.—
325	Civil engineering; mechanical handling equipment	147	53	36.1	24952	21706.5	87.—
413	Dairy products	134	58	43.8	53432	47222.5	88.4
422	Animal and poultry foods	177	64	36.2	54663	51825.—	94.8
427	Brewing and malting	231	64	27.7	45667	38887.3	85.2
431	Wool industry	236	48	20.3	21046	13458.1	63.9
432	Cotton industry	310	50	16.1	26643	19095.3	71.7
438	Floor coverings	215	57	26.5	26990	24004.2	88.9
472	Paper and board	311	59	18.3	17709	17514.2	98.9
483	Plastics	439	90	20.5	23953	22082.8	92.2

centrated, because few firms represent high sales percentages. This feature is not bound with the selected industries we investigate, but seems quite normal for the whole manufacturing sector of Belgium (Jegers 1982).

The maximum-likelihood estimators of the parameters and its standard errors of model (3.2) have been estimated by applying a combination of three minimization methods (a Monte Carlo searching technique, a simplex method, and a variable metric method). Further discussion of these methods can be found in our previous article (Meeusen and van den Broeck 1977a).

Table 3-2 presents the parameter values for the various selected industries. As one can see, the elasticities of labor production are fairly high and very significant. On the other hand, the elasticities of capital production are rather small and in most cases not significant at the 5 percent level. Even for the sector of civil engineering and mechanical handling equipment the capital elasticity equals practically zero. It seems very improbable that capital stock has little or no effect on production and a possible explanation for this result—in spite of the careful screening—might be the quality of the capital data of the financial accounts. A dynamic analysis of the capital data to find out the behaviour of depreciation rates applied by the firms (fiscal versus economical) is a possible way to correct the capital variable. Further research into this is required. The efficiency parameter for each industry is significant at the 5 percent level, except for the sector of concrete, cement, or plaster products. For this sector it appears that there are no efficiency differences. The nature of the products manufactured by this industry, the relatively simple technology, and the protected market (no foreign competition) may explain why all the selected firms of this sector lie practically on the production frontier. A dynamic analysis of this industry might give a more conclusive answer. The average efficiency of the other industries fluctuates between 0.8926 (civil engineering; mechanical equipment) and 0.7351 (brewing and malting), which seems reasonable.

It is also interesting to note the fairly low regression standard errors relative to the efficiency parameters, which can be seen as the result of the use of three-digit classification for efficiency analysis. To calculate the individual efficiencies for each firm, we calculate the total error (w) in each firm per industry. Together with the industry parameters, they are inserted in the mean of the conditional distribution (3.5) to give an efficiency measure for each firm of the selected industries (see chapter appendixes).

Apart from NACE-sector 243, the upper efficiency limit fluctuates between 0.9622 and 0.9085 (inefficiency between 3.78% and 9.15%) and the lower efficiency limit between 0.6335 and 0.2056 (inefficiencies between

36.65% and 79.44%). The latter is abnormally low and responsible for the low efficiency average of the brewing and malting sector. Inspection of the calculated total errors (w) confronts us with the phenomenon of outliers. Simple elimination of the largest outlier on the low efficiency level (minus value for w) gives us a new lower efficiency limit, namely 0.7716 and 0.4636; but brewing and malting still keep the lowest efficiency measure (see chapter appendixes).

The regression of individual efficiency with the size of the firm, expressed in gross value added terms (10^9 BF), for the four models we adopt to describe the efficiency-size relationship gives us some idea about the structure of the latter. The comparison of the results of each model for the fourteen industries gives us overwhelming support for model (3.7). Twelve out of fourteen industries are positively related and significant at the 5% level. Only the pharmaceutical industry and paper and board are not significant. The poorest results come from the parabolic model, where only clay products and the wool industry are significant at the 5% level. In both industries, the relationship shows a maximum, which suggests the existance of a zone where firms are less inefficient (clay products ± 150 billion BF (value added) and wool industry ± 330 billion BF (value added).

Inspection of the results of the fourteen industries shows us that building and refractory clays, clay products, and brewing and malting suggest a relatively strong correlated relation between efficiency and size for model (3.7). The size elasticity of efficiency ranges from 0.12 to 0.08, which means that for each 1% increase in size, efficiency will also increase by 0.12%. The parabolic model also gives good results for clay products but the power model appears to be better ($R^2 = 0.4184$). The explanatory power of model (3.7) for dairy products, the wool industry, and floor covering is still satisfactory because more than 20% is explained by the model. The size elasticity of efficiency of these sectors lies between 0.07 and 0.03. As we mentioned earlier, the parabolic model for the wool industry is also significant, but the power model appears to be more relevant because it explains better the relation between efficiency and size ($R^2 = 0.2584$).

Less satisfactory are the results with regard to tools and finished metal goods, civil engineering, animal and poultry food, the cotton industry and plastics, but the size elasticities still range from 0.07 to 0.016.

Only pharmaceutical products and paper and board show no size relation at all. However, the biggest firm of both industries achieves one of the highest efficiency levels and the smallest firm a relatively low level. The efficiency pattern with respect to size seems to be erratic for these industries.

Table 3-2 Results of the Stochastic Cobb-Douglas Production Function Frontier for 14 Selected 3-digit Industries of the Belgian Manufacturing Sector (1978)

NACE Code	*Industry (Number of Firms)*	*Constant*
231	building and refractory clays (42)	0.6326 (0.6005)*
241	clay products (44)	−0.5936 (0.4033)
243	concrete, cement, or plaster products (101)	0.6339 (0.0348)
257	pharmaceutical products (37)	−0.5286 (0.5150)
316	tools and finished metal goods (115)	0.3809 (0.1825)
325	civil engineering; mechanical handling equipment (53)	−0.3298 (0.3401)
413	dairy products (58)	−0.5263 (0.0228)
422	animal and poultry foods (64)	0.3492 (0.3721)
427	brewing and malting (64)	0.6340 (0.6161)
431	wool industry (48)	−1.0780 (0.4855)
432	cotton industry (50)	−0.7564 (0.3767)
438	floor covering (57)	−0.2116 (0.4428)
472	paper and board (59)	0.4325 (0.4229)
483	plastics (90)	0.5655 (0.4879)

*Asymptotic standard errors are in parentheses.

Table 3-2 (*Continued*)

Elasticities of Production				
Labor	*Capital*	σ	*Efficiency Parameter* λ	*Efficiency* $\bar{\varepsilon} = \frac{1}{1 + \lambda}$
0.8862	0.0254	0.2540	0.3553	0.7378
(0.0649)	(0.0449)	(0.0463)	(0.0849)	
0.9215	0.0933	0.2417	0.3244	0.7551
(0.0328)	(0.0347)	(0.0491)	(0.0814)	
0.8122	0.0835	0.2708	0.0085	0.9916
(0.0018)	(0.0025)	(0.0102)	(0.0706)	
0.8853	0.1059	0.2522	0.2704	0.7872
(0.0579)	(0.0449)	(0.0506)	(0.0830)	
0.8700	0.0209	0.1845	0.1377	0.8790
(0.0355)	(0.0264)	(0.0415)	(0.0142)	
0.9422	0.0	0.2111	0.1203	0.8926
(0.0273)	—	(0.0278)	(0.0472)	
0.8762	0.1154	0.2387	0.1792	0.8480
(0.0031)	(0.0037)	(0.0000)	(0.0348)	
0.7772	0.1609	0.3159	0.1912	0.8395
(0.0533)	(0.0521)	(0.0362)	(0.0616)	
0.8304	0.0899	0.3748	0.3604	0.7351
(0.0680)	(0.0518)	(0.0482)	(0.0800)	
0.9227	0.0909	0.2277	0.2168	0.8218
(0.0718)	(0.557)	(0.0574)	(0.0856)	
0.9420	0.0522	0.1470	0.3273	0.7534
(0.0450)	(0.0437)	(0.0347)	(0.0701)	
0.8844	0.0808	0.2540	0.3041	0.7668
(0.0452)	(0.0370)	(0.0362)	(0.0656)	
0.8126	0.0887	0.2244	0.1483	0.8709
(0.0430)	(0.0299)	(0.0419)	(0.0723)	
0.8460	0.0440	0.2915	0.2226	0.8179
(0.0604)	(0.0504)	(0.0302)	(0.0535)	

If we disregard the statistical significance of the estimated models, we could say that the overall relation between efficiency and size is positive— that is, the bigger the firm the greater the efficiency, or the smaller the inefficiency.

All the signs of the coefficients suggest the same positive relationship. This is a surprising result because a lot of researchers believe that big firms are more afflicted by bureaucratic rules which demotivate personnel and spoil human relations within the firm and are thus less efficient. If we consider size as an aggregate variable for these phenomena, it seems that for the industries under consideration the reverse is true. However, we have to question this conclusion, because the explanatory power of the models employed are, in general, modest. Most models are not even significant. That does not apply to model (3.7), where for brewing and malting as much as 42% of the variance has been explained.

A possible explanation for the relationship revealed by this research may be the production nature of the industries. Most of the industries manufacture products that lend themselves more or less easily to mass production. Such production can be organized in a better way by a bigger firm, so that its resources are more efficiently used, despite the bigger organization. The paper and board sector, however, seems to be an exception so that further research is certainly required.

3.4. Conclusion

From the four different models we have used to find a relation between stochastic technical efficiencies for each firm and the size of the firm for fourteen selected industries out of 113 three-digit industries of the Belgian manufacturing sector for 1978, the power function would appear to be the most relevant. This functional model describes best the efficiency-size relation. The size-elasticity of efficiency fluctuates between 0.12 and 0.016 and is constant within each industry. However, its explanatory power is moderate (between 42% and 7% for the significant sectors).

Other explanatory variables have to be found to explain the efficiency differences, because some of the industries have a very weak or no relation at all with firm size. A dynamic analysis should be considered for the same selected industries to investigate the validity of the present results. Nevertheless it does not seem irrelevant to employ a power relation model (3.7) in further research into the efficiency-size relationship.

Notes

1. Royal Decree of 8 October 1976 concerning Company Financial Accounts, *Belgisch Staatsblad* 19 October 1976 (cf. Lefebvre 1982).

2. NACE: *Nomenclature générale des Activités économiques dans les Communautés Européennes* (General Industrial Classification of Economic Activities within the European Communities).

References

Aigner, D. J., C. A. K. Lovell, and P. Schmidt. 1977. "Formulation and Estimation of Stochastic Frontier Production Function Models." *Journal of Econometrics* 6:21–37.

Farrell, M. 1957. "The Measurement of Productive Efficiency." *Journal of the Royal Statistical Society,* ser. A, 120:253–290.

Försund, F., and L. Hjalmarsson. 1979. "Generalized Farrell Measures of Efficiency: An Application to Milk Processing in Swedish Dairy Plants. *Economic Journal* 89:294–315.

Jegers, M. 1982. "De verdeling van meerdere grootte- en rentabiliteitsindicatoren op verschillende aggregatieniveaus van de Belgische economie in 1977 (The distribution of several measures of dimension and profitability for different aggregation levels of the Belgian economy in 1977), working paper no. 82/10, University of Antwerp (RUCA), 1–13.

Jegers, M., W. Buijink. 1983. "The quality of a new source of financial accounting data in Belgium: An exploratory analysis." Paper presented at the Workshop on Accounting and Financial Information, European Institute for Advanced Studies in Management, Brussel, 6–7 June, 1–41.

Jondrow, J., C. A. K. Lovell, I. S. Materov, and P. Schmidt. 1982. "On the Estimation of Technical Inefficiency in the Stochastic Frontier Production Function Model." *Journal of Econometrics* 19:233–238.

Kopp, R. 1981. "The Measurement of Productive Efficiency: A Reconsideration." *Quarterly Journal of Economics* 96(3): 477–503.

Lefebvre C. 1982. "Development of Belgian Accounting Standards within the European Economic Community Framework," *International Journal of Accounting* 17(1): 103–132.

Leibenstein, H. 1965. "Allocative Efficiency vs. X-efficiency." *American Economic Review* 56:392–415.

Materov, I. 1981. "K probleme polnoy identifikatsii modeli stokhasticheskikh granits proizvodstva (On Full Identification of the Stochastic Production Frontier Model)." *Ekonomika i Matematicheskie Metody* 17:784–788.

Meeusen, W., and J. Van den Broeck. 1977a. "Efficiency Estimation from Cobb-Douglas Production Functions with Composed Error." *International Economic Review* 18:435–444.

Meeusen, W., and J. Van den Broeck. 1977b. "Technical Efficiency and Dimension of the Firm: Some Results on the Use of Frontier Production Functions." *Empirical Economics* 2(2):109–122.

Nationaal Instituut voor de Statistiek (Koninkrijk België). 1980. *Sociale Statistieken,* no. 3:12–23.

Pitt, M. M., and L. F. Lee. 1981. "The Measurement and Sources of Technical Inefficiency in the Indonesian Weaving Industry." *Journal of Development Economics* 9:43–64.

Timmer, C. 1971. "Using a Probabilistic Frontier Production Function to Measure Technical Efficiency. *Journal of Political Economy* 79:176–794.

Van den Broeck, J. 1978. "De substitutie-elasticiteiten in de secundaire sector van België 1955–1970. (The Elasticity of Substitution in the Belgian Manufacturing Sector, 1955–1970)," *Cahiers Economiques de Bruxelles,* no. 77, 49–69.

Van den Broeck, J. 1981. "Outliers and the Probabilistic Approach of Frontier Production Functions Estimation, working paper 81/06, Universiteit Antwerpen, R.U.C.A., 1-7.

Van den Broeck, J., F. Försund, L. Hjalmarsson, and W. Meeusen. 1980. "On the Estimation of Deterministic and Stochastic Frontier Production Functions." *Journal of Econometrics* 13:83–100.

APPENDIX 3A

Tests to Select Firms and Industries

- gross value added $\geqslant$ 100,000 BF
- total capital $\geqslant$ 500,000 BF
- total wages $\geqslant$ 1,000,000 BF
- seventeen quality tests, such as total assets equal total liabilities, summation of total assets greater than zero, summation of total liabilities greater than zero, summation of sub-items must equal total of item under consideration, etc. (see Jegers and Buijink 1983).

Data

- Gross value added: operating income minus cost of trade stock, raw materials, consumables and supplies, and miscellaneous goods and services
- Capital: net tangible fixed assets (land and buildings; installations, machines, and equipment, furniture, and rolling stock;

construction in progress and advance payments: fixed assets held on long lease; Other tangible fixed assets).

- Labor: remuneration

APPENDIX 3B

Total Error (w_i) *and Individual Efficiency* ($\varepsilon_i = 1/1 + \lambda_i$) *for Each Firm in Selected Three-digit Industries of Belgium—1978 (increasing size order)*

Table 3B-1. Building Materials and Refractory Clays (42)

No.	*Total Error* (w_i)	*Efficiency* $1/(1 + \lambda_i)$
1	2.8743	0.2708
2	0.1071	0.8490
3	0.9041	0.5799
4	0.3839	0.7716
5	0.1957	0.8279
6	0.4945	0.7320
7	1.2267	0.4890
8	−0.0400	0.8771
9	0.1772	0.8326
10	−0.2773	0.9085
11	0.4187	0.7596
12	0.6331	0.6788
13	0.2465	0.8142
14	0.4094	0.7628
15	0.1263	0.8447

(*continued*)

Table 3B-1. (*Continued*)

No.	*Total Error* (w_i)	*Efficiency* $1/(1 + \lambda_i)$
16	0.5376	0.7157
17	0.3929	0.7685
18	0.1182	0.8466
19	0.6521	0.6714
20	0.3475	0.7837
21	−0.3116	0.9120
22	−0.1810	0.8975
23	0.1991	0.8270
24	0.7342	0.6401
25	0.6329	0.6789
26	0.4197	0.7592
27	0.7015	0.6525
28	0.3842	0.7715
29	0.3214	0.7920
30	0.4098	0.7626
31	0.6166	0.6852
32	0.4592	0.7450
33	−0.3170	0.9125
34	0.3212	0.7921
35	0.1998	0.8268
36	−0.3629	0.9168
37	0.1089	0.8486
38	0.2553	0.8118
39	0.4088	0.7630
40	0.0726	0.8563
41	0.0772	0.8554
42	−0.1542	0.8940

Table 3B-2. Clay Products (44)

No.	*Total Error* (w_i)	*Efficiency* $1/(1 + \lambda_i)$
1	2.3606	0.3144
2	1.0646	0.5306
3	0.4848	0.7389
4	0.8081	0.6130
5	0.6333	0.6801

Table 3B-2. (*Continued*)

No.	*Total Error* (w_i)	*Efficiency* $1/(1 + \lambda_i)$
6	0.2159	0.8289
7	0.6478	0.6743
8	0.1166	0.8536
9	0.7838	0.6219
10	0.4717	0.7440
11	0.4178	0.7641
12	0.5720	0.7046
13	0.3726	0.7802
14	0.5419	0.7166
15	0.1484	0.8462
16	0.3724	0.7803
17	0.1774	0.8390
18	0.1574	0.8440
19	−0.4220	0.9275
20	−0.1298	0.8973
21	0.0456	0.8685
22	0.4110	0.7666
23	0.8538	0.5968
24	0.0559	0.8665
25	−0.0293	0.8821
26	0.1947	0.8345
27	−0.0235	0.8811
28	0.4238	0.7619
29	−0.2820	0.9152
30	0.1211	0.8526
31	0.4359	0.7574
32	0.3634	0.7834
33	−0.3725	0.9235
34	−0.0304	0.8823
35	0.3133	0.8000
36	−0.0811	0.8904
37	−0.0931	0.8921
38	0.2001	0.8331
39	0.3180	0.7985
40	0.1578	0.8439
41	0.7011	0.6533
42	0.3390	0.7916
43	0.1210	0.8526
44	0.3346	0.7930

Table 3B-3. Concrete, Cement, or Plaster Products (101)

No.	*Total Error* (w_i)	*Efficiency* $1/(1 + \lambda_i)$	*No.*	*Total Error* (w_i)	*Efficiency* $1/(1 + \lambda_i)$
1	0.6253	0.9909	51	−1.0425	0.9925
2	0.3467	0.9912	52	0.2853	0.9913
3	0.4322	0.9911	53	0.1442	0.9914
4	−0.0021	0.9916	54	0.2462	0.9913
5	0.2081	0.9914	55	0.0923	0.9915
6	0.4853	0.9911	56	−0.0543	0.9916
7	0.4828	0.9911	57	−0.3943	0.9919
8	−0.3020	0.9919	58	0.2392	0.9913
9	0.4649	0.9911	59	0.1053	0.9915
10	0.1572	0.9914	60	−0.2933	0.9919
11	0.2081	0.9914	61	−0.2364	0.9918
12	−0.0088	0.9916	62	0.1779	0.9914
13	0.0905	0.9915	63	0.2152	0.9914
14	0.4565	0.9911	64	0.2021	0.9914
15	−0.8253	0.9923	65	0.1903	0.9914
16	0.2787	0.9913	66	−0.5114	0.9920
17	0.1586	0.9914	67	0.1051	0.9915
18	0.3941	0.9912	68	0.0724	0.9915
19	−0.0824	0.9917	69	−0.0556	0.9916
20	0.1394	0.9914	70	0.0817	0.9915
21	0.1481	0.9914	71	0.1028	0.9915
22	−0.0598	0.9916	72	0.0404	0.9915
23	0.2045	0.9914	73	0.0293	0.9916
24	−0.1545	0.9917	74	0.0069	0.9916
25	0.1073	0.9915	75	0.0717	0.9915
26	0.3132	0.9913	76	0.1660	0.9914
27	−0.4112	0.9920	77	−0.1036	0.9917
28	0.1110	0.9915	78	0.1186	0.9915
29	−0.2406	0.9918	79	−0.3026	0.9919
30	−0.1240	0.9917	80	0.4057	0.9912
31	−0.5160	0.9920	81	−0.0699	0.9916
32	−0.4343	0.9920	82	−0.0034	0.9916
33	0.2832	0.9913	83	−0.0204	0.9916
34	0.1232	0.9915	84	−0.0597	0.9916
35	−0.1805	0.9917	85	−0.1064	0.9917
36	−0.1493	0.9917	86	−0.0132	0.9916
37	0.2085	0.9914	87	−0.1561	0.9917
38	0.1287	0.9915	88	0.1145	0.9915
39	−0.1441	0.9917	89	0.0398	0.9915
40	0.0361	0.9915	90	0.1027	0.9915

Table 3B-3. *(Continued)*

No.	*Total Error* (w_i)	*Efficiency* $1/(1 + \lambda_i)$	*No.*	*Total Error* (w_i)	*Efficiency* $1/(1 + \lambda_i)$
41	−0.1176	0.9917	91	0.0976	0.9915
42	−0.2220	0.9918	92	0.1743	0.9914
43	0.1720	0.9914	93	−0.2209	0.9918
44	−0.1244	0.9917	94	0.1295	0.9915
45	−0.2376	0.9918	95	−0.1768	0.9917
46	−0.3618	0.9919	96	−0.1017	0.9917
47	0.3418	0.9912	97	−0.4098	0.9920
48	0.0428	0.9915	98	0.0471	0.9915
49	−0.0106	0.9916	99	−0.1860	0.9918
50	−0.2066	0.9918	100	−0.2683	0.9918
			101	−0.4005	0.9919

Table 3B-4. Pharmaceutical Products (37)

No.	*Total Error* (w_i)	*Efficiency* $1/(1 + \lambda_i)$
1	0.6127	0.6266
2	0.5363	0.6554
3	0.0514	0.8253
4	0.4266	0.6979
5	0.1627	0.7931
6	1.7705	0.3640
7	−0.1555	0.8708
8	0.1347	0.8017
9	0.0768	0.8184
10	0.5215	0.6611
11	1.0778	0.4868
12	−0.0765	0.8555
13	0.1664	0.7919
14	0.2060	0.7790
15	0.4133	0.7031
16	0.3137	0.7410
17	0.5029	0.6683
18	0.5067	0.6668
19	0.4150	0.7025
20	0.7291	0.5856

(continued)

Table 3B-4. *(Continued)*

No.	*Total Error* (w_i)	*Efficiency* $1/(1 + \lambda_i)$
21	−0.0277	0.8448
22	0.0928	0.8139
23	−0.4263	0.9085
24	0.3270	0.7361
25	0.6484	0.6137
26	0.3440	0.7297
27	−0.0302	0.8454
28	0.7099	0.5921
29	0.3682	0.7205
30	0.4065	0.7057
31	0.4407	0.6925
32	0.1903	0.7842
33	−0.1734	0.8740
34	0.4885	0.6739
35	0.2248	0.7727
36	0.1718	0.7902
37	−0.2879	0.8917

Table 3B-5. Civil Engineering; Mechanical Handling Equipment (53)

No.	*Total Error* (w_i)	*Efficiency* $1/(1 + \lambda_i)$
1	0.9948	0.6151
2	0.1726	0.8980
3	0.3111	0.8706
4	−0.5815	0.9587
5	−0.0647	0.9282
6	−0.0614	0.9279
7	0.1735	0.8979
8	0.1925	0.8946
9	0.2494	0.8840
10	0.3932	0.8496
11	0.3164	0.8694
12	0.0631	0.9141
13	0.1064	0.9082
14	−0.3102	0.9465
15	0.5373	0.8029

Table 3B-5. *(Continued)*

No.	*Total Error* (w_i)	*Efficiency* $1/(1 + \lambda_i)$
16	0.3674	0.8566
17	−0.3696	0.9497
18	0.0716	0.9130
19	0.1437	0.9027
20	0.2741	0.8788
21	−0.0755	0.9292
22	0.1781	0.8971
23	0.0847	0.9112
24	0.1853	0.8959
25	0.1832	0.8962
26	0.1641	0.8994
27	0.1917	0.8948
28	0.0310	0.9180
29	0.1342	0.9041
30	0.2124	0.8911
31	−0.3334	0.9478
32	0.1621	0.8997
33	0.0113	0.9203
34	0.2867	0.8761
35	0.1587	0.9003
36	0.1400	0.9033
37	0.1661	0.8991
38	0.1085	0.9079
39	0.4365	0.8369
40	0.2462	0.8845
41	0.1156	0.9069
42	0.0246	0.9188
43	0.1994	0.8934
44	0.3344	0.8650
45	0.3256	0.8672
46	0.1024	0.9088
47	−0.0466	0.9265
48	0.3882	0.8510
49	−0.1088	0.9322
50	−0.0870	0.9303
51	−0.0737	0.9291
52	−0.2476	0.9426
53	−0.2009	0.9395

Table 3B-6. Tools and Finished Metal Goods (115)

No.	*Total Error* (w_i)	*Efficiency* $1/(1 + \lambda_i)$	*No.*	*Total Error* (w_i)	*Efficiency* $1/(1 + \lambda_i)$
1	0.3620	0.8350	59	0.0218	0.9241
2	0.1163	0.9021	60	0.1473	0.8958
3	0.3532	0.8382	61	0.2008	0.8837
4	1.2409	0.5016	62	0.1710	0.8907
5	0.2358	0.8748	63	−0.0745	0.9305
6	0.4518	0.7996	64	0.1435	0.8966
7	−0.4052	0.9560	65	0.3546	0.8377
8	0.0087	0.9200	66	−0.2499	0.9465
9	−0.3350	0.9521	67	0.1565	0.8939
10	0.7674	0.6572	68	−0.0143	0.9231
11	0.2538	0.8698	69	0.0309	0.9167
12	0.3229	0.8486	70	0.0564	0.9127
13	0.3153	0.8512	71	0.1628	0.8925
14	0.2263	0.8773	72	0.0965	0.9058
15	0.4778	0.7884	73	−0.0419	0.9267
16	−0.1361	0.9370	74	0.2113	0.8811
17	0.1287	0.8997	75	0.0868	0.9075
18	0.5327	0.7638	76	0.3231	0.8486
19	0.2864	0.8603	77	−0.0619	0.9291
20	0.2685	0.8656	78	0.2370	0.8744
21	0.1911	0.8861	79	−0.0522	0.9279
22	−0.2824	0.9488	80	0.0962	0.9059
23	0.1731	0.8902	81	0.1251	0.9004
24	0.2076	0.8820	82	0.1486	0.8956
25	0.3142	0.8515	83	0.1510	0.8951
26	0.4866	0.7846	84	0.1641	0.8922
27	0.1080	0.9037	85	0.2714	0.8648
28	0.3491	0.8397	86	−0.0580	0.9286
29	0.2043	0.8829	87	0.0847	0.9079
30	−0.1761	0.9406	88	0.0544	0.9130
31	0.4272	0.8099	89	−0.0091	0.9224
32	0.1971	0.8846	90	0.8544	0.6220
33	0.0069	0.9202	91	0.3008	0.8558
34	0.4418	0.8038	92	−0.1575	0.9390
35	0.3392	0.8431	93	0.1666	0.8917
36	−0.0224	0.9242	94	0.1483	0.8956
37	−0.2124	0.9437	95	0.2780	0.8628
38	0.1047	0.9043	96	−0.0091	0.9224
39	0.3495	0.8395	97	0.0453	0.9145
40	0.3348	0.8446	98	0.1744	0.8899

Table 3B-6. *(Continued)*

No.	*Total Error* (w_i)	*Efficiency* $1/(1 + \lambda_i)$	*No.*	*Total Error* (w_i)	*Efficiency* $1/(1 + \lambda_i)$
41	−0.0829	0.9315	99	0.1866	0.8871
42	0.0879	0.9073	100	−0.1783	0.9408
43	0.1279	0.8998	101	0.1025	0.9047
44	0.4402	0.8045	102	−0.4307	0.9573
45	0.1241	0.9006	103	−0.0348	0.9258
46	0.9110	0.6009	104	0.1185	0.9017
47	0.2825	0.8615	105	−0.0473	0.9273
48	0.0694	0.9106	106	0.0344	0.9162
49	−0.0090	0.9224	107	0.1213	0.9011
50	0.0423	0.9149	108	−0.0535	0.9281
51	0.1614	0.8928	109	−0.0801	0.9312
52	−0.1423	0.9376	110	−0.0789	0.9310
53	0.2497	0.8710	111	0.0297	0.9169
54	−0.0280	0.9249	112	−0.2260	0.9447
55	0.2086	0.8818	113	−0.1325	0.9366
56	0.2778	0.8629	114	0.0595	0.9122
57	0.3782	0.8291	115	−0.5442	0.9622
58	0.2339	0.8753			

Table 3B-7. Dairy Products (58)

No.	*Total Error* (w_i)	*Efficiency* $1/(1 + \lambda_i)$
1	1.6656	0.4260
2	0.2510	0.8561
3	0.2213	0.8626
4	0.0568	0.8921
5	0.1619	0.8744
6	0.2314	0.8604
7	0.2401	0.8585
8	0.2500	0.8563
9	0.2222	0.8624
10	0.1963	0.8678
11	0.3117	0.8416
12	0.2296	0.8608
13	0.7667	0.6823

(continued)

Table 3B-7. *(Continued)*

No.	*Total Error* (w_i)	*Efficiency* $1/(1 + \lambda_i)$
14	0.3340	0.8358
15	0.1922	0.8686
16	0.2155	0.8638
17	0.2454	0.8574
18	0.4579	0.7993
19	−0.1025	0.9124
20	0.2002	0.8670
21	0.3976	0.8180
22	−0.0419	0.9054
23	0.1785	0.8713
24	0.1752	0.8719
25	0.2827	0.8488
26	0.2867	0.8478
27	0.3154	0.8407
28	−0.0875	0.9108
29	0.2272	0.8613
30	0.1425	0.8780
31	−0.0878	0.9108
32	0.2090	0.8652
33	0.1485	0.8769
34	0.2065	0.8657
35	0.0193	0.8975
36	−0.4170	0.9379
37	0.1076	0.8840
38	−0.1165	0.9139
39	0.2119	0.8646
40	0.3078	0.8426
41	0.4503	0.8017
42	0.1913	0.8688
43	−0.0344	0.9045
44	0.1568	0.8754
45	−0.3262	0.9320
46	−0.1055	0.9127
47	0.1375	0.8789
48	0.0290	0.8961
49	0.3182	0.8400
50	0.0986	0.8855
51	0.1864	0.8697
52	0.0131	0.8983
53	−0.1001	0.9121

Table 3B-7. *(Continued)*

No.	*Total Error* (w_i)	*Efficiency* $1/(1 + \lambda_i)$
54	0.1715	0.8726
55	0.1902	0.8690
56	0.0057	0.8993
57	0.1969	0.8676
58	0.1187	0.8822

Table 3B-8. Animal and Poultry Foods (64)

No.	*Total Error* (w_i)	*Efficiency* $1/(1 + \lambda_i)$
1	0.4850	0.8070
2	0.3898	0.8267
3	0.3790	0.8288
4	0.6310	0.7716
5	−0.0886	0.8926
6	0.5858	0.7833
7	0.5574	0.7903
8	0.3986	0.8250
9	0.1819	0.8612
10	0.0208	0.8814
11	0.4941	0.8050
12	−0.2929	0.9093
13	0.4946	0.8049
14	0.1923	0.8597
15	1.7645	0.4459
16	0.0094	0.8826
17	−0.5050	0.9224
18	0.1949	0.8593
19	0.2849	0.8454
20	0.3566	0.8330
21	0.3904	0.8266
22	0.6253	0.7731
23	−0.4010	0.9164
24	0.5986	0.7800
25	0.1691	0.8630
26	0.3990	0.8249

(continued)

Table 3B-8. (*Continued*)

No.	*Total Error* (w_i)	*Efficiency* $1/(1 + \lambda_i)$
27	0.0621	0.8766
28	−0.1611	0.8991
29	0.4346	0.8178
30	0.3569	0.8329
31	−0.3380	0.9124
32	0.6057	0.7782
33	0.2470	0.8515
34	0.4206	0.8206
35	0.3130	0.8407
36	0.3529	0.8336
37	0.2126	0.8567
38	0.2845	0.8455
39	0.1580	0.8645
40	0.4124	0.8223
41	0.4736	0.8095
42	0.0060	0.8830
43	−0.2500	0.9062
44	0.4067	0.8234
45	−0.1079	0.8944
46	−0.6996	0.9317
47	0.1503	0.8655
48	0.1580	0.8645
49	0.4429	0.8160
50	0.3251	0.8386
51	0.4073	0.8233
52	−0.2316	0.9048
53	−0.2638	0.9072
54	−0.6784	0.9308
55	−0.5103	0.9227
56	0.1161	0.8700
57	−0.0462	0.8884
58	0.3051	0.8421
59	0.2907	0.8445
60	0.2233	0.8551
61	−0.1873	0.9012
62	0.2714	0.8477
63	−0.0155	0.8853
64	−0.0267	0.8864

Table 3B-9. Brewing and Malting (64)

No.	*Total Error* (w_i)	*Efficiency* $1/(1 + \lambda_i)$
1	4.2524	0.2056
2	1.0219	0.5988
3	0.8682	0.6443
4	0.2220	0.8028
5	0.7587	0.6762
6	0.5394	0.7351
7	0.6847	0.6970
8	0.5717	0.7270
9	0.7017	0.6922
10	0.9407	0.6228
11	0.4850	0.7483
12	0.6238	0.7134
13	0.7216	0.6867
14	0.8509	0.6494
15	0.4908	0.7469
16	0.5913	0.7219
17	−0.7372	0.9042
18	−0.8450	0.9101
19	0.4938	0.7462
20	−0.2907	0.8710
21	0.3126	0.7858
22	0.1425	0.8164
23	0.3284	0.7826
24	0.5039	0.7438
25	0.2303	0.8013
26	−0.2484	0.8668
27	0.5405	0.7348
28	0.2146	0.8041
29	0.7641	0.6746
30	0.8433	0.6516
31	−1.0188	0.9183
32	0.0590	0.8293
33	0.1876	0.8088
34	0.8040	0.6631
35	0.0941	0.8240
36	0.0515	0.8304
37	0.3209	0.7841
38	0.4462	0.7573

(*continued*)

Table 3B-9. *(Continued)*

No.	*Total Error* (w_i)	*Efficiency* $1/(1 + \lambda_i)$
39	0.4314	0.7607
40	0.6175	0.7151
41	0.6883	0.6960
42	0.3237	0.7835
43	0.2607	0.7958
44	0.2716	0.7937
45	0.2784	0.7924
46	−0.4298	0.8832
47	0.4272	0.7616
48	0.4279	0.7614
49	0.1243	0.8193
50	0.0904	0.8246
51	0.5986	0.7200
52	0.0098	0.8363
53	0.1488	0.8153
54	0.4528	0.7558
55	0.3595	0.7762
56	−0.2034	0.8622
57	0.1834	0.8096
58	0.2120	0.8046
59	−0.1286	0.8538
60	0.0604	0.8291
61	−0.0208	0.8404
62	0.2164	0.8038
63	0.1338	0.8178
64	0.0080	0.8365

Table 3B-10. Wool Industry (48)

No.	*Total Error* (w_i)	*Efficiency* $1/(1 + \lambda_i)$
1	0.9736	0.5764
2	1.3482	0.4741
3	0.7198	0.6709
4	0.1733	0.8623
5	0.5658	0.7343
6	0.1616	0.8649

Table 3B-10. *(Continued)*

No.	*Total Error* (w_i)	*Efficiency* $1/(1 + \lambda_i)$
7	0.3018	0.8289
8	0.2527	0.8427
9	0.2763	0.8362
10	−0.2310	0.9231
11	0.2919	0.8318
12	−0.5536	0.9456
13	0.6734	0.6899
14	0.0945	0.8787
15	0.0494	0.8869
16	0.2548	0.8421
17	0.5368	0.7460
18	0.1133	0.8750
19	−0.0177	0.8977
20	0.0242	0.8911
21	−0.3996	0.9366
22	0.4054	0.7956
23	0.0789	0.8817
24	0.3408	0.8170
25	0.4346	0.7852
26	0.5693	0.7327
27	0.0718	0.8829
28	0.1517	0.8671
29	0.0102	0.8934
30	0.4167	0.7916
31	0.1025	0.8772
32	0.3166	0.8245
33	−0.1162	0.9109
34	0.1400	0.8696
35	0.2880	0.8329
36	0.1307	0.8715
37	0.1846	0.8597
38	0.0903	0.8795
39	−0.1817	0.9182
40	0.4255	0.7885
41	−0.2397	0.9239
42	0.0084	0.8937
43	0.2038	0.8551
44	0.0100	0.8934
45	0.2055	0.8547

(continued)

Table 3B-10. *(Continued)*

No.	*Total Error* (w_i)	*Efficiency* $1/(1+\lambda_i)$
46	0.4167	0.7916
47	0.0839	0.8807
48	0.2460	0.8445

Table 3B-11. Cotton Industry (50)

No.	*Total Error* (w_i)	*Efficiency* $1/(1+\lambda_i)$
1	2.5983	0.2831
2	0.3406	0.7781
3	0.2039	0.8449
4	0.3335	0.7818
5	0.3102	0.7939
6	1.2229	0.4636
7	0.1617	0.8624
8	0.2557	0.8210
9	0.7658	0.5883
10	0.3387	0.7791
11	0.2410	0.8280
12	0.2734	0.8124
13	0.3211	0.7882
14	0.0013	0.9119
15	0.1552	0.8649
16	0.3422	0.7773
17	0.5365	0.6799
18	−0.1787	0.9425
19	0.3453	0.7757
20	0.4747	0.7093
21	−0.0547	0.9236
22	0.4257	0.7339
23	0.0648	0.8954
24	0.2814	0.8084
25	0.4533	0.7199
26	0.3024	0.7978
27	0.0509	0.8993
28	0.1236	0.8766
29	1.1953	0.4697

Table 3B-11. (*Continued*)

No.	*Total Error* (w_i)	*Efficiency* $1/(1 + \lambda_i)$
30	−0.0874	0.9294
31	0.0885	0.8882
32	0.0283	0.9053
33	0.4038	0.7451
34	0.5691	0.6652
35	−0.0367	0.9201
36	−0.1849	0.9432
37	0.3111	0.7934
38	0.3332	0.7820
39	0.8731	0.5534
40	0.7217	0.6040
41	0.2409	0.8281
42	−0.1895	0.9438
43	0.0714	0.8934
44	0.0535	0.8986
45	0.1925	0.8498
46	0.4237	0.7349
47	0.2632	0.8174
48	0.1579	0.8638
49	0.0645	0.8955
50	0.1774	0.8561

Table 3B-12. Floor Coverings (57)

No.	*Total Error* (w_i)	*Efficiency* $1/(1 + \lambda_i)$
1	3.1083	0.2567
2	1.2050	0.5018
3	0.0184	0.8724
4	−0.1185	0.8933
5	0.4586	0.7562
6	0.2758	0.8146
7	0.5532	0.7214
8	0.1847	0.8382
9	0.3652	0.7878
10	0.0013	0.8753

(*continued*)

Table 3B-12. *(Continued)*

No.	*Total Error* (w_i)	*Efficiency* $1/(1 + \lambda_i)$
11	0.6724	0.6755
12	0.4052	0.7747
13	0.2109	0.8318
14	0.4974	0.7423
15	0.8585	0.6060
16	0.6273	0.6929
17	0.2945	0.8093
18	0.5866	0.7086
19	−0.0414	0.8822
20	0.1634	0.8432
21	0.2982	0.8082
22	0.1795	0.8395
23	−0.1958	0.9029
24	0.6143	0.6980
25	0.5422	0.7256
26	0.0831	0.8604
27	0.4995	0.7415
28	0.0116	0.8736
29	0.2917	0.8101
30	0.1349	0.8496
31	0.0961	0.8578
32	0.2737	0.8152
33	−0.1899	0.9022
34	0.4223	0.7689
35	−0.1859	0.9018
36	0.0679	0.8633
37	0.1748	0.8406
38	0.3103	0.8047
39	0.0952	0.8579
40	0.3589	0.7898
41	0.4693	0.7524
42	0.3872	0.7807
43	−0.2985	0.9137
44	0.3142	0.8035
45	0.3269	0.7997
46	0.5213	0.7334
47	−0.0232	0.8794
48	−0.7587	0.9438
49	0.6748	0.6745
50	0.3354	0.7971

Table 3B-12. (*Continued*)

No.	*Total Error* (w_i)	*Efficiency* $1/(1 + \lambda_i)$
51	0.2984	0.8082
52	0.3366	0.7968
53	0.3839	0.7818
54	−0.2277	0.9065
55	0.1678	0.8422
56	−0.0278	0.8801
57	0.2422	0.8237

Table 3B-13. Paper and Board (59)

No.	*Total Error* (w_i)	*Efficiency* $1/(1 + \lambda_i)$
1	0.2827	0.8621
2	0.3973	0.8321
3	0.3746	0.8386
4	0.9148	0.6335
5	0.0786	0.9001
6	0.3033	0.8573
7	0.2922	0.8599
8	0.5396	0.7849
9	0.3585	0.8431
10	0.2532	0.8688
11	0.2067	0.8784
12	−0.3253	0.9397
13	0.2427	0.8710
14	0.2296	0.8738
15	0.0804	0.8999
16	0.3534	0.8445
17	−0.1514	0.9266
18	0.1460	0.8895
19	−0.2027	0.9310
20	0.2596	0.8673
21	0.2107	0.8776
22	0.2417	0.8712
23	0.0472	0.9046
24	−0.3375	0.9405

(*continued*)

Table 3B-13. (*Continued*)

No.	*Total Error* (w_i)	*Efficiency* $1/(1 + \lambda_i)$
25	0.2781	0.8632
26	0.0423	0.9053
27	0.0434	0.9051
28	0.2577	0.8678
29	0.4304	0.8221
30	0.0179	0.9085
31	−0.0545	0.9171
32	−0.1280	0.9245
33	0.2546	0.8685
34	−0.0628	0.9180
35	0.2745	0.8640
36	0.2836	0.8619
37	0.3867	0.8352
38	−0.0311	0.9144
39	−0.0028	0.9111
40	0.0486	0.9044
41	0.1946	0.8807
42	0.7221	0.7120
43	0.0941	0.8978
44	−0.2153	0.9320
45	−0.2342	0.9334
46	0.3623	0.8420
47	0.6991	0.7216
48	−0.3870	0.9434
49	0.2476	0.8700
50	−0.0677	0.9185
51	0.1186	0.8940
52	−0.3953	0.9439
53	0.6746	0.7318
54	0.0882	0.8987
55	0.1748	0.8844
56	−0.0548	0.9171
57	0.0465	0.9047
58	−0.0565	0.9173
59	−0.0905	0.9208

Table 3B-14. Plastics (90)

No.	*Total Error* (w_i)	*Efficiency* $1/(1 + \lambda_i)$	*No.*	*Total Error* (w_i)	*Efficiency* $1/(1 + \lambda_i)$
1	0.7674	0.6949	46	0.3451	0.8198
2	2.3919	0.3322	47	0.2984	0.8300
3	0.6209	0.7441	48	0.5146	0.7764
4	0.2846	0.8329	49	0.4062	0.8053
5	0.4023	0.8063	50	0.7514	0.7004
6	0.5485	0.7665	51	−0.0213	0.8825
7	0.8508	0.6654	52	0.4014	0.8065
8	0.3694	0.8142	53	0.4250	0.8006
9	0.7119	0.7140	54	0.3624	0.8159
10	0.0326	0.8755	55	0.1575	0.8566
11	0.4048	0.8057	56	−0.0004	0.8798
12	0.2633	0.8372	57	0.3797	0.8118
13	0.5401	0.7690	58	0.1995	0.8493
14	0.4690	0.7891	59	0.2613	0.8376
15	0.2654	0.8368	60	−0.5489	0.9270
16	0.2641	0.8371	61	0.3511	0.8185
17	−0.5240	0.9256	62	0.3016	0.8294
18	0.5802	0.7569	63	−0.0899	0.8906
19	−0.3035	0.9107	64	0.2462	0.8406
20	−0.1267	0.8945	65	0.0133	0.8781
21	0.0354	0.8751	66	0.2410	0.8416
22	0.9914	0.6161	67	0.4375	0.7974
23	0.5098	0.7778	68	0.0461	0.8736
24	0.0335	0.8754	69	−0.5268	0.9258
25	0.1986	0.8495	70	0.1932	0.8504
26	0.4907	0.7831	71	0.2559	0.8387
27	0.0646	0.8710	72	−0.1230	0.8941
28	−0.5325	0.9261	73	0.4853	0.7846
29	−0.0489	0.8859	74	0.2901	0.8318
30	−0.4245	0.9195	75	−0.3190	0.9119
31	−0.1502	0.8970	76	0.1743	0.8537
32	−0.2954	0.9100	77	0.2094	0.8475
33	0.2260	0.8444	78	0.4271	0.8001
34	0.3643	0.8154	79	0.4465	0.7951
35	0.0291	0.8760	80	0.2571	0.8385
36	0.5000	0.7805	81	0.3261	0.8241
37	0.0711	0.8701	82	0.0425	0.8741
38	0.3050	0.3286	83	−0.4371	0.9203
39	0.4216	0.8015	84	0.0949	0.8665

(*continued*)

Table 3B-14. (*Continued*)

No.	*Total Error* (w_i)	*Efficiency* $1/(1 + \lambda_i)$	*No.*	*Total Error* (w_i)	*Efficiency* $1/(1 + \lambda_i)$
40	0.3088	0.8278	85	0.0368	0.8749
41	0.3251	0.8243	86	0.2508	0.8397
42	0.1972	0.8497	87	−0.0795	0.8894
43	0.3767	0.8125	88	0.0370	0.8749
44	0.3264	0.8240	89	−0.1791	0.8998
45	0.1483	0.8581	90	−0.5923	0.9294

APPENDIX 3C

Regression Results of the Relationship Efficiency:Size for Selected Belgian Three-digit Industries—1978 (standard errors below estimates)

1. Building and refractory clays

$$E = \underset{(2.2589)}{74.2884} + \underset{(0.0149)}{0.0312S} \qquad R^2 = 0.0993$$

$$\ln E = \underset{(0.0868)}{3.9764} + \underset{(0.0218)}{0.0929 \ln S} \qquad R^2 = 0.3120$$

$$\ln E = \underset{(0.0387)}{4.2853} + \underset{(0.000255)}{0.000472S} \qquad R^2 = 0.0788$$

$$E = \underset{(2.9652)}{72.1482} + \underset{(0.0529)}{0.0876S} - \underset{(0.000115)}{0.000128S^2} \qquad R^2 = 0.1268$$

*Lung-Fai Wong and Vernon W. Ruttan are research assistant and professor, respectively, in the Department of Agricultural and Applied Economics at the University of Minnesota, St. Paul. The authors wish to thank Willis Peterson and Karen Brooks for their helpful suggestions. The authors are also indebted to Anna Burger, Elizabeth Clayton, Anton Malish, Todor Popov, Philip Raup, Anthony Tang, Karl-Eugen Wadekin, Augustyn Wos, and Michael Wyzan for their comments on methodology and the accuracies of data. This project is partially supported and funded by the Minnesota Experiment Station.

2. Clay products

$$E = \underset{(2.6095)}{74.3140} + \underset{(0.0252)}{0.0504S} \qquad R^2 = 0.0870$$

$$\ln E = \underset{(0.0875)}{3.8790} + \underset{(0.0215)}{0.1184} \ln S \qquad R^2 = 0.4184$$

$$\ln E = \underset{(0.0414)}{4.2831} + \underset{(0.000399)}{0.000796S} \qquad R^2 = 0.0864$$

$$E = \underset{(3.4275)}{65.0589} + \underset{(0.0772)}{0.3196S} - \underset{(0.000299)}{0.001086S^2} \qquad R^2 = 0.3097$$

3. Concrete, cement, or plaster products

$$E = \underset{(0.0027)}{99.1541} + \underset{(0.000009)}{0.00002S} \qquad R^2 = 0.0445$$

$$\ln E = \underset{(0.0001)}{4.5964} + \underset{(0.00003)}{0.00008} \ln S \qquad R^2 = 0.0845$$

$$\ln E = \underset{(0.00003)}{4.5967} + \underset{(0.0944(e^{-06}))}{0.2029(e^{-06})S} \qquad R^2 = 0.0445$$

$$E = \underset{(0.0033)}{99.1525} + \underset{(0.000031)}{0.000045S} - \underset{(0.0177(10^{-6}))}{0.0148(10^{-6})S^2} \qquad R^2 = 0.0513$$

4. Pharmaceutical products

$$E = \underset{(2.0677)}{71.5295} + \underset{(0.0035)}{0.0060S} \qquad R^2 = 0.0796$$

$$\ln E = \underset{(0.1090)}{4.1165} + \underset{(0.0224)}{0.0346} \ln S \qquad R^2 = 0.0641$$

$$\ln E = \underset{(0.0324)}{4.2555} + \underset{(0.000054)}{0.000085S} \qquad R^2 = 0.0657$$

$$E = \underset{(2.5081)}{71.3280} + \underset{(0.0102)}{0.0074S} - \underset{(0.0000036)}{0.0000005S^2} \qquad R^2 = 0.0801$$

5. Tools and finished metal goods

$$E = \underset{(0.7546)}{86.9929} + \underset{(0.0042)}{0.0126S} \qquad R^2 = 0.0747$$

$$\ln E = \underset{(0.0311)}{4.3555} + \underset{(0.0074)}{0.0300} \ln S \qquad R^2 = 0.1262$$

$$\ln E = \underset{(0.0100)}{4.4615} + \underset{(0.000055)}{0.000150S} \qquad R^2 = 0.0614$$

$$E = \underset{(0.9871)}{85.9360} + \underset{(0.01220)}{0.0314S} - \underset{(0.000017)}{0.000028S^2} \qquad R^2 = 0.0965$$

6. Civil engineering; mechanical handling equipment

$$E = \underset{(0.7124)}{89.3352} + \underset{(0.0013)}{0.0016S} \qquad R^2 = 0.0290$$

$$\ln E = \underset{(0.0314)}{4.4271} + \underset{(0.0074)}{0.0162}\ \ln S \qquad R^2 = 0.0864$$

$$\ln E = \underset{(0.0090)}{4.4906} + \underset{(0.000017)}{0.000019S} \qquad R^2 = 0.0241$$

$$E = \underset{(0.8757)}{88.6968} + \underset{(0.0062)}{0.0092S} - \underset{(0.000002)}{0.000002S^2} \qquad R^2 = 0.0580$$

7. Dairy products

$$E = \underset{(1.0925)}{85.3041} + \underset{(0.0059)}{0.0083S} \qquad R^2 = 0.0348$$

$$\ln E = \underset{(0.0336)}{4.3248} + \underset{(0.085)}{0.0343}\ \ln S \qquad R^2 = 0.2275$$

$$\ln E = \underset{(0.0165)}{4.4400} + \underset{(0.000088)}{0.000114S} \qquad R^2 = 0.0287$$

$$E = \underset{(1.3118)}{84.2026} + \underset{(0.0210)}{0.0383S} - \underset{(0.000040)}{0.000059S^2} \qquad R^2 = 0.0719$$

8. Animal and poultry foods

$$E = \underset{(0.8840)}{84.3080} + \underset{(0.0031)}{0.0037S} \qquad R^2 = 0.0232$$

$$\ln E = \underset{(0.0376)}{4.3549} + \underset{(0.0096)}{0.0216}\ \ln S \qquad R^2 = 0.0752$$

$$\ln E = \underset{(0.0127)}{4.4303} + \underset{(0.000044)}{0.000048S} \qquad R^2 = 0.0184$$

$$E = \underset{(1.0383)}{83.5544} + \underset{(0.0095)}{0.0160S} - \underset{(0.000005)}{0.000007S^2} \qquad R^2 = 0.0519$$

9. Brewing and malting

$$E = \underset{(1.3710)}{75.3123} + \underset{(0.0025)}{0.0049S} \qquad R^2 = 0.0555$$

$$\ln E = \underset{(0.0574)}{3.9583} + \underset{(0.0124)}{0.0832}\ \ln S \qquad R^2 = 0.4198$$

$$\ln E = \underset{(0.0261)}{4.3059} + \underset{(0.000049)}{0.000074S} \qquad R^2 = 0.0358$$

$$E = \underset{(1.5556)}{73.8947} + \underset{(0.0073)}{0.0174S} - \underset{(0.000003)}{0.000005S^2} \qquad R^2 = 0.1040$$

10. Wool industry

$$E = \underset{(1.6754)}{81.7689} + \underset{(0.0105)}{0.0161S} \qquad R^2 = 0.0488$$

$$\ln E = \underset{(0.0515)}{4.2209} + \underset{(0.0123)}{0.0491} \ln S \qquad R^2 = 0.2584$$

$$\ln E = \underset{(0.0232)}{4.3937} + \underset{(0.000145)}{0.000227S} \qquad R^2 = 0.0506$$

$$E = \underset{(2.1097)}{79.1088} + \underset{(0.0275)}{0.0665S} - \underset{(0.000051)}{0.000101S^2} \qquad R^2 = 0.1248$$

11. Cotton industry

$$E = \underset{(2.0857)}{78.2882} + \underset{(0.0050)}{0.0047S} \qquad R^2 = 0.0180$$

$$\ln E = \underset{(0.0901)}{4.0623} + \underset{(0.0209)}{0.0702} \ln S \qquad R^2 = 0.1908$$

$$\ln E = \underset{(0.0334)}{4.3388} + \underset{(0.000080)}{0.000072S} \qquad R^2 = 0.0166$$

$$E = \underset{(2.5281)}{76.8166} + \underset{(0.0166)}{0.0209S} - \underset{(0.000006)}{0.000007S^2} \qquad R^2 = 0.0396$$

12. Floor covering

$$E = \underset{(1.6595)}{78.4644} + \underset{(0.0074)}{0.0091S} \qquad R^2 = 0.0267$$

$$\ln E = \underset{(0.0636)}{4.0904} + \underset{(0.0155)}{0.0703} \ln S \qquad R^2 = 0.2720$$

$$\ln E = \underset{(0.0285)}{4.3457} + \underset{(0.000127)}{0.000146S} \qquad R^2 = 0.0232$$

$$E = \underset{(1.9038)}{77.0909} + \underset{(0.0179)}{0.0309S} - \underset{(0.000016)}{0.000022S^2} \qquad R^2 = 0.0577$$

13. Paper and board

$$E = \underset{(0.9638)}{86.7805} + \underset{(0.0060)}{0.0079S} \qquad R^2 = 0.0293$$

$$\ln E = \underset{(0.0437)}{4.4037} + \underset{(0.0104)}{0.0160} \ln S \qquad R^2 = 0.0401$$

$$\ln E = \underset{(0.0119)}{4.4608} + \underset{(0.000074)}{0.000092S} \qquad R^2 = 0.0260$$

$$E = \underset{(1.2896)}{86.3788} + \underset{(0.0150)}{0.0144S} - \underset{(0.000019)}{0.000009S^2} \qquad R^2 = 0.0332$$

14. Plastics

$$E = \underset{(0.9893)}{81.4239} + \underset{(0.0059)}{0.0155S} \qquad R^2 = 0.0823$$

$$\ln E = \underset{(0.0509)}{4.2036} + \underset{(0.0121)}{0.0514} \ln S \qquad R^2 = 0.1695$$

$$\ln E = \underset{(0.0154)}{4.3920} + \underset{(0.000092)}{0.000217S} \qquad R^2 = 0.0600$$

$$E = \underset{(1.2548)}{80.2139} + \underset{(0.0138)}{0.0359S} - \underset{(0.000016)}{0.000024S^2} \qquad R^2 = 0.1068$$

4 SOURCES OF DIFFERENCES IN AGRICULTURAL PRODUCTIVITY GROWTH AMONG SOCIALIST COUNTRIES

Lung-Fai Wong and Vernon W. Ruttan*

4.1. Introduction

Ever since the emergence of collectivization, the efficiency of agriculture of centrally planned economies (CPE) has been of great interest to economists. The recent increase of food purchases by socialist countries in the international market has renewed this interest. In particular, the production efficiency of socialist agriculture has drawn the concern of economists, their conclusions, however, are mixed.

Judging from the growth of agricultural production, D. Gale Johnson has pointed out "From a number of viewpoints the agriculture of most CPE performed well from about 1950 to the mid-1970s" (Johnson 1982, 845). Michael Wyzan has argued that "the empirical evidence suggests that Soviet decisions in the sphere of agricultural production, contrary to the conventional wisdom, are well-founded technologically" (Wyzan 1981,

*Lung-Fai Wong and Vernon W. Ruttan are research assistant and professor, respectively, in the Department of Agricultural and Applied Economics at the University of Minnesota, St. Paul. The authors wish to thank Willis Peterson and Karen Brooks for their helpful suggestions. The authors are also indebted to Anna Burger, Elizabeth Clayton, Anton Malish, Todor Popov, Philip Raup, Anthony Tang, Karl-Eugen Wadekin, Augustyn Wos, and Michael Wyzan for their comments on methodology and the accuracies of data. This project is partially supported and funded by the Minnesota Experiment Station.

475). But other researchers have insisted that agriculture in socialist countries is less efficient than in capitalist countries. Michael Ellman concluded that "the growth of agricultural productivity under state socialism has been very unsatisfactory from a Marxist-Leninist standpoint" (Ellman 1981, 988).

It becomes clear that evaluation of agriculture in socialist countries varies depending on the criteria economists use and the focus of their studies. Up to now, most studies have focused on agrarian policies and performance in a particular country or region. A quantitative comparative analysis of the differences, and the sources of differences, in agricultural productivity growth among socialist countries has not been available.

In this chapter, we will investigate the sources of agricultural productivity growth in nine socialist countries; Bulgaria, Czechoslovakia, East Germany, Hungary, Poland, Romania, Yugoslavia, the Soviet Union, and China. A detailed discussion of agrarian policies in these countries is, however, beyond the scope of the chapter. We (a) first compare the growth of aggregate production, labor productivity, and land productivity among countries; (b) estimate a cross-country metaproduction function for the countries included in our study; (c) use the estimated coefficients to account for the sources of labor and land productivity growth within and among countries.

In order to enable us to perform a multicountry comparative analysis, we converted all input and output measures to comparable units (see the chapter appendix for sources of data and the conversion procedure). All of our analysis is done at the national level.

4.2. Growth in Agricultural Production

A summary of the aggregate agricultural output growth indexes for the several countries for 1950–1979 is presented in table 4-1. The year 1960 was chosen as the base year for comparison purposes in order to avoid any bias in growth rate that might have resulted from the disruption and recovery after World War II. It also allowed us to concentrate on the period of economic reform in the USSR and in the Eastern European countries after the death of Stalin.

The growth indexes presented in table 4-1 may not be a good measure of performance, but they represent the different growth patterns of the socialist countries. Among the Eastern European countries, Hungary, Romania, and Yugoslavia can be classified as the fast-growth countries. Growth rates of agricultural production in these countries are in the range of 3.04 to 3.89%. These three countries are also characterized by their success in maintaining a relatively steady growth rate over the last two decades.

Bulgaria, Czechoslovakia, East Germany, and Poland are the slow-growth countries. Their growth rates are in the range of 1.85 to 2.56%. Except Poland, these countries experienced some stagnation during the early sixties. Poland apparently had been able to maintain steady growth in the sixties. But since 1975, Poland's 1.85% growth rate has been the smallest among the socialist countries.

Russian agricultural output expanded 60 percent during the same period. Although the 2.86% growth rate fell short of what had been planned, Soviet agricultural performance compares favorably with East Germany and Poland.

Among the nine socialist countries, China is the least well-fed nation. But the rate of growth in agricultural output in China has been high.[1] China achieved a 4.76% growth rate which resulted in a more than doubling of its aggregate agricultural production in the last two decades. This rapid growth occurred in spite of the disappointing "Three Red Flags" campaign and damage from drought and flood in the early sixties. Also, during the turmoil period of the Cultural Revolution, agricultural production was less than anticipated. Not until 1972 did Chinese agriculture resume its rapid growth rate.

Agriculture in the socialist countries has a relatively satisfactory performance when evaluated in terms of overall growth rates. The average growth rate for the seven Eastern European countries was 2.75 for the period of 1960–1979, and the overall average growth for all nine countries is 2.99. This is not low in terms of the historical performance of other developed countries. But this does not necessarily imply that their performance was satisfactory of from either a per worker food production or a per area food production perspective.

4.3. Growth in Labor and Land Productivity

The two partial productivities, output per worker and output per hectare—measured in wheat units—are presented for the nine socialist countries for the period of 1950–1979 in tables 4-2 and 4-3. As shown in table 4-2, East Germany had the highest level of labor productivity, and Hungary the second highest level of labor productivity. They were followed by Czechoslovakia, Bulgaria, the Soviet Union, Poland, Yugoslavia, Romania, and China.

Three general patterns can be observed. First, the three most industrialized countries—East Germany, Hungary, and Czechoslovakia—had the highest level of labor productivity. Second, the differences in labor productivity among these countries are large and are growing. In 1960, labor productivity in East Germany was 13.6 times that of China. This

Table 4-1 Indexes of Aggregate Agricultural Production (1960 = 100)

Year	*BUL*	*CZE*	*GDR*	*HUN*	*POL*	*ROM*	*YUG*	*USSR*	*PRC*
1950	62	88	69	75	81	58	50	73	82
1951	87	88	82	92	72	78	75	66	90
1952	66	87	86	64	72	70	44	75	104
1953	83	97	86	84	74	85	78	74	107
1954	69	88	90	77	81	79	64	76	111
1955	78	96	83	92	79	96	84	85	119
1956	72	103	85	83	90	75	67	95	125
1957	86	98	88	98	91	96	100	91	129
1958	85	95	91	92	93	80	82	104	133
1959	102	94	86	108	92	104	112	99	115
1960	100	100	100	100	100	100	100	100	100
1961	96	97	76	95	111	104	96	106	98
1962	100	94	88	100	100	96	100	107	104
1963	101	104	88	103	108	100	107	101	116
1964	115	106	93	106	111	105	115	120	131
1965	120	91	98	109	113	115	106	114	142
1966	141	107	98	116	118	132	128	134	154
1967	138	109	108	118	124	130	124	131	157
1968	128	115	107	118	129	127	120	137	153

1969	133	117	99	126	123	131	132	132	155	
1970	134	118	103	119	125	114	121	149	173	
1971	138	125	102	137	121	141	134	148	178	
1972	152	130	113	147	132	159	132	141	177	
1973	145	138	113	151	141	149	138	170	192	
1974	135	144	124	161	142	153	158	159	200	
1975	147	137	117	159	139	156	156	142	210	
1976	157	134	112	155	143	196	165	168	215	
1977	145	145	121	170	132	190	173	163	218	
1978	152	153	127	176	144	193	162	179	238	
1979	164	142	127	167	140	201	166	160	259	
Growth	3.13	1.88	1.62	2.95	2.48	3.60	3.72	3.22	3.29	(1950–1979)
rate	2.50	2.56	2.03	3.37	1.85	3.89	3.04	2.86	4.76	(1960–1979)

Sources:

Indexes for the USSR and Eastern Europe are USDA estimates. 1950–67 indexes are derived from *Indexes of Agricultural Production in Eastern Europe and Soviet Union 1950–68.* USDA, ERS Foreign 273, Washington D.C.: July 1969, page 1. 1968–69 indexes are derived and computed from *Agricultural Statistics of Eastern Europe and the Soviet Union 1950–70.* USDA, ERS Foreign 349, Washington D.C.: June 1973, page 28. 1970–79 indexes are derived from *Indexes of Agricultural and Food Production for Europe and the USSR, average 1961–65 and Annual 1970 through 1979.* USDA Economic, Statistics and Cooperation Service, Statistical Bulletin No. 635, Washington D.C.: June 1980, page 5.

Indexes for the USSR and Eastern Europe are calculated by Laspeyres' base-weighted aggregate formula. The weights used are estimates of the 1961–65 average prices received by farmers in Western Europe.

Indexes for China are official figures published in the *Annual Economic Report of China.* Beijing: 1981, page VI–10. Indexes for 1950–69 are calculated at constant price of 1957, and for 1970–79 are calculated at constant price of 1970.

Table 4-2 Labor Productivity, Wheat Units per Labor Unit

Year	*BUL*	*CZE*	*GDR*	*HUN*	*POL*	*ROM*	*YUG*	*USSR*	*PRC*
1950	2.43	6.69	11.36	5.27	6.08	1.67	1.68	5.51	1.31
1951	3.54	6.95	13.51	6.53	5.42	2.29	2.52	4.96	1.42
1952	2.76	7.15	14.02	4.61	5.42	2.04	1.50	5.68	1.63
1953	3.45	8.31	14.12	6.42	5.58	2.48	2.75	5.65	1.67
1954	2.90	7.41	14.43	5.96	6.12	2.29	2.25	5.85	1.71
1955	3.24	7.95	12.81	6.97	5.98	2.60	3.00	6.60	1.81
1956	2.95	8.66	13.71	6.16	6.83	2.11	2.43	7.44	1.87
1957	3.59	8.56	14.71	7.18	6.92	2.66	3.69	7.19	1.93
1958	3.46	8.54	15.21	6.83	7.09	2.19	3.08	8.29	1.97
1959	4.38	9.15	15.27	8.18	7.03	2.82	4.28	7.67	1.69
1960	4.69	10.69	19.86	7.99	7.65	2.64	3.88	8.00	1.46
1961	4.53	11.00	15.48	8.08	8.46	2.85	3.82	8.70	1.42
1962	5.06	10.96	17.93	8.89	7.61	2.64	4.02	8.93	1.49
1963	5.28	12.27	17.94	9.60	8.21	2.76	4.38	8.57	1.63
1964	6.19	12.78	18.85	10.26	8.39	2.91	4.79	10.10	1.81

1965	7.37	11.18	20.25	10.71	8.70	3.14	4.70	9.52	1.91	
1966	8.95	13.20	20.63	11.46	9.11	3.69	5.64	11.28	2.02	
1967	8.90	13.72	23.10	11.72	9.62	3.65	5.57	11.14	2.02	
1968	8.67	14.69	25.47	11.64	10.04	3.58	5.49	11.74	1.93	
1969	9.49	15.15	24.57	14.18	9.58	3.71	6.15	11.47	1.91	
1970	9.97	15.39	25.70	13.63	9.76	3.21	5.75	13.06	2.07	
1971	10.72	16.52	25.58	15.88	9.47	4.03	6.49	13.07	2.08	
1972	12.07	18.24	29.46	17.43	10.42	4.56	6.53	12.48	2.02	
1973	11.99	19.88	30.07	18.48	11.10	4.29	6.96	15.00	2.13	
1974	11.56	20.91	34.34	20.34	11.12	4.42	8.13	14.02	2.17	
1975	13.46	20.37	33.78	20.62	11.64	4.56	8.19	12.69	2.22	
1976	15.12	19.99	33.28	20.44	12.21	5.79	8.84	15.05	2.22	
1977	14.55	22.08	37.04	22.78	11.50	5.67	9.46	14.73	2.20	
1978	15.65	23.71	39.82	23.61	12.81	5.84	9.04	16.20	2.37	
1979	16.89	22.17	40.82	22.24	12.89	6.16	9.45	14.62	2.52	
Growth	6.89	4.49	4.23	5.51	2.97	3.77	5.61	3.92	1.52	(1950–1979)
rate	6.90	4.45	4.79	6.11	2.69	4.50	5.04	3.45	2.48	(1960–1979)

Sources: see appendix 4A.

Table 4-3 Land Productivity, Wheat Units per Hectare

Year	*BUL*	*CZE*	*GDR*	*HUN*	*POL*	*ROM*	*YUG*	*USSR*	*PRC*
1950	1.18	1.97	2.58	1.50	1.61	0.73	0.69	0.28	0.66
1951	1.67	1.98	3.06	1.85	1.44	0.98	1.02	0.26	0.75
1952	1.27	1.96	3.22	1.29	1.44	0.88	0.59	0.29	0.89
1953	1.60	2.26	3.23	1.71	1.48	1.07	1.03	0.29	0.95
1954	1.33	2.02	3.38	1.56	1.62	1.00	0.83	0.29	1.02
1955	1.52	2.17	3.13	1.88	1.58	1.22	1.08	0.33	1.08
1956	1.40	2.34	3.21	1.70	1.80	0.95	0.85	0.37	1.13
1957	1.69	2.24	3.32	2.01	1.82	1.20	1.27	0.35	1.15
1958	1.68	2.16	3.45	1.89	1.86	0.99	1.04	0.40	1.19
1959	1.97	2.15	3.26	2.22	1.84	1.28	1.42	0.38	1.03
1960	1.92	2.35	3.79	2.07	1.99	1.23	1.27	0.39	0.88
1961	1.84	2.24	2.87	1.98	2.22	1.28	1.21	0.41	0.86
1962	1.91	2.18	3.33	2.11	2.01	1.17	1.27	0.41	0.91
1963	1.93	2.42	3.34	2.18	2.18	1.22	1.37	0.39	1.01
1964	2.17	2.61	3.51	2.25	2.24	1.28	1.47	0.46	1.12

1965	2.25	2.13	3.72	2.32	2.31	1.39	1.36	0.44	1.22	
1966	2.64	2.51	3.72	2.48	2.41	1.59	1.64	0.52	1.32	
1967	2.56	2.57	4.10	2.52	2.55	1.57	1.60	0.50	1.33	
1968	2.37	2.71	4.14	2.53	2.65	1.52	1.55	0.53	1.25	
1969	2.40	2.76	3.85	2.70	2.56	1.57	1.70	0.50	1.32	
1970	2.42	2.79	4.00	2.56	2.60	1.37	1.56	0.57	1.47	
1971	2.50	2.96	3.96	2.95	2.52	1.69	1.74	0.56	1.51	
1972	2.74	3.09	4.39	3.17	2.77	1.91	1.72	0.54	1.51	
1973	2.64	3.29	4.39	3.27	2.97	1.79	1.81	0.65	1.59	
1974	2.45	3.43	4.82	3.51	3.00	1.84	2.07	0.61	1.69	
1975	2.69	3.28	4.54	3.47	2.95	1.87	2.05	0.54	1.78	
1976	2.75	3.22	4.35	3.39	3.04	2.35	2.18	0.64	1.78	
1977	2.54	3.49	4.70	3.73	2.81	2.28	2.29	0.62	1.86	
1978	2.66	3.69	4.94	3.88	3.07	2.31	2.14	0.68	1.97	
1979	2.87	3.44	4.94	3.71	3.00	2.41	2.20	0.61	2.14	
Growth	2.75	2.12	1.78	3.29	2.76	3.38	3.72	3.14	3.10	(1950–1979)
rate	1.99	2.73	2.21	3.67	2.24	3.76	3.29	2.76	4.49	(1960–1979)

Sources: See appendix 4A.

ratio grew to 16.2 by 1979—a 20% jump. Third, even though there has been much discussion of the favorable effects of decentralization, the labor productivity data cannot be interpreted as supporting the hypothesis that the less centralized countries (Hungary, Poland, Yugoslavia, Romania) have out performed the more centralized countries.

Land productivity, measured in wheat units per hectare, is presented in table 4-3. The three industrialized countries also had the highest level of land productivity. The differences in land productivity among countries are smaller than the differences in labor productivity and are shrinking over time. Apparently it has been easier to improve labor productivity than to improve land productivity. With the exception of China, none of these countries has been able to double their land productivity over the last 20 years.

In spite of the common perception that agricultural production in socialist countries is rather slow, our data indicate that the labor productivity of the nine socialist countries (including the highly populated China) has increased by at least 60% for the period of 1960–1979. We also noted that industrial inputs played an increasingly important role in agricultural production. For example, from 1960 to 1979, the consumption of chemical fertilizer in both Romania and China increased by fifteen times. The number of tractors in Yugoslavia and China increased ten and thirteen times, respectively.

Except for China, the growth rate of labor productivity has been faster than the growth rate of land productivity. Despite the fact that the total agricultural area in the Eastern European countries has decreased (or remained unchanged), the USSR and Eastern European countries have emphasized mechanical technology to increase their labor productivity, while China has concentrated on labor-intensive technology to intensify land use.

4.4. The Cross-Country Metaproduction Function

The partial productivities indicate significant differences in the pattern of productivity growth among these socialist countries. In order to understand the sources of these differences, we have estimated a cross-country metaproduction function for these countries.[2] Three categories—resource endowments, technical inputs, and human capital—are considered as possible sources of productivity changes, or, of productivity differences. Resource endowments include labor, land, and internal capital accumulation in the form of land reclamation and development, such as livestock inventories. Technical inputs include the chemical devices and the biological and chemical materials purchased from the industrial sector. Human capital generally includes education, skill, knowledge, and capacity embodied in the population of the agricultural sector. In this study, because of the lack of variation over time and among countries in the general education level, we concentrate on the capacity of agricultural research instead.

The input variables used in the estimation are agricultural labor (*N*), land (*L*), fertilizer (*F*), machinery (*M*), livestock (*S*), and agricultural research (*R*). The dependent variable is aggregate agricultural output (*Y*) measured in wheat units (see appendix 4A for definitions and sources). The production function we are estimating is the unrestricted Cobb-Douglas production form specified as follows:

$$Y = e^{a}N^{b1}A^{b2}F^{b3}M^{b4}L^{b5}R^{b6} \tag{4.1}$$

Earlier estimations have shown strong evidence of existence of multicollinearity, which is not unexpected in a cross-section time series model. Two methods are being used to correct this problem. The principal components method was employed to reduce the problem of correlation among variables. Three-year averages were also used to reduce the correlation that generated from the time series data.

Because the different measuring units used in the independent variables would cause high sensitivity for transformation of the components, all analyses therefore were done on the correlation matrix which, in effect, normalized all variables.[3] The choices of principal components are based on the criteria that at least 95% of variances can be explained.

Six types of regressions are estimated. The first one includes all nine countries from the period of 1950 to 1979 and annual data of the five conventional variables, *N,L,F,M,*S. As shown in table 4-4, all estimated coefficients for regression 1 are positive and statistically significant, except for the livestock coefficient which has an extremely low *t*-ratio. Elsewhere, other studies also experienced the problem of negative or insignificant livestocks coefficients (Clayton 1980; Brooks 1983).

Regressions 2 to 6 use data from a smaller number of countries and employ the three-year averages. They are based on data for only the seven years for which agricultural research data are available. Hence, East Germany is excluded because of incomplete data for the variable for agricultural research. Also, only those years that have data for all six variables are used in these regressions, which reduces the total number of observations to fifty-six, mostly from the period of 1959 to 1979. Comparing

Table 4-4 Comparison of Agricultural Production Functions for Socialist Countries[a]

Regression No.	*R1*	*R2*	*R3*	*R4*
Model	*Wong*	*Wong*	*Wong*	*Wong*
No. of Countries	*9*	*8*	*8*	*8*
		(Eastern Europe, USSR, PRC)		
Deg. of Freedom	*266*	*52*	*52*	*52*
Labor	0.223[b]	0.199[b]	0.225[b]	0.23[b]
	(0.009)	(0.011)	(0.010)	(0.012)
Land	0.143[b]	0.135[b]	0.129[b]	0.145[b]
	(0.005)	(0.007)	(0.008)	(0.003)
Fertilizer	0.177[b]	0.257[b]	0.208[b]	0.165[b]
	(0.009)	(0.019)	(0.02)	(0.006)
Machinery	0.122[b]	0.119[b]	0.054[b]	0.08[b]
	(0.015)	(0.02)	(0.019)	(0.015)
Livestock	0.233	0.206	0.20	0.204
	(1.27)	(1.29)	(1.29)	(1.29)
Research & Ext.			0.097[b]	0.084[b]
			(0.01)	(0.01)
Tech. Educ.				
Trend				0.078
				(0.054)
Climate				
Sum of coeff.	0.898	0.916	0.913	0.908
R^2	0.98	0.99	0.99	0.99
R^2 adjust.	0.98	0.99	0.99	0.99

[a]Figures in parentheses are standard errors.

[b]Asterisk indicates the significance of estimates compared to standard errors.

Sources:

R1 to R6: See appendix 4A.

R7: Hayami and Ruttan (1971, p. 93).

R8: Kawagoe, Hayami, and Ruttan (1983, table 2).

R9: Clayton (1980, p. 455).

R10: Johnson and Brooks (1983, p. 147).

Table 4-4 *(Continued)*

R5	*R6*	*R7*	*R8*	*R9*	*R10*
Wong	*Wong*	*Hayami & Ruttan*		*Clayton*	*Brooks*
4	*4*	*37*	*43*	*1*	*11*
Less-Cntl	*Centlz*	*(1971)*	*(1983)*	*(15 SOVIET REPUBLICS)*	
24	*24*	*29*	*32*	*60*	*292*
0.063[b]	0.222[b]	0.451[b]	0.436[b]	0.37[b]	0.37[b]
(0.018)	(0.006)	(0.074)	(0.042)	(0.05)	(0.034)
0.15[b]	0.138[b]	0.088	0.091[b]	0.20[b]	0.65[b]
(0.024)	(0.002)	(0.062)	(0.012)	(0.05)	(0.049)
0.085[b]	0.208[b]	0.112	0.195[b]	0.21[b]	0.34[b]
(0.011)	(0.004)	(0.059)	(0.012)	(0.03)	(0.016)
0.126	0.078[b]	0.071	0.109[b]	0.14[b]	−0.30[b]
(0.779)	(0.009)	(0.065)	(0.004)	(0.06)	(0.078)
0.145[b]	0.207	0.247[b]	0.195[b]	0.05	−0.14[b]
(0.015)	(1.47)	(0.089)	(0.01)	(0.09)	(0.056)
0.134[b]	0.068[b]				
(0.012)	(0.007)				
		0.182[b]	0.064[b]		
		(0.057)	(0.006)		
0.197[b]	−0.003				0.0002
(0.037)	(0.039)				(0.0019)
					0.02[b]
					(0.003)
0.703	0.921	1.15	1.026	0.97	0.92
0.88	0.99		0.97	0.99	
0.87	0.99	0.95	0.93		0.993

regression 2 to regression 1, only the fertilizer coefficient is significantly different. Although it cannot provide us with additional information, regression 2 provides a base for comparison of regressions 2 to 4.

Regressions 3 and 4 include man-years in agricultural research in an attempt to capture the effect of technical change. With the inclusion of agricultural research in regression 3, the magnitude of the machinery coefficient drops more than 50 percent. The magnitude of the fertilizer coefficient drops slightly. Other variables remain quite stable. The significance of the coefficient indicates that agricultural research in these countries has made a significant contribution to agricultural production. The factor share of agricultural research may even be greater than that of machinery.

Regression 4 is similar to regression 2, but a time-trend variable is added. This variable is included in an attempt to capture some of the unexplained residual effects of technological change or other infrastructure investments not captured by agricultural research. Its lack of significances suggests that most of the changes have been explained by the other six variables.

In order to investigate different economic production patterns between centralized and less-centralized agricultures, we separate the four less-centralized countries, Hungary, Poland, Romania, and Yugoslavia, from our samples. The results of regression of the less-centralized countries in regression 5 are quite different than the results in regressions 1 to 4. The differences are even more obvious when compared with regression 6 which includes only the four centralized countries, Bulgaria, Czechoslovakia, the Soviet Union, and China. The estimated coefficients in regression 6 are very similar to those in regression 3, but are very distinct from regression 5.

First of all, the smaller coefficient for the labor and fertilizer variables in regression 5 suggests that farmers in the less-centralized countries tended to utilize their labor and purchased inputs more efficiently. On the other hand, the larger research coefficient indicates that agricultural research in the less-centralized countries has a higher factor share than it does in the centralized countries. Third, the significance of the trend coefficient suggests that there are additional sources of changes that are not explained by those conventional inputs.

It may be of interest to compare our results with some results obtained by other scholars. Regression 7 to 10 presented estimates by Hayami and Ruttan; Clayton; and Johnson and Brooks. Hayami's and Ruttan's estimates are based on a group of developed countries and developing countries for the period of 1955 to 1980. The estimates of Clayton and Johnson and Brooks are for the 15 Soviet Republics for the period of 1960–1975 and 1960–1979 respectively. Compared with their results, our estimates have smaller labor coefficients, but the other coefficients are surprisingly close. Thus, considering the crudeness of the data, we feel reasonably comfortable with our results.

Comfortable or not, we are sensitive to a number of problems that we are not yet able to overcome. On the output side, we included outputs from both the state farms and private farms. This should not cause any serious problem per se because our input variables also include the private sector. It causes some problems only when we are not able to account for the laborers that work in the garden plots, and hence, overestimate the labor productivity. As illustrated in appendix 4A, our output series used the price structure of nonsocialist countries to aggregate individual commodities. Had we had the complete data on price structure for the nine socialist countries, we might have had more efficient estimates.

The problems of data quality also appear in the input variables. The nine countries cover a large geographic area starting from a latitude of 20 degrees north to 70 degrees north. Hence without adjusting for the soil quality and climate conditions, it is questionable whether an accurate land coefficient can be obtained. As for the industrial inputs, the quality of technical inputs such as fertilizer and machinery is related to institutional structure which varies among countries. Although we realize that it takes some time for the effect of agricultural research to show up in the production process, we do not impose any time lags for the agricultural research variables. This should not cause too many biases on other estimated coefficients since agricultural research has been increasing.[4]

4.5. Accounting for Productivity Changes

As stated earlier, our primary interest in the production coefficients is to use them in accounting for changes in labor and land productivity in these socialist countries between 1960 and 1979. The results we obtained from estimating a cross-country time series production function can be interpreted as the metaproduction function for these socialist countries. The sum of the estimated coefficients indicates that the assumption of a linear homogeneous production function is not too unreasonable.[5] Combined with the Euler theorem, this implies that the percentage differences in output per labor unit over time can be expressed as the sum of percentage differences in conventional and nonconventional inputs per labor unit, weighted by their respective production elasticities.

Based on the results presented in table 4-4, the following set of adjusted coefficients are adopted for the growth-accounting procedure: 0.25 for labor, 0.15 for land, 0.2 for fertilizer, 0.1 for machinery, 0.2 for livestock, and 0.1 for agricultural research. We will use these adjusted production elasticities to find out the sources of changes in labor and land productivities from 1960 to 1979 for all the nine socialist countries. We will also use U.S. data to do a cross-country comparison of differences in labor productivity for 1979 and Japan data to do a cross-country comparison of differences in land productivity. The United States is chosen for the labor productivity comparison because it has achieved exceptionally high levels of labor productivity; Japan is chosen for the land productivity comparison because it has achieved exceptionally high levels of land productivity. The growth-accounting results are presented in tables 4-5 through 4-8.

In table 4-5, figures in the "percent" columns represent the percentage changes in agricultural *labor productivity* from 1960 to 1979. For example, the percentage changes in labor productivity are computed from the changes of labor productivity during the period of 1960–1979 divided by the labor productivity in 1979. Other entries in the "percent" columns account for the percentage changes of factor/labor ratios during the same period. The "index" columns account for the percentage of productivity changes that can be explained by the respective factor inputs, with the first row being set to 100. For example, the change in labor productivity between 1960 and 1979 in Bulgaria is 72.22% of the 1979 productivity level. Of this 72.22%, 21.29 (or 29% of the 72.22) is attributable to the changes in resource endowments in Bulgaria.

The "index" columns are constructed for the purpose of comparison. As shown in the "index" columns, 17 to 29% (depending on individual countries) of the change in labor productivity can be explained by the change in resource endowment during the period of 1960–1979. This indicates that the increase in land/labor ratios and the livestock/labor ratios account only for a quarter of the increase in labor productivity. The negative percentages for China are due to a decrease in the land/labor ratio.

Interestingly enough, the total change in fertilizer and machinery explained 34–59% of the increase in labor productivity. This can have an important policy implication. It suggests that industrial inputs have been the major sources of growth of labor productivity in socialist countries—particularly the sizeable contribution from fertilizer.

The changes in agricultural research explained at least 10 percent of the increase of labor productivity. Although agricultural research in Poland and China explained up to 20% of the changes, it is still quite low. Another study showed that human capital accounted for 35% of the differences in labor productivity among a group of developing and developed countries (Hayami and Ruttan 1971, 97).

Several generalizations are worth mentioning here. In all the countries, fertilizer is the single most important source for the changes in labor productivity. On the other hand, machinery is not as important as most people might have expected. Following fertilizer, agricultural research is the second most important source for the changes in labor productivity. This is especially so in Poland and China and somewhat less so in other socialist countries. It suggests that other socialist countries are capable of increasing their labor productivity by investing more in agricultural research. The importance of land and livestock is quite evenly distributed among countries, except China whose land/labor ratio has been decreasing rather than increasing. All together, the five factor/labor ratios totally explained 70% or mroe of the changes in labor productivity. The unexplained portion may be caused by other factors such as technological change or shifting of policy. In the case of Poland, one might interpret it as all labor productivity changes are explained by the six factor/labor ratios.

The growth accounting for changes in *land productivity* for the same period is presented in table 4-6. In general, except for China, the percentage changes of land productivity are less than for labor productivity, and are less than 50% of the current productivity level. Moreover, because the labor/land ratio experienced a sizeable decline, it contributed negatively to the changes of land productivity. For example, the negative figure in the labor factor for Bulgaria can be explained as follows: had the labor/land ratio remained unchanged in that period, Bulgaria would have had another 35% increase in land productivity.

Next to Bulgaria, East Germany has the largest percentage decrease in the labor/land ratio. The industrialization process in East Germany has drawn a large number of workers away from the agricultural sector. As a result of this, East Germany has the lowest increase in land productivity; about half of what the Hungarians and Romanians had achieved.

The three less-centralized countries—Hungary, Romania, and Yugoslavia—had a relatively large increase in land productivity. This also supports the result of regression 5 in the estimation of the metaproduction function, which suggested that less-centralized countries tend to use their labor more efficiently and hence obtain a higher increase in land productivity.

The reason for the positive labor percentage in China is obvious. Unlike all Eastern European countries and the Soviet Union, which had a sizeable decrease in the number of agricultural laborers, the Chinese had positive growth in agricultural labor. And this, combined with other factors, has made the percentage changes of China's land productivity the largest among the nine socialist countries.

Again, as in the case of changes in labor productivity, the increase in fertilizer/land ratio is also the single most important source for the changes in land productivity for all nine countries. The machinery/land ratio in Hungary has a surprisingly low change rate and makes a small contribution to change of land productivity. In contrast, agricultural

Table 4-5. Accounting for Changes in Agricultural Labor Productivity Among Socialist Countri (60 vs 79)

	BULGARIA		CZECH-OSLAVAKIA		E. GERMANY		HUNGARY	
Country	*percent*	*index*	*percent*	*index*	*percent*	*index*	*percent*	*index*
Changes in labor productivity (%)	72.22	100	51.78	100	51.35	100	64.09	100
Resource endowment	21.29	29	12.77	25	14.99	29	14.63	23
Land	8.75	12	4.40	8	5.50	11	5.34	8
Livestock	12.54	17	8.37	16	9.49	18	9.28	14
Technical inputs	24.79	34	20.93	40	18.89	37	22.51	35
Fertilizer	18.27	25	16.11	31	12.68	25	18.69	29
Machinery	6.52	9	4.83	9	6.22	12	3.82	6
Research & Ext.	8.82	12	7.84	15	8.26	16	8.37	13
Explained total	54.90	76	41.54	80	42.14	82	45.50	71
Unexplained total	17.32	24	10.24	20	9.21	18	18.59	29

Accounting formula: $$\frac{\Delta(Y/N)}{(Y/N)_0} = 0.15\frac{\Delta(L/N)}{(L/N)_0} + 0.2\frac{\Delta(S/N)}{(S/N)_0} + 0.2\frac{\Delta(F/N)}{(F/N)_0} + 0.1\frac{\Delta(M/N)}{(M/N)_0} + 0.1\frac{\Delta(R/N)}{(R/N)_0} + \text{unexplained}.$$

research is an important source for explanation of changes of land productivity. It explained as much as 31 percent of the land productivity changes in East Germany.

Two more observations can be made from table 4-6. Agricultural research in Eastern Europe and the Soviet Union is in general a more important source for the changes of land productivity than for changes in labor productivity. The reverse holds for China. But it is still relatively lower than its effect in other nonsocialist countries. The zero percentage in the unexplained row for Poland again supports the notion that a large share of the productivity changes, both land and labor, can be explained by the changes of conventional inputs and agricultural research.

Table 4-5. *(Continued)*

POLAND		*ROMANIA*		*YUGOSLAVIA*		*USSR*		*CHINA*	
percent	*index*	*percent*	*index*	*percent*	*index*	*percent*	*index*	*percent*	*index*
40.61	100	57.06	100	58.92	100	45.27	100	42.01	100
8.60	21	10.67	19	10.23	17	8.91	20	−3.50	−8
1.60	4	2.42	4	4.28	7	1.98	4	−6.12	−15
7.00	17	8.25	14	5.95	10	6.92	15	2.62	6
23.95	59	24.65	43	25.09	43	23.73	52	22.66	54
15.94	39	18.94	33	16.35	28	18.45	41	18.19	43
8.01	20	5.71	10	8.74	15	5.29	12	4.47	11
8.04	20	8.48	15	6.33	11	6.65	15	8.90	21
40.59	100	43.80	77	41.65	71	39.29	87	28.06	67
0.01	0	13.26	23	17.28	29	5.97	13	13.95	33

4.6. Comparison of Productivity Differences

Besides examining the sources for changes in labor productivity and land productivity among the nine socialist countries, it is interesting to examine the sources of differences in productivity between socialist and nonsocialist countries as of 1979. The results of a comparison of *labor productivity* between the socialist countries and the United States as of 1979 are summarized in table 4-7. As shown on the first row, labor productivity is substantially higher in U.S. agriculture. Of the large differences, about one-third can be explained by the differences in resource endowments and one-third can be explained by the differences in technical inputs. Differences in agricultural research explained less than 10 percent of the differences in labor productivity. This is quite low relative to the comparisons with LDC's in which human capital accounted for 35 percent of the differences in labor productivity (Hayami and Ruttan 1971, 91). The small differences in agricultural research indicate that it has little effect in reducing the labor productivity gap between socialist countries and the United States. Second, it indicates that the contribution of agricultural

Table 4-6. Accounting for Changes in Agricultural Land Productivity Among Socialist Countrie (60 vs 79).

	BULGARIA		*CZECH-OSLAVAKIA*		*E. GERMANY*		*HUNGARY*	
Country	*percent*	*index*	*percent*	*index*	*percent*	*index*	*percent*	*index*
Changes in land productivity (%)	33.28	100	31.77	100	23.22	100	44.23	100
Resource endowment	−32.97	−99	−6.82	−21	−11.04	−48	−10.47	−24
Labor	−35.04	−105	−10.37	−33	−14.46	−62	−13.83	−31
Livestock	2.08	6	3.55	11	3.41	15	3.35	8
Technical inputs	17.48	53	17.17	54	12.47	54	18.37	42
Fertilizer	15.84	48	14.49	46	8.45	36	17.97	41
Machinery	1.65	5	2.68	8	4.03	17	0.40	1
Research & Ext.	7.17	22	6.94	22	7.25	31	7.47	17
Explained total	−8.32	−25	17.29	54	8.68	37	15.36	35
Unexplained total	41.60	125	14.49	46	14.54	63	28.87	65

Accounting formula: $$\frac{\Delta(Y/L)}{(Y/L)_0} = 0.25\frac{\Delta(N/L)}{(N/L)_0} + 0.2\frac{\Delta(S/L)}{(S/L)_0} + 0.2\frac{\Delta(F/L)}{(F/L)_0} + 0.1\frac{\Delta(M/L)}{(M/L)_0} + 0.1\frac{\Delta(R/L)}{(R/L)_0} + \text{unexplained.}$$

research systems to labor productivity in these socialist countries is as important as is the case in U.S. agriculture.

Table 4-8 summarizes the results of comparing *land productivity* between the socialist countries and Japan as of 1979. The difference in labor/land ratio is the most important source in explaining the differences of land productivity, and fertilizer is the second. The agricultural research ratio is as important as livestock and machinery in the explanation of differences of land productivity. For the majority of countries, except China, about 80% of differences in land productivity can be explained by the differences in resource endowments, technical inputs, and agricultural research. Differences in these three categories explained only 62% of the land productivity differences between Japan and China. This suggests that there is more than factor/land ratios in the explanation of differences in land productivity between these two countries.

Table 4-6. *(Continued)*

POLAND		*ROMANIA*		*YUGOSLAVIA*		*USSR*		*CHINA*	
percent	*index*	*percent*	*index*	*percent*	*index*	*percent*	*index*	*percent*	*index*
33.52	100	48.81	100	42.52	100	36.92	100	58.81	100
2.46	7	1.19	2	−9.65	−23	1.12	3	14.90	25
−2.98	−9	−4.80	−10	−9.98	−23	−3.81	−10	7.24	12
5.45	16	6.00	12	0.34	1	4.93	13	7.66	13
23.23	69	23.62	48	23.13	54	22.78	62	24.79	42
15.46	46	18.73	38	14.89	35	18.21	49	18.71	32
7.77	23	4.89	10	8.24	19	4.57	12	6.08	10
7.81	23	8.19	17	4.86	11	6.14	17	9.22	16
33.50	100	33.01	68	18.34	43	30.04	81	48.90	83
0.01	0	15.81	32	24.17	57	6.88	19	9.91	17

4.7. Summary

The results we have presented above provide insight into the sources of agricultural productivity growth in socialist countries. We found that chemical fertilizer is the single most important factor for the increase in land productivity and labor productivity. But this may not be so in the future. As Karen Brooks has commented with reference to the aggregate production in Soviet, "Higher yields can be obtained in the USSR with greater fertilizer use, but the current levels of fertilizer use suggest that most areas of USSR are already on quite a flat portion of the fertilizer response curve and that increased yield can be obtained in this way only at high cost" (Johnson and Brooks 1983, 142).

Our comparison of centralized and less-centralized socialist countries suggests that farmers in less-centralized agricultures tend to utilize labor more efficiently. Although our data shows that centralized agricultures tended to emphasize the use of machinery, we are not able to demonstrate whether less-centralized agriculture is more efficient than centralized agriculture, or vice versa.

Agricultural research is clearly an important source of productivity changes and differences for the socialist countries. But it is a less impor-

Table 4-7. Accounting for Agricultural Labor Productivity Differences, Socialist vs USA (1979)

	BULGARIA		*CZECH-OSLAVAKIA*		*E. GERMANY*		*HUNGARY*	
Country	*percent*	*index*	*percent*	*index*	*percent*	*index*	*percent*	*index*
Difference in labor productivity (%)	92.20	100	89.76	100	81.14	100	89.73	100
Resource endowment	33.02	36	32.18	36	30.44	38	33.03	37
Land	14.53	16	14.48	16	14.34	18	14.52	16
Livestock	18.49	20	17.70	20	16.10	20	18.51	21
Technical inputs	27.96	30	25.74	29	24.30	30	26.61	30
Fertilizer	18.14	20	16.10	18	14.82	18	16.75	19
Machinery	9.82	11	9.64	11	9.48	12	9.85	11
Research & Ext.	7.82	8	−0.31	0	3.78	5	6.85	8
Explained total	68.80	75	57.62	64	58.52	72	66.48	74
Unexplained total	23.40	24	32.14	36	22.62	28	23.24	26

Accounting formula: $$\frac{\Delta(Y/N)}{(Y/N)_{US}} = 0.15\frac{\Delta(L/N)}{(L/N)_{US}} + 0.2\frac{\Delta(S/N)}{(S/N)_{US}} + 0.2\frac{\Delta(F/N)}{(F/N)_{US}} + 0.1\frac{\Delta(M/N)}{(M/N)_{US}} + 0.1\frac{\Delta(R/N)}{(R/N)_{US}} + \text{unexplained.}$$

tant source for the explanation of productivity differences between socialist and nonsocialist countries.

This study provides a quantitative comparative analysis of the productivity growth among socialist countries. An important part of the changes in labor productivity and land productivity among socialist countries and the differences in productivity among the U.S. and Japan and socialist countries have been accounted for. We have not, however, included intrastructure, institutional changes, and policy changes as sources of differences in productivity.

Notes

1. The growth rate in the Chinese agricultural production is biased upward on two counts. First, the indexes are computed using, as the base year, 1960 which is the worst year in the recent history of Chinese agriculture. Accordingly, indexes for other years were exaggerated.

Table 4-7. *(Continued)*

POLAND		*ROMANIA*		*YUGOSLAVIA*		*USSR*		*CHINA*	
percent	*index*	*percent*	*index*	*percent*	*index*	*percent*	*index*	*percent*	*index*
94.05	100	97.16	100	95.63	100	93.23	100	98.83	100
33.09	35	34.09	35	33.70	35	30.99	33	34.64	35
14.66	16	14.79	15	14.66	15	13.09	14	14.91	15
18.43	20	19.30	20	19.04	20	17.90	19	19.73	20
27.84	30	29.43	30	29.04	30	28.06	30	29.53	30
18.23	19	19.50	20	19.37	20	18.36	20	19.54	20
9.61	10	9.92	10	9.66	10	9.71	10	9.99	10
7.17	8	8.49	9	8.56	9.	7.05	8	9.85	10
68.10	72	72.01	74	71.30	75	66.10	71	74.02	75
25.95	28	25.14	26	24.34	25	27.14	29	24.82	25

Second, the official growth indexes are computed using three different constant prices: 1950–1956 used the constant price of 1952, 1957–1969 used the constant price of 1957, and 1970–1979 used the constant price of 1970. As a result of these nonunified constant prices, the reported indexes are not consistent and are biased upward. But the growth rates are not biased, as they were computed by estimating a linear regression of a natural exponential function.

2. Metaproduction function can be defined as the envelope of the production points of all the most efficient countries. It describes a technology frontier that other countries can reach by borrowing or by adaptive research, and by investment in human capital, in extension, and in rural infrastructure (Binswanger and Ruttan 1978, 46). In the context of our study, it represents the envelope of the production function of the nine socialist countries.

3. Principal components regression is a form of restricted least square. Since it is sensitive to transformation, it is necessary to use the correlation matrix for the computation of components. Because of this, we need to normalize (or center) the retained components such that unity variance of the components can be obtained. It is recognized that principal component regression is only an ad hoc solution to the multicollinearity problem and is not an unbiased estimation. It is not uncommon, however, for this procedure to be used in the estimation of cross-country metaproduction function (Mundlak and Hellinghausen 1982, 664–672). In this study, dropping variables is not consistent with production theory. However, other statistical procedures such as ridge regression and first differences have been attempted to reduce the multicollinearity problem. The results obtained using these other procedures were inferior to results obtained using the principal components.

4. If we can assume that agricultural research has been increasing at a constant rate, then using only the current-year agricultural research as the agricultural research variable biases upward the expected value of the estimated constant term of the production function. It does

Table 4-8. Accounting for Agricultural Land Productivity Differences, Socialist vs Japan (1979

	BULGARIA		*CZECH-OSLAVAKIA*		*E. GERMANY*		*HUNGARY*	
Country	*percent*	*index*	*percent*	*index*	*percent*	*index*	*percent*	*index*
Difference in land productivity (%)	76.49	100	71.84	100	59.60	100	69.64	100
Resource endowment	32.90	43	29.86	42	26.74	45	33.24	48
Labor	21.48	28	21.79	30	22.50	38	21.55	31
Livestock	11.42	15	8.07	11	4.25	7	11.70	17
Technical inputs	22.68	30	16.07	22	15.49	26	17.89	26
Fertilizer	13.13	17	6.89	10	6.43	11	8.25	12
Machinery	9.56	12	9.17	13	9.06	15	9.64	14
Research & Ext.	9.46	12	7.65	11	8.90	15	9.23	13
Explained total	65.04	85	53.57	75	51.12	86	60.36	87
Unexplained total	11.45	15	18.27	25	8.47	14	9.27	13

Accounting formula: $$\frac{\Delta(Y/L)}{(Y/L)_J} = 0.25\,\frac{\Delta(N/L)}{(N/L)_J} + 0.2\,\frac{\Delta(S/L)}{(S/L)_J} + 0.2\,\frac{\Delta(F/L)}{(F/L)_J} + 0.1\,\frac{\Delta(F/L)}{(F/L)_J} + 0.1\,\frac{\Delta(R/L)}{(R/L)_J} + \text{unexplained.}$$

not, however, bias the expected value of the estimated coefficients of the conventional inputs (Bredahl and Peterson 1976, 685).

5. Compared with the coefficients estimated by other scholars, the sums of the coefficients of the conventional inputs in regressions 1 to 6 are relatively smaller and are less than one. This may be caused either by misspecification or by the bias characteristic of principal component procedure.

References

Binswanger, Hans P., and Vernon W. Ruttan. 1978. *Induced Innovation—Technology, Institutions and Development.* Baltimore: The Johns Hopkins University Press.

Bredahl, Maury, and Willis Peterson. 1976. "The Productivity and Allocation of Research: U.S. Agricultural Experiment Stations." *American Journal of Agricultural Economics* 58(4):684–692.

Clayton, Elizabeth. 1980. "Productivity in Soviet Agriculture." *Slavic Review* 39:446–458.

Table 4-8. *(Continued)*

POLAND		*ROMANIA*		*YUGOSLAVIA*		*USSR*		*CHINA*	
percent	*index*	*percent*	*index*	*percent*	*index*	*percent*	*index*	*percent*	*index*
75.46	100	80.32	100	81.97	100	94.99	100	82.46	100
28.00	37	27.73	35	32.72	40	41.19	43	19.83	24
20.18	27	16.91	21	20.17	25	24.13	25	7.40	9
7.82	10	10.82	13	12.54	15	17.05	18	12.43	15
19.72	26	25.34	32	25.66	31	28.33	30	21.34	26
11.07	15	15.77	20	16.82	21	18.51	19	11.46	14
8.65	11	9.56	12	8.84	11	9.82	10	9.88	12
9.03	12	9.14	11	9.51	12	9.82	10	9.81	12
56.75	75	62.21	77	67.89	83	79.33	84	50.99	62
18.71	25	18.11	23	14.08	17	15.66	16	31.47	38

Ellman, Michael. 1981. "Agricultural Productivity Under Socialism." *World Development* 9:979–989.

Hayami, Yujiro, and Vernon W. Ruttan. 1971. *Agricultural Development: An International Perspective.* Baltimore: The Johns Hopkins University Press.

Johnson, D. Gale. 1982. "Agriculture in the Centrally Planned Economies." *American Journal of Agricultural Economics* 64(5):845–853.

Johnson, D. Gale, and Karen M. Brooks. 1983. *Prospects for Soviet Agriculture in the 1980's.* Bloomington, IN: Indiana University Press.

Kawagoe, Toshihiko, Yujiro Hayami, and Vernon W. Ruttan. 1983. "Agricultural Productivity Differences Among Countries Revisited." Monograph, August.

Kozlowski, Z. 1975. "Agriculture and the Economic Growth of East European Socialist Countries." In Lloyd Reynolds, *Agriculture and Development Theory.* New Haven: Yale, University Press, 411–450.

Mundlak, Yair and René Hellinghausen. 1982. "The Intercountry Agricultural Production Function: Another View," *American Journal of Agricultural Economics,* 64(4):664–672.

Tang, Anthony, and Bruce Stone. 1980. *Food Production in PRC.* Washington, D.C.: International Food Policy Research Institute.

Wadekin, Karl-Eugen. 1982. *Agrarian Policies in Communist Europe.* Totowa, NJ: Littlefield Adams (Allanheld, Osmun & Co.).

Wyzan, Michael. 1981. "Empirical Analysis of Soviet Agricultural Production and Policy." *American Journal of Agricultural Economics* 63(3):475–483.

APPENDIX 4A
Data and Sources

Data used in this report are pooled from a large number of books and reports published during the period of 1950–1980. When there are missing data, especially in the early 1950s, interpolations are used. The definition and code sources of data are reported below.

OUTPUT is defined as the geometrical mean of the gross agricultural outputs net of intermediate products converted to wheat units weighted by the U.S., Japan, and India price structure. Data for agricultural output are derived from FAO, *Food Balance Sheets,* Rome, 1980, page 183-997. Data for prices were prepared and reported in Yujiro Hayami, *An International Comparison of Agricultural Production and Productivities,* Technical Bulletin 277-1971, Agricultural Experiment Station, University of Minnesota, St. Paul, 1971.

LABOR is defined as economically active populations including all working farmers, their wives working in agriculture, helping family members, and hired labor, measured in full-time many years.

Figures for Bulgaria, Czechoslavkia, East Germany, Hungary, Poland, and Yugoslavia, are derived from Thad Alton, Elizabeth Bass, Gregor

Lazarcik, Wasoyl Znayenko, and Joseph Bombelles, "Agricultural Output, Expenses, and Depreciation Gross Product, and Net Product in Eastern Europe: 1965, 1970, and 1975–1981," Research Project on National Income in East Central Europe, OP-71, New York, 1982.

Figures for Romania are derived from *Annual Statistic al Republic Socialiste Romania,* and FAO, *Production Yearbook.* Figures for USSR are derived from ILO, *Yearbook of Labor Statistics.* International Labor Organization, Geneva, Switzerland. Figures for China are derived from Anthony Tang and Bruce Stone, *Food Production in the PRC,* IFPRI, Research Report No. 15, Washington, D.C.: 1980.

LAND is defined as the total area of arable land, permanent crop land, permanent pasture, and meadows. Figures are derived from USDA, *Agricultural Statistics of Eastern Europe and the Soviet Union 1950–70,* Washington, D.C., 1973; and FAO, *Production Yearbook,* Rome, various issues.

FERTILIZER Is defined as the gross weight of total consumption of nitrogeneous fertilizer, phosphate, and potash. Figures are derived from FAO, *Fertilizer Yearbook.* Figures for Bulgaria for 1950–1955 are derived from OP-39. Figures for Poland for 1950–1957 are derived from OP-37. Figures for Romania are derived from *Statistical al Republic Socialiste Romania, 1981* and OP-38. Figures for USSR for 1950–1955 are interpolated. Figures for China are derived from Tang and Stone, *Food Production in PRC* and *China Agricultural Yearbook 1980,* Beijing.

MACHINE is defined as the total horsepower of wheel and crawler tractors (excluding the garden tractors) used in agriculture. Assuming larger tractors have 30 h.p., small tractors have 5 h.p. Tractor numbers are derived from FAO, *Production Yearbook.* Tractor numbers for East Germany for 1950–1957 are derived from *Statistiches Jahrbuch ddr,* East Berlin, 81. Tractor numbers for USSR for 1950–1955 are derived from Central Statistical Administration, *The USSR Economy, A Statistical Abstract,* London, 1957. Tractor numbers for China are derived from *China Agricultural Yearbook, 1980,* Beijing.

LIVESTOCK is defined as the aggregate unit of all animals, weighted by the FAO conversion factors. Conversion factors are: camels 1.1; buffalo, horse, and mules 1.0; cattle and asses 0.8; pigs 0.2; sheep and goats 0.1; poultry 0.01. Livestock numbers are derived from FAO, *Production Yearbook.*

AGRICULTURAL RESEARCH defined as scientist man-years of man-power involved in agricultural research. Figures are derived from Ann Judd, James Boyce, and Robert Evenson, "Investment in Agricultural Supply," monograph, Economic Growth Center, Yale University. 1982; and Boyce and Evenson, *National and International Agricultural Research and Extension Programs,* A/D/C, New York, 1975.

5 COST PRESSURES AND RELATIVE PRODUCTIVITY IN CANADIAN TELECOMMUNICATIONS FIRMS

Michael Denny
and
Alain de Fontenay

5.1. Introduction

Recent work on regional or interspatial productivity measures has improved our capabilities of interpreting relation productivity levels across firms.[1] In an earlier paper, we reported some preliminary results of applying these methods to three large Canadian telecommunications firms.[2] These firms are relatively unique because they have all developed and made public detailed productivity studies. The public data from these studies have been used to make the comparisons.[3]

This chapter reports the results of making these comparisons with an improved data set not available earlier. There remain some differences in the data, and these are discussed in the chapter appendix.

Our results indicate first that the *level* and rate of growth of productivity vary significantly across the companies. Second, telecommunications firms have had very high rates of productivity growth compared to firms in other industries.[4] However, telecommunications firms have experienced a slowdown in productivity growth during the seventies.

The relative productivity levels measure the extent to which more resources are required to produce a given output bundle in one firm than another. These are measured at a point in time. Since accidental factors may play a large role in the measurement during a given year, the availability of a time series of annual measures is reassuring. The annual relative productivity values do fluctuate but they also display significant differences among companies through time. The efficiency or productivity levels are driven through time by the relative growth rates of productivity. Consequently, the two productivity measures are linked.

The inflationary difficulties of the 1970s created cost pressures for these firms. Here, we extend our earlier analysis by linking productivity prices and profits. Telephone rates are regulated in Canada; and the regulatory activity during this decade was a mixture of reform due to technological change and increasing competition, combined with responses to the inflationary pressure on prices.

The differential growth in the firms' productivities translated into different pressures on the regulatory agencies. Alberta Government Telephones (AGT) was able to offset most of the inflationary cost pressures during the 1970s through productivity growth. The latter was sufficiently large that prices grew slowly and the income of the corporation grew rapidly. The other firms in the study were not as successful in achieving rapid productivity increases that would offset the cost pressures.

5.2. Productivity: Inter- and Intrafirm

Productivity is usually defined as output per unit of input. A wide variety of special definitions exists depending on how output and input are defined. We will concentrate on *total factor productivity,* (TFP). Output is measured as gross output and all inputs are included in the input measure.

The growth in productivity through time is usually the focus of most productivity studies. We are interested in productivity because it measures our capability of producing output per unit of our restricted resources. It is the resource constraint that makes increasing productivity one of the key goals of any society.

To measure the rate of growth of productivity, consider a firm that produces n outputs Q_i using m inputs X_j. The productivity growth rate, $T\dot{F}P$ is defined by,

$$T\dot{F}P = \tfrac{1}{2}\sum_i (s_{it} + s_{it-1})(\log Q_{it} - \log Q_{it-1}) - \tfrac{1}{2}\sum_j (s_{jt} + s_{jt-1}) \cdot (\log X_{jt} - \log X_{jt-1}) \tag{5.1}$$

The rate of productivity growth equals the difference between the weighted rates of growth of the outputs and the weighted rates of growth of the inputs. The weights are the shares of output i, s_i, and input j, s_j in the revenues and costs of the firm.

This particular definition of TFP is convenient for our purposes although other definitions are possible. This definition has many desirable features when one wishes to interpret the productivity measure.

For example, suppose the firm had a production function that indicated the outputs it could produce with any bundle of inputs.

$$H(Q_1,Q_2, \ldots, X_1, X_2, \ldots, t) = 0 \tag{5.2}$$

Due to technical change, t in equation (5.2), the production function shifts. If there is technical progress then the outputs that can be produced using any bundle of inputs will increase. This is an increase in productivity. Diewert (1976) has shown that our definition of productivity, equation (5.1), is exactly identical to shifts in a particular production function for equation (5.2) when certain conditions are met. If it is possible to approximate (5.2) with a translog production function then (5.1) will be an exact measure of technical change given the conditions. The conditions required are that the input and output quantities be chosen competitively and that economies of scale equal one. To the extent that these conditions are not met, Denny and Fuss (1980) and Denny, Fuss and May (1981) have shown exactly what the productivity measure (5.1) includes. That is, there are a set of limiting conditions under which $\dot{TFP}$ defined by (5.1) is equivalent to technical change. More importantly, $\dot{TFP}$ may correspond to technical change plus the effects of scale and noncompetitive input and output choices. Empirically, it may be difficult to sort out these separate items. It is clear that we can specify exactly how they will enter into productivity measurement.[5]

The conceptualization of interfirm relative productivity levels is entirely the same as the development above for productivity for a single firm. The logarithmic relative productivity level between any two firms, s and r, may be defined as,

$$\theta_{rs} = \tfrac{1}{2} \sum_i (s_{ir} + s_{is})(\log Q_{ir} - \log Q_{is}) - \tfrac{1}{2} \sum_j (s_{jr} + s_{js})(\log X_{jr} - \log X_{js}) \tag{5.3}$$

To simplify the interpretation define, $E_{rs} \equiv \exp(\theta_{rs})$, which is the relative productivity level in firm r compared to that in firm s. The logarithmic relative productivity level equals the weighted difference in the logarithms of outputs minus the weighted difference in the logarithms of inputs.

A similar cost efficiency measure can be defined

$$\gamma_{rs} = C_r - C_s - \tfrac{1}{2}\sum_j (S_{jr} + s_{js})(\log w_{jr} - \log w_{js})$$
$$- \tfrac{1}{2}(s_{ir} + s_{is})(\log Q_{ir} - \log Q_{is})$$

It can be shown (Caves et al. 1982) that θ_{rs} has the following approximate interpretation. The value of θ_{rs} equals the average of the relative output levels of the firms, r and s evaluated at the two observed input levels of the firms. The relative output levels produced by the firm at the same input level is a convenient measure of the relative productivity levels. Since we do not observe the firms at the same input level, is is useful to relate the measure θ_{rs} to this concept.

This is called an approximate interpretation because it is conditional on the true production functions being adequately approximated by a translog function.

5.3. Productivity Growth

The growth rate of TFP has varied sharply over time and among companies. Table 5-1 shows the TFP growth rates for British Columbia Telephones (BC Tel.), Alberta Government Telephones (AGT), and Bell Canada (Bell). At AGT, TFP growth has been swifter than at the other companies. From 1972–1978, TFP growth averaged 6.1% at AGT and 3.9% at Bell and BC Tel.

The indexes of TFP for each company (Table 1) indicate the extent to which the rapid growth at AGT cumulates to provide a much higher index level.

TFP is one component of labor productivity. The labor productivity evidence in table 5-2 provides a modified picture of the performance of the three companies. Labor productivity grows because TFP grows and because of growth in the quantity of other factors, capital and materials, used per unit of labor. The second component we will refer to as the aggregate factor intensity growth.[6] While BC Tel. and Bell had equal average TFP growth rates, BC Tel. had a faster growth rate of labor productivity than Bell. This faster growth was achieved by a more rapid rise in aggregate factor intensity at BC Tel. than at Bell. AGT's labor productivity rose the most rapidly but this was entirely due to AGT's TFP growth.

Table 5-1. TFP Growth Rates for Canadian Telephone Companies

	Annual Rates of Growth of TFP (percentages)			*TFP Indexes (1972 = 100)*		
	BC Tel.	*AGT*	*BELL*	*BC Tel.*	*AGT*	*BELL*
1967	—	—	5.9	—	69.8	86.8
1968	—	8.3	4.3	—	75.9	90.6
1969	—	8.9	2.9	—	82.9	93.3
1970	—	5.6	3.7	—	87.7	96.8
1971	—	4.4	−0.5	—	91.6	96.3
1972	—	8.8	3.7	100.0	100.0	100.0
1973	2.9	9.0	4.7	102.9	109.4	104.8
1974	5.9	12.8	4.4	109.1	124.4	109.5
1975	6.0	5.5	6.9	115.9	131.4	117.3
1976	4.4	1.1	1.0	121.0	132.8	118.5
1977	−2.2	4.1	0.7	118.4	138.3	119.4
1978	3.0	10.2	2.3	122.0	153.1	122.2
1979	2.5	—	2.2	125.1	—	114.9

Source: See appendix 5A.

Table 5-2. Labor Productivity (1972 = 100.0)

	AGT	*BC Tel.*	*BELL*
1967	55.0	—	66.3
1968	69.4	—	74.4
1969	78.1	—	80.8
1970	82.9	—	86.2
1971	88.6	—	92.5
1972	100.0	100.0	100.0
1973	109.7	104.2	105.4
1974	126.7	111.9	109.7
1975	137.2	131.4	122.3
1976	151.1	150.8	125.5
1977	153.7	159.9	129.6
1978	176.2	157.1	131.7
1979	—	149.2	133.9

Source: See appendix 5C.

AGT's factor intensity growth was not larger than BC Tel.'s by any substantial amount although it did exceed that of Bell.

The comparisons of the relative productivity and cost efficiency levels in the three companies can be found in tables 5-3 and 5-4.

The entries in these tables should be read in the following manner. The first row in table 5-3 states that in 1967, the productivity level at Bell Canada was 34% higher than at AGT. The same results may be stated in terms of cost efficiency. The cost of producing output in Bell was only 74.6% of the costs of producing output at AGT in 1967.

Due to the higher productivity growth rate at AGT compared to Bell, there has been a swift reversal of the initial situation. The productivity level at Bell, in 1978, was 11% lower than at AGT.

Table 5-4 compares AGT and Bell to BC Tel. from 1972–1978. The movements in the relative efficiency levels are not quite as dramatic over this shorter time period. BC Tel. and Bell have had productivity levels that are roughly equivalent throughout the period. AGT has made significant gains relative to BC Tel., just as it did relative to Bell.

Two of the three companies have productivity levels that are roughly equivalent and the third, AGT, had the lowest productivity level in the early 1970s and the highest by the late 1970s.

To provide some guidance, an interpretation of these numbers is required. Productivity is normally thought of as measuring output per unit of input. In our case, inputs are measured as the aggregate of all the different inputs. The relative productivity levels are the ratio of the productivity in one firm over the productivity in another firm. It is tempting to interpret either the firm productivity indexes or the relative productivity levels in an unduly simple manner. It is safest to keep firmly in mind that knowing what the temperature is outside or the level of profits or productivity does *not* tell you why that particular value or level has been reached. Our results clearly indicate that AGT uses fewer real resources to produce output than the other companies and that this has been a recent phenomenon.

5.4. Productivity and Cost Pressures

The primary importance of productivity growth from the firm's point of view is its crucial role in the growth of profits and the survival of the firm in an inflationary environment. It is useful to link productivity growth to the cost pressures and output price changes of the firm. This is par-

Table 5-3. Relative Efficiency of Bell Compared to AGT

	Productivity *BELL*	*AGT*	*Cost Efficiency* *BELL*
1967	134.1	100	74.6
1968	129.6	100	77.1
1969	122.6	100	81.6
1970	120.8	100	82.8
1971	115.5	100	86.6
1972	110.4	100	90.6
1973	105.8	100	94.6
1974	97.3	100	102.8
1975	99.4	100	100.6
1976	99.5	100	100.5
1977	96.3	100	103.9
1978	88.9	100	112.4

Table 5-4. Relative Efficiency of AGT and Bell Compared to BC Tel.

	Productivity			*Cost Efficiency*	
	AGT	*BELL*	*BC Tel.*	*AGT*	*BELL*
1972	89.3	98.8	100	112.0	101.2
1973	94.9	100.7	100	105.4	99.4
1974	101.8	99.5	100	98.2	100.5
1975	101.3	101.0	100	98.7	99.0
1976	98.2	98.1	100	101.8	102.0
1977	104.9	101.2	100	95.3	98.8
1978	113.0	100.5	100	88.5	99.4

ticularly true when management is trying to understand the consequences of productivity for the firm.

The rate of growth of output prices, $\dot{P}$, must equal the difference between the rate of growth of input prices, $\dot{W}$, minus the rate of growth of total factor productivity, $T\dot{F}P$.[7] This may be written,

$$\dot{P} = \dot{W} - T\dot{F}P \tag{5.4}$$

Intuitively, this equation states that unless cost pressures, due to input price increases, are offset by the growth of productivity they must ultimately lead to output price increases or the demise of the firm.

The treatment of profits in the measurement of cost pressures requires careful explanation. Divide total costs into capital costs (assumed to be owned by the firm) and all other costs. The capital costs can be measured as the opportunity cost of capital to the firm or as the actual capital costs, that is, net income or profits. When the opportunity cost of capital is used in measuring W, we will call this *gross* cost pressure. *Net* cost pressure will be measured by including the actual capital costs in W.

The use of the terminology, gross and net, arises from the following consideration. As noncapital input prices rise, these may be offset by increases in productivity, increases in output prices, or a *reduction in profits*. In the short run, the latter is very important. In the long run, it is less important provided the firm survives. Gross cost pressure corresponds to the case in which one of the ways to temporarily absorb cost increases is through a change in actual or measured profits.[8] Net cost pressures combine the gross cost pressure with the change in profits to focus on the net pressure on changes in output prices and productivity.

In table 5-5, evidence is presented for AGT and Bell Canada on net cost pressure in the form of the percentage increase in the aggregate input price. The columns entitled productivity relief indicate the percentage of the net cost pressure that was absorbed by the growth in productivity.

Table 5-5. Productivity and Cost Pressures

	Cost Pressures (%)		*Productivity Relief (%)*	
	AGT	*BELL*	*AGT*	*BELL*
1968	12.4	4.1	67	103
1969	9.2	3.5	97	85
1970	5.1	7.0	110	53
1971	4.5	2.3	98	−23
1972	9.1	5.9	96	63
1973	9.6	7.1	94	65
1974	12.9	6.3	100	70
1975	8.9	11.1	62	62
1976	15.5	7.0	69	15
1977	9.9	5.4	41	13
1978	11.0	9.9	92	24
1979	13.1	8.5	99	26

For example, in 1967, aggregate input prices were increasing at an annual rate of 12.4% at AGT and 4.1% at Bell Canada. Two-thirds (67%) of this cost pressure at AGT was absorbed by productivity growth. At Bell Canada, more than one hundred percent (103%) of the cost pressure was absorbed by productivity growth.

Over the period, 1968–1979, one can observe the very important role that productivity growth has had in absorbing cost pressures. For AGT, productivity growth has been sufficiently high that pressure on output prices has been relatively slight in more years. For Bell Canada, the situation is worse. In eight years for AGT and only two years for Bell, more than 80% of the cost pressures were offset by productivity increases. Since 1975, productivity growth has only been able to absorb about 20% of the cost pressure generated. The proportion of cost pressures that impact on output prices has become much larger at Bell than it used to be and much larger than it is at AGT. Unless productivity growth can be increased at Bell, that firm will require more rapid price increases for any given level of cost pressure. It is important to remember that table 5-5 does not standardize the cost pressures. AGT has had faster rising aggregate input prices (net cost pressures) than Bell. For AGT, the degree of productivity relief achieved has required higher rates of productivity growth than would be necessary at Bell where the net cost pressures have been slower.

The growth in a firm's gross income can be evaluated with the following expression:

$$\dot{P} + T\dot{F}P + s_K\dot{K} - s_v\dot{W}_v = s_K V\dot{K} \tag{5.5}$$

The growth in income ($V\dot{K}$) is positively affected by the growth in prices ($\dot{P}$), productivity ($T\dot{F}P$), and the capital stock ($\dot{K}$).[9] Income growth is impeded by the growth in the prices of noncapital inputs ($\dot{W}_v$).

For AGT, the evidence for this breakdown is shown in table 5-6. Output price increases have not contributed to the growth in income except in the few years in which rate increases were granted. The growth in the capital stock has been quite rapid. Its contribution to earnings has been almost large enough to offset the negative effects of rising input prices. Rapid productivity growth has provided the major impetus for rising earnings.

For Bell Canada, there exists a much longer public record. In Table 5-7, evidence is shown for 1953–1978. Price increases have played a relatively minor role, until 1970, in the growth of Bell's income. In the 1970s and particular after 1974, that income would hardly have grown without price increases. Productivity growth within Bell has been very high relative to other industries and even some telephone companies. However, it is much

Table 5-6. Decomposition of Growth Rates of Value of Gross Income: AGT

	% Change	*Contribution to % Change by*			
Year	$SK \cdot \dot{VK}$ = *Growth of VK*	$\dot{P}$	$\dot{TFP}$	$SK \cdot \dot{K}$	$SV \cdot \dot{WV}$
1968	13.2	4.1	8.3	4.6	−3.9
1969	8.6	0.3	8.9	4.4	−4.9
1970	5.2	−0.5	5.6	3.7	−3.6
1971	4.2	0.1	4.4	3.9	−4.2
1972	9.4	0.4	8.8	3.9	−3.5
1973	8.2	0.6	9.0	2.8	−4.2
1974	9.8	0	12.8	3.3	−6.4
1975	6.8	3.4	5.5	6.0	−8.1
1976	14.9	14.4	1.1	6.4	−7.0
1977	11.0	5.9	4.1	4.6	−3.5
1978	11.4	0.9	10.2	3.7	−3.3

lower than AGT's productivity growth. For this reason, they have had to seek a stream of rate increases. The cost pressures from increases in non-capital input prices was higher during the 1970s although lower than the CPI growth. The failure of productivity growth, in the 1970s, to remain high, or to rise to offset rising costs, meant that output price changes have been necessary to sustain growth in the firm's income.

This section has illustrated the impact of productivity growth on the prices and incomes of the firms. This type of analysis is relatively easy and can certainly be extended. It is very useful for purposes of explaining the importance of productivity gains to the regulator and to the management of firms.

5.5. Summary

The very rapid growth in productivity in the telecommunications industry can mask substantial variation within the industry. AGT has moved in a decade from being 10% less efficient to being 30% more efficient. This is a very dramatic shift and we would like to know why it has occurred. It is hoped that further research may untangle the sources of this differential productivity growth.

Table 5-7. Decomposition of Growth Rate of the Value of Gross Income: Bell

	% Change	Contribution to % Change by			
Year	$SK \cdot \dot{VK}$	$\dot{P}$	$\dot{TFP}$	$SK \cdot \dot{K}$	$SV \cdot \dot{WV}$
1953	4.0	0.7	2.8	3.9	−3.4
1954	2.7	0	0.7	3.6	−1.6
1955	3.9	0.3	0.9	4.2	−1.6
1956	4.0	0	1.5	4.1	−1.6
1957	6.4	0.1	4.2	4.2	−2.0
1958	4.4	0.8	2.2	4.3	−3.0
1959	11.4	5.6	5.2	4.3	−3.7
1960	7.9	2.9	3.2	4.3	−2.7
1961	3.2	−2.6	4.4	4.0	−2.5
1962	5.8	−1.6	5.2	3.7	−1.6
1963	3.9	0.4	0.6	3.8	−1.0
1964	5.9	0	3.3	3.7	−1.1
1965	5.6	−0.1	3.3	3.6	−1.3
1966	4.4	−0.8	3.4	3.9	−2.1
1967	6.5	−0.4	5.9	4.1	−3.1
1968	4.9	−0.1	4.3	4.0	−3.2
1969	4.5	0.5	2.9	3.9	−2.9
1970	7.0	3.3	3.7	3.6	−3.6
1971	3.3	2.9	−0.5	3.6	−2.7
1972	5.7	2.2	3.7	3.6	−3.8
1973	7.5	2.5	4.7	3.2	−2.8
1974	4.9	1.8	4.4	3.3	−4.6
1975	8.0	4.3	6.9	3.8	−7.0
1976	5.7	5.9	1.0	3.7	−4.9
1977	3.8	4.7	0.7	3.0	−4.6
1978	9.1	7.6	2.3	2.2	−3.0

Notes

1. This work was begun by Jorgenson and Nishimizu (1978) and extended by Caves et al. (1982); Denny, Fuss, and May (1981); Denny, de Fontenay, and Werner (1981); Denny, Fuss, and Waverman (1981); and Denny and Fuss (1983).

2. See Denny, de Fontenay, and Werner (1983). An earlier unpublished paper by the same authors was available as a working paper.

3. This data is periodically updated and presented to regulatory hearings at the CRTC and Alberta Public Utilities Board. The output measures are not explicitly adjusted for quality change. However, the companies offer a very similar range of services and there is no

evidence that output quality differentials affect the results. The share of capital is measured residually in this study. Alternative measures have been used but they do not alter the basic pattern of results although the exact magnitudes change.

4. Total factor productivity growth in telecommunications has been roughly three times larger than in total manufacturing over the last three decades.

5. More extensive developments of this material and that in the following paragraph may be found in the references listed in note one.

6. Factor intensity growth in a cost share weighted aggregate of the rates of growth of the capital-labor and materials-labor ratios. In telecommunications, the first ratio is far more important than the second.

7. The equality of total revenues equal total costs is being assumed in this statement.

8. There is no explicit causality in these relations. Rapid exogenous increases in factor prices, not offset by productivity change, will lead to short-run profit declines and/or price increases. However the rate of productivity growth is partially endogenous and partially exogenous to the firm.

9. The growth in the capital stock simply provides an increase in the asset base on which income may be earned.

References

Caves, D. W., L. Christensen, and W. E. Diewert. 1982. "Multilateral Comparisons of Output Input and Productivity Using Superlative Index Numbers." *Economic Journal* 92(March): 73–86.

Denny, M., and M. Fuss. 1983. "A General Approach to Intertemporal and Interspatial Productivity Comparisons." *Journal of Econometrics* 23:315–330.

Denny, M., A. de Fontenay, and M. Werner. 1981. "Total Factor Productivity in Telecommunications Utility as a Measure of Efficiency and as a Regulatory Tool." *Proceedings of Third International Conference on Analysis, Forecasting and Planning for Public Utilities,* Paris.

Denny, M., A. de Fontenay, and M. Werner. 1983. "Comparing the Efficiency of Firms: Canadian Telecommunications Companies." In L. Courville, A. de Fontenay and R. Dobell (eds.), *Economic Analysis of Telecommunications,* Amsterdam: North-Holland.

Denny, M., M. Fuss, and J. D. May. 1981. "Intertemporal Changes in Regional Productivity in Canadian Manufacturing." *Canadian Journal of Economics* (August): 390–408.

Denny, M. and M. Fuss. 1980. "Intertemporal and Interpartial Comparisons of Cost Efficiency and Productivity," Institute for Policy Analysis working paper no. 818, University of Toronto.

Denny, M., M. Fuss, and L. Waverman. 1981. "The Measurement and Interpretation of Total Factor Productivity in Regulated Industries, with an Application to Canadian Telecommunications." In T. G. Cowing and R. E. Stevenson (eds.), *Productivity Measurement in Regulated Industries.* New York: Academic Press, 179–218.

Diewert, W. E. 1976. "Exact and Superlative Index Numbers." *Journal of Econometrics* 4:115–146.

Jorgenson, D. W., and M. Nishimizu. 1978. "U.S. and Japanese Economic Growth 1952–74: An International Comparison." *Economic Journal* 88:1–44.

Kravis, I. 1976. "A Survey of International Comparisons of Productivity." *Economic Journal* 86 (March): 1–44.

Kravis, I., A. Heston, and R. Summers. 1978. *United Nations International Comparison Project: Phase II International Comparison of Real Product and Purchasing Power.* Baltimore: Johns Hopkins Press.

Kravis, I., Z. Kenessey, A. Heston, and R. Summers. 1975. *A System of International Comparisons of Gross Product and Purchasing Power.* Baltimore: Johns Hopkins Press.

Walters, D. 1968. *Canadian Income Levels and Growth: An International Perspective.* Staff Study No. 23, Economic Council of Canada. Ottawa: Queen's Printer.

Walters, D. 1970. *Canadian Growth Revisited, 1950–67.* Staff Study No. 28, Economic Council of Canada. Ottawa: Queen's Printer.

West, E. C. 1971. *Canada-United States Price and Productivity Differences in Manufacturing Industries, 1963.* Staff Study No. 28, Economic Council of Canada. Ottawa: Queen's Printer.

APPENDIX 5A
Data Sources

The comparisons in this chapter are based on the public data bases of the three companies considered. In a small but crucial number of incidents the companies have provided extra data which were very helpful. The purpose of this appendix is to identify the exact public data series that was used.

For Bell Canada, the data were taken from a recent productivity submission to the CRTC: Bell Canada, *Information Requested by National Anti-Poverty Organization, March 30, 1981,* Bell (NAPO) 30 Mar. 81-612, CRTC.

For BC Telephone, the data were taken from the submission to the CRTC: BC Telephone, *Total Factor Productivity Study: Data Description and Methodology,* by J. T. M. Lee, BC Tel. (NAPO) 80-08-01-406, CRTC.

For AGT, data in current dollars were supplied by the company, and the corresponding constant dollar data appear in the CRTC submission by AGT, Saskatchewan Telecommunications and Manitoba Telephone Systems in the CNCP-Bell Canada interconnect case: *Some Economic Aspects of Interconnection,* Evidence in Chief, H. Harries, economic witness.

To indicate the nature of the variables, the following section will describe the major outputs and inputs for each company.

Bell Canada

Labor

The quantity equals the unweighted man-hours (*MH*) (unadjusted man-hours from table 6 of NAPO 30 Mar. 81). The price index, *PL*, is generated by dividing total labor compensation (*TLE*) (Table 6 NAPO 30 Mar. 81) by unadjusted man-hours, $PL = TLE/MH\$$.

Capital

The total average gross stock of physical capital in current $ divided by constant $ series (table 7 NAPO 30 Mar. 81) yields the asset price series. This asset price series was renormalized in 1972 and the renormalized price was divided into current $ total average gross stock of capital to yield a constant dollar gross capital series in 1972 $.

The value of the capital services was generated residually by subtracting total labor compensation (table 6, NAPO) and current $ cost of materials (table 3 NAPO) from total revenue (table 1 NAPO 30 Mar. 81):

$$VK = TR - PM * M - PL * L$$

The service price of capital was arrived at by dividing the 1972 constant $ gross capital series into the value of capital services.

Materials

The current $ cost of materials, services, rents, and supplies divided by constant $ cost of materials, etc. (from table 3 NAPO 30 Mar. 81) to arrive at a price index. This price series is renormalized in 1972. The renormalized series is divided into the current $ cost of materials to provide a constant $ material series.

Output

The output quantity is a divisia index with the output price = 1.0 in 1972. The components in the divisia index are the prices and quantities of local service, message toll, other toll, directory advertising, and miscellaneous. Current and constant \$ amounts for these categories appear in tables 1 and 2 of NAPO 30 Mar. 81. The price series for each classification were found by dividing current \$ series by the corresponding constant \$ series.

B.C. TELEPHONE

Labor

Table A-13 of (BC Tel. NAPO 80-08-01-406) provides expensed labor hours and expensed wages, benefits, and taxes for the following classifications; management, clerical operators, occupational, engineers, salesmen, service rep., technicians, and draftsmen. The quantity of labor is the simple, unweighted sum of the expensed labor hours of all these categories. The price of labor was obtained by dividing this quantity of labor into the unweighted sum of the expensed wages of all the categories.

$$PL = \frac{\sum_i \text{wages}_i}{\sum_i \text{labor hours}_i}$$

Capital

The value of capital services equals the sum of the financial charges (Total line in table A-4), depreciation (Total line in table A-5), property tax (Total line in table A-6) for Okanagan Tel. and the financial expense (Total line in table A-7), depreciation expense (Total line in table A-8) and property taxes (total line in table A-9) for BC Tel.

The capital quantity series equals the reproduction cost of capital in table A-11, adjusted to 1972 \$.

The price of capital services was generated by dividing the value of capital services series by the capital series.

Materials

The value of materials is generated residually. It is found by subtracting total expensed wages (see above) and the value of capital services (see above) from total revenue (see above).

This value of materials series is deflated by a renormalized (1972) materials price index equal to the StatsCan GNE deflator to yield a constant 1972 $ series for materials.

Output

The output price and quantity series is a divisia index (price = 1.0 in 1972) of the disaggregated output categories given in tables A-1 and A-2. The quantity series is given in table A-2 while the corresponding revenues are given in table A-1. A price series is generated for each category by dividing the quantity series into the revenue series.

Alberta Government Telephones

Labor

The current $ value of labor (from Harries' testimony) is divided by the man-hour series (Interconnection Evidence, appendix 4, table 1) to arrive at a price series for labor.

Capital

The value of capital services in current $ (from Harries' testimony) is divided by the constant 1972 $ average gross capital series to yield a price of capital services. This series is constructed by dividing the current $ gross capital series (Harries' testimony) by the constant 1971 $ gross capital series (Interconnection Evidence) which yields an asset price series. The asset price series is renormalized in 1972 and then divided into current $ gross capital to arrive at the constant 1972 $ gross capital series.

Materials

The current dollar value of materials (in Harries' letter of Dec. 4, 1980) is divided by the constant 1971 $ value of materials (provided in Interconnection Evidence appendix 4, table 1) to arrive at a price series. This price series is renormalized in 1972 and a constant $ material series is found by dividing current $ value materials by the renormalized price series.

Output

The output quantity series is produced by dividing gross revenue in current $ (Harries' letter) by gross revenue in constant 1971 $ (Interconnection Evidence) to yield an output price series. The output price is renormalized in 1972 then divided into current $ gross revenue to yield a constant 1972 $ output series.

6 ALLOCATIVE INEFFICIENCY IN THE AIRLINE INDUSTRY: A CASE FOR DEREGULATION*

Robin C. Sickles

6.1. Introduction

During the 1970s and early 1980s, the U.S. airline industry underwent substantial changes—the two most important of which were the accelerated rate of increase in energy prices and the Air Deregulation Act of 1978. Supporters of deregulation argued, among other things, that a new economic climate would enhance the ability of the airlines to adjust to changes in the economic environment on both the supply and demand side, to operate in an efficient fashion, and to provide for a competitive environment that would reduce monopoly profits. An implicit presumption in these arguments was that inefficiencies of one sort or another existed prior to deregulation.

This chapter examines the degree to which the airline industry was allocatively inefficient in the period of the 1970s preceding deregulation. Subsequent research will focus on modeling the transition through the

*Funding for this research was supported by NSF grant DAR 80-12982. An earlier draft of this chapter was presented at the Conference on Current Issues in Productivity at Rutgers The State University of New Jersey.

deregulatory period. We utilize a very rich panel of firm-specific quarterly data which has been analyzed elsewhere (Sickles 1985; Schmidt and Sickles 1984). We lean heavily on the work of Lovell and Sickles (1983) in specifying and estimating allocative inefficiency in joint production. Regulatory constraints are not explicitly modeled, and thus one source of inefficiency could be constrained profit-maximizing behavior due to regulated output markets. Our modeling of technology and introduction of inefficiency directly into the profit function allows us to use Hotelling's lemma to generate a system of profit maximizing output supply and input demand equations from which allocative inefficiency and substitution and transformation possibilities can be identified. Furthermore, the cost of allocative inefficiency—forgone profits—can be calculated and its time path can be examined.

Section 6.2 reviews and outlines the model of efficient and inefficient technology. Section 6.3 briefly discusses the data set on which our analysis is based. Section 6.4 presents the statistical model. We consider a two-output four-input production process. In section 6.5, our estimates are presented. Section 6.6 concludes.

6.2. Efficient and Inefficient Production Technology

This section is based on the model of Lovell and Sickles (1983). For a more detailed discussion see the referenced article. We consider a production unit employing inputs $x = (x_1, \ldots, x_n) \geqslant 0$ to produce outputs $y = (y_1, \ldots, y_m) \geqslant 0$. The set of all technologically feasible input-output vectors is given by the production possibilities set T, which is assumed to satisfy the following regularity conditions:

T.1: T is a nonempty subset of Ω^{m+n}, and if $(y, -x) \in T$ then $y \geqslant 0$, $x \geqslant 0$.
T.2: T is a closed set which is bounded from above.
T.3: T is a convex set.
T.4: If $(y, -x) \in T$, then $(y', -x') \in T$ for all $0 \leqslant y' \leqslant y$, $x' \geqslant x$.

We assume that the production unit takes output prices $p = (p_1, \ldots, p_m) > 0$ and input prices $w = (w_1, \ldots, w_n) > 0$ as given, and attempts to adjust outputs and inputs so as to solve

$$\sup_{y,x} \{py - wx\colon (y, -x) \in T\}$$

If $(y^0,-x^0)$ solves this problem, then the production unit's profit function is $\pi(p,w) = py^0 - wx^0$, where π satisfies the following regularity conditions:

π.1: $\pi(p,w)$ is a real valued function defined for all $(p,w) > 0$.
π.2: $\pi(p,w)$ is nondecreasing in p and nonincreasing in w.
π.3: $\pi(\lambda p,\lambda w) = \lambda\pi(p,w)$ for all $\lambda > 0$.
π.4: $\pi(p,w)$ is a convex function in (p,w).

The profit function results are useful for two reasons. First, there exists a duality relationship between a production possibilities set T satisfying {T.1–T.4} and a profit function π satisfying {π.1–π.4}, and so π and T provide equivalent representations of the technology of a profit maximizing production unit.[1] Second, Hotelling's lemma states that profit maximizing output supply and input demand equations can be obtained directly from the profit function by means of

$$\nabla_p\pi(p,w) = y(p,w), \qquad \nabla_w\pi(p,w) = -x(p,w),$$

at all $(p,w) > 0$ for which $\pi(p,w)$ is differentiable. The supply and demand equations inherite their properties directly from properties {π.1–π.4} of the profit function.

We now incorporate inefficiency into the model. The production unit is said to be *allocatively inefficient* if it operates at the wrong point on the boundary of its production possibilities set, given the output and input prices it faces and given its behavioral objective of profit maximization. Allocative inefficiency leads to a failure to maximize profit. Although we do not provide estimates of technical inefficiency we can incorporate it into our model.[2] The production unit is paid to be *technically inefficient* if it operates on the interior of its production possibilities set, so that for observed input-output vector $(y,-x) \in T$ there exists $(y',-x') \in T$ such that $(y',-x') \geqslant (y,-x)$. Since $(py' - wx') > (py - wx)$, technical inefficiency also leads to a failure to maximize profit.

The generalized Leontief profit function (Diewert, 1971) and its corresponding system of output supply and input demand equations can be modified to incorporate our two inefficiency measures in the following way. Allocative inefficiency is modeled, following Toda (1976) and Atkinson and Halvorsen (1980), by assuming that the production unit adjusts output supplies and input demands to the wrong price ratios. Technical inefficiency is modeled by adjusting the intercepts so as to permit a divergence between actual and profit maximizing output supplies and input demands. Specifically, our modified generalized Leontief profit function is written as

$$\pi(q,\phi,\theta) = \sum_{i=1}^{6} (A_{ii} - \phi_i)q_i + \sum_{i=1}^{5} \sum_{\substack{j=2 \\ j>i}}^{6} A_{ij}(\theta_{ij}^{-1/2} + \theta_{ij}^{1/2})q_i^{1/2}q_j^{1/2}$$

where $q \equiv (p_1,p_2,w_1,w_2,w_3,w_4)$.

The output supply and input demand equations are given by

$$z_i(q,\phi,\theta) = (A_{ii} - \phi_i) + \sum_j A_{ij}[\theta_{ij}q_i/q_j]^{-1/2} \qquad (i = 1,\ldots,6)$$

where $z' = [y_1,y_2,-x_1,-x_2,-x_3,-x_4]$

In the modified generalized Leontief system the parameters $\phi_i \geqslant 0$ measure the underproduction of outputs ($i = 1,2$) and the excessive usage of inputs ($i = 3,4,5,6$) attributable to technical inefficiency. The components of ϕ are expressed in the same units as are the components of $(y,-x)$, and can be converted into percentages if necessary. Thus the parameter vector ϕ provides a nonneutral measure of technical inefficiency, even if all components of ϕ are equal. This is in contrast to the Debreu (1951)-Farrell (1957) measure, which is neutral.[3] The parameters $\theta_{ij} > 0, j > i$, are pure numbers that measure the ratio of perceived to actual price ratios. They capture what Schmidt and Lovell (1979) refer to as the systematic component of allocative inefficiency. Thus $\theta_{ij} \gtreqless 1$ implies that the perceived price ratio exceeds, equals, or falls below the actual price ratio, so that the corresponding commodity mix is inefficiently small, allocatively efficient, or inefficiently large. The effect of technical inefficiency alone on profit is given by the difference

$$\pi(q) - \pi(q,\phi) = \sum_{i=1}^{6} \phi_i q_i$$

which is zero if $\phi_i = 0$, for all i, and positive otherwise. The effect of allocative inefficiency alone on profit is given by the difference

$$\pi(q) - \pi(q,\theta) = \sum_{i=1}^{5} \sum_{\substack{j=2 \\ j>i}}^{6} A_{ij}q_i^{1/2}q_j^{1/2} \cdot [2 - (\theta_{ij}^{-1/2} + \theta_{ij}^{1/2})]$$

which is zero if all $\theta_{ij} \neq 1$. If any $\theta_{ij} \neq 1$ then $[\pi(q) - \pi(q,\theta)] \geqslant 0$ by virtue of the convexity property π.4, with equality holding if and only if the corresponding $A_{ij} = 0$.

Thus far we have ignored the fact that the production unit faces only six market prices, and only five independent market price ratios, although we have used fifteen independent θ_{ij}'s to model allocative inefficiency. Clearly the market price ratios can be expected to be consistent, in the sense that any five independent price ratios can be used to determine the remaining ten price ratios. In this analysis we assume that the perceived price ratios as modeled by $[\theta_{ij}(q_i/q_j)]$ are also consistent.

Consistent allocative inefficiency is specified by constraining the preceding model. Perceived price ratios must satisfy

$$[\theta_{ij}(q_i/q_j)] \cdot [\theta_{jk}(q_j/q_k)] = \theta_{ik}(q_i/q_k), \qquad i < j < k$$

which, given consistency of market price ratios, requires that

$$\theta_{ik} = \theta_{ij} \cdot \theta_{jk}, \qquad i < j < k$$

which reduces the number of independent allocative inefficiency parameters from fifteen to five. Writing the constrained vector as $\bar{\theta}$, it remains the case that $[\pi(q) - \pi(q,\bar{\theta}) = 0$ if $\bar{\theta} = 1$, and that $[\pi(q) - \pi(q,\bar{\theta}) \geqslant 0]$ if any $\bar{\theta}_{ij} \neq 1$, again by virtue of the convexity property π.4. The only real effect of forcing allocative inefficiency to be consistent is to blur the distinctions among output mix, input mix, and scale types of allocative inefficiency.

An illustration of the costs of technical and allocative inefficiency using this decomposition is given in figure 6-1 for a single output, single input production unit. A technically and allocatively inefficient production unit operates at point A on the interior of its production possibilities set T. It would be technically (but not allocatively) inefficient if it used less (ϕ_3) of input x_1 to produce more (ϕ_1) of output y_1 at point B on the boundary of T. It would also earn greater profit, although not maximum profit, since point B remains allocatively inefficient. It would be both technically and allocatively efficient, and earn maximum profit, if it altered its scale of operation by moving to point C on the boundary of T. Since $0 < \theta < 1$ the movement from B to C involves an increase in the scale of operation.

6.3. Data

We will give a brief discussion of the input and output aggregates. For more detailed coverage see Sickles (1984). The data are by airline by quarter from 1970 I through 1978 III. The airlines are: American, Alleghany, Braniff, Continental, Delta, Eastern, Frontier, North Central, Ozark, Piedmont, United, and Western.

Information on expenses and headcounts were used to develop divisia

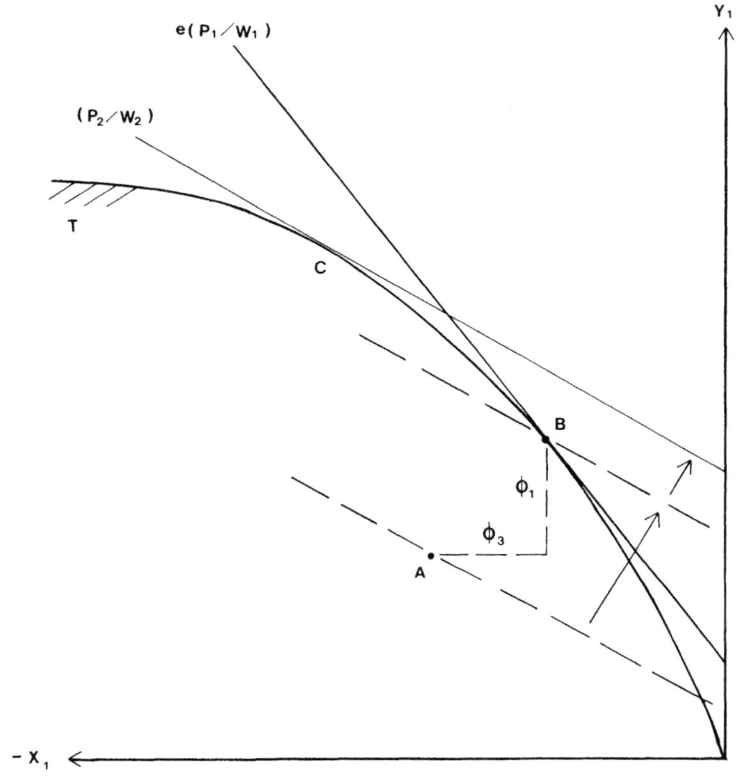

Figure 6-1. Technical and Allocative Inefficiency Illustrated

quantity and price indices for employment. The employment classes are pilots, flight attendants, machinists, passenger/cargo and aircraft handlers, and other personnel. Labor related expenses such as insurance, pension, and payroll taxes were allocated to each class on the basis of its expense share.

The capital input was developed by constructing four categories of expenses which were directly or indirectly identified with capital. The expense categories are flight equipment purchased and rented, ground equipment purchased, ground equipment rented, and landing fees. Quantity indexes for flight equipment purchased and rented were calculated by imputing to purchased aircraft the rental price of a comparably configured aircraft in a fashion similar to Caves, Christensen, and Tretheway (1981). We adjusted for differing aircraft utilization rates by scaling the capital quantity on the bases of average hours ramp-to-ramp relative to the maximum average usage over the period.

The last two input categories are energy and materials. For the energy input we combined information on the quantity of fuel (in gallons) with direct energy expenses. Materials is comprised of many broad classes of residual inputs which are themselves aggregates of 56 different accounts. The categories include advertising, communications, insurance, outside services, supplies, utilities, passenger food, commissions, and other operating and nonoperating expenses.

Capacity ton-mile passenger and freight output indexes were calculated from data on total capacity ton-mile and capacity ton-miles for first class and coach. Price deflators for the three categories were derived from the revenue output accounts. Our measure of output is transferred space and we assume that unused space is wastage.

6.4. Statistical Model

We estimate the system of output supply and input demand equations outlined in section 6.2 by nonlinear seemingly unrelated regressions (Gallant 1975). We allow for serial correlation in the errors, which is not constrained to be the same across equations. In the notation developed below y and x are generic variables denoting the endogeneous and exogenous variables, not output and input quantities, and θ_i is the parameter vector for the ith equation.

Let $G(=6)$ be the number of equations. The system can be written as

$$y_{ti} = \alpha_i + f_i(x_{ti}; \theta_i) + u_{ti}, \qquad i = 1, \ldots, G$$

$$u_{ti} = \rho^i u_{t-1,i} + \varepsilon_{ti}, \qquad |\rho^i| < 1 \ \forall_i$$

where x_{ti} are $k_i \times 1$ vectors, θ_i are $p_i \times 1$ vectors, and α_i are scalars. The G-variate errors $(\varepsilon_{t1}, \ldots, \varepsilon_{tG})'$ are assumed to be independent, to have distribution functions with mean $\phi_i (i = 1, \ldots, G)$ and positive definite covariance matrix Σ, and to always be of the same sign. The standard interpretation of the equation is that the systematic part gives the "optimum" value of y_{ti} and the nonsystematic part arises out of random shocks identifying technical inefficiencies of one sort or another (see, e.g., Aigner and Chu 1968). The technical inefficiencies correspond to an underproduction of outputs and an overutilization of inputs, and cause profit to be less than maximum. Thus the disturbances u_{ti} are all of the same sign, in this case nonpositive.

Assume that ρ_i is known. We can write each equation as

$$P_i y_i = P_i \alpha_i + P_i f_i(\theta) + \varepsilon_i, \qquad i = 1, \ldots, G$$

where

$$y_i = [y_{1i}, y_{2i}, \ldots, y_{Ti}]'$$

$$f_i(\theta_i) = [f_i(x_{1i}; \theta_i), f_i(x_{2i}; \theta_i), \ldots f_i(x_{Ti}; \theta_i)]'$$

$$\varepsilon_i = (\varepsilon_{1i}, \varepsilon_{2i}, \ldots, \varepsilon_{Ti})'$$

and where P_i is such that

$$P_i P_i' = \Lambda_i^{-1}, \qquad \Lambda_i = E[u_i, u_i'].$$

The complete system is then

$$y^* = \alpha^* + f(\theta)^* + \varepsilon$$

where

$$y^* = [(P_1 y_1)', \ldots, (P_G y_G)']'$$

$$\alpha^* = (P_1 \alpha_1, P_2 \alpha_2, \ldots, P_G \alpha_G)'$$

$$f(\theta)^* = [P_1 f_1'(\theta_1), P_2 f_2'(\theta_2), \ldots, P_G f_G'(\theta_G)]'$$

$$\theta = (\theta_1', \ldots, \theta_G')$$

$$\varepsilon = (\varepsilon_1', \varepsilon_2', \ldots, \varepsilon_G')$$

Define $\mu = \alpha^* + \phi$ and let $\delta = (\mu, \theta)$, $g(\delta) = \mu + f(\theta)$. If we specify the covariance matrix for ε as $\Sigma \otimes I_T$ then the limiting distribution of $\tilde{\delta}$ is

$$\sqrt{T}(\tilde{\delta} - \delta) \rightarrow N(0, \Omega^{-1})$$

where

$$\Omega = (T^{-1}) G'(\delta)(\Sigma^{-1} \otimes I) G(\delta)$$

$$G(\delta) = \text{diag}\,[G_1(\delta_1), G_2(\delta_2), \ldots, G_G(\delta_G)]$$

$$G_i(\delta_i) = \partial g_i(\delta_i)/\partial \delta_i$$

and where $\tilde{\delta}$ is obtained by minimizing

$$S(\delta) = (T^{-1})[y^* - g(\delta)]'\textstyle\sum^{-1} \otimes I[y^* - g(\delta)]$$

over δ. As a practical matter, $P_i(i = 1, \ldots, 6)$ and Σ are unknown. We thus use a four-step procedure to estimate δ. The first step involves consistently estimating the residuals u_i by ordinary least squares on each equation separately. From the estimated residuals we can form consistent estimates of the ρ_i and thus can form P_i. In the third step the residual vectors e_i are formed. The fourth step involves estimation of Σ by

$$\tilde{\sigma}_{ij} = (T^{-1})e_i'e_j,\ i,j = 1, \ldots, G$$

Identification of average technical inefficiency from estimates of the μ_i could be accomplished in the following fashion. Greene (1980) has shown that, regardless of the distribution of the disturbances, if the x_{ti} are well behaved and the errors are distributed identically and independently, then consistent estimates of the intercept terms α_i^* are given by the order statistics of the consistent residuals for each equation. Because the estimating equations are driven from a maximum profit frontier, the consistent order statistics are given by $e_{i(1)} = \max(e_{ti})$, where e_{ti} are the estimated residuals. Thus estimated average technical efficiency is given by

$$\phi_i = e_{i(1)} \quad \text{and} \quad \hat{\alpha}_i^* = \hat{\mu}_i - \phi_i$$

This argument is valid only if the white noise component of u_{ti} is identifying the technical inefficiency. Thus the proof of Greene must be amended to allow for dependent errors. We put forth as a conjecture but do not prove that the consistent order statistics of the distribution of the dependent errors u_{ti} can be derived from $\tilde{u}_{i(1)} = \min(\tilde{u}_{ti})$ where $\tilde{u}_{ti}$ are consistent estimates of u_{ti}. This would allow average technical inefficiency to be estimated, although we are not yet certain if the estimates are consistent. For this and for the reason cited in note 2 we will focus on allocative inefficiency in the empirical work to follow.

6.5. Empirical Results

Each equation of the system of output supplies and input demands was augmented by a set of seasonal dummies and two proxies for networking differences between carriers—load factor and average stage length. We also included a time trend in each equation to account for output augmenting (diminishing) and/or input diminishing (augmenting) technical change. The estimation results are given in table 6-1. We first note that the allocative inefficiency parameters are nonunity and several are significantly so. The test of nonunitary $\bar{\theta}_{ij}$'s yielded *t*-statistics of 0.13, 0.16, 1.73, 1.66, 4.16, and a χ^2 of 19.2 suggesting significant allocative inefficiency. Technical change was output augmenting for passenger and cargo, input saving for labor, capital, and energy, and input using for materials. The yearly rates of technical change at average values of outputs and inputs are 2.7, 1.5, 0.5, 2.3, 1.9, 2.7.

The cost of inefficiency (forgone profits) due to suboptimal allocative decisions is plotted in figure 6-2 as a function of time. We have deflated the quarterly industry figures by the Producer Price Index to get an idea of the real opportunity cost of allocative inefficiency to the industry. The industry aggregates are smoothed using a four degree polynomial spline between points. Several conclusions can be drawn from the figure. First real industry lost profits ($ millions) trended upward during the 1970s although a slight dip is found at the end of the sample period. We will examine the post-1978 period in future research. The upward trending in lost profits could be due to the increased level of operation experienced by the majority of carriers during the period and a relatively constant degree of inefficiency although there is nothing in our model that would force the level of inefficiency to be constant. Second the rather dramatic spike in the lost profits profile after the first oil price shock indicates substantial inefficiency relative to other periods. It appears that the industry was able to adjust in a little over a year along an upward trend either by altering operating procedures or by modifying the configuration of its fleet.

6.6. Conclusions

This chapter has outlined an econometric model that allows for the identification and estimation of allocative and technical efficiency in joint production. We have presented estimates of the former of these inefficiencies for the U.S. airline industry using a rich quarterly panel of 12 carriers. We have found that significant allocative inefficiencies existed from 1970

Table 6-1. Estimation Results

Variable: Equation (i)	*Estimate*	*t-statistic*
A11	−159.630	−58.760
A12	9.367	3.436
A13	−24.914	−5.292
A14	15.184	1.439
A15	4.475	0.282
A16	−6.863	−1.307
A22	−17.857	−9.354
A23	5.812	0.743
A24	5.722	0.978
A25	4.073	1.497
A26	−1.885	−0.506
A33	82.223	18.907
A34	−0.947	−0.299
A35	0.017	0.008
A36	−0.761	−0.372
A44	−9.404	−5.898
A45	−3.145	−0.756
A46	−15.479	−9.959
A55	13.027	3.128
A56	−7.590	−5.057
A66	46.828	5.761
$\bar{\theta}_{12}$	1.210	1.791
$\bar{\theta}_{23}$	1.199	0.932
$\bar{\theta}_{34}$	0.562	1.899
$\bar{\theta}_{45}$	2.371	2.837
$\bar{\theta}_{56}$	0.259	1.450
Time (1)	2.533	1.717
Time (2)	0.357	0.123
Time (3)	−0.107	1.062
Time (4)	−0.137	−0.911
Time (5)	−0.177	−0.526
Time (6)	0.261	1.387
Stagel (1)	0.971	2.203
Stagel (2)	0.219	1.218
Stagel (3)	−0.213	−1.912
Stagel (4)	−0.016	−1.032
Stagel (5)	−0.076	−1.586
Stagel (6)	−0.079	−1.604
Load F (1)	163.000	161.760
Load F (2)	−42.239	−40.073

(*continued*)

Table 6-1. *(Continued)*

Variable: Equation (i)	*Estimate*	*t-statistic*
Load F (3)	−116.320	−58.467
Load F (4)	−2.923	−2.369
Load F (5)	−9.959	−3.607
Load F (6)	−52.186	−21.090
Spring (1)	−0.492	−0.074
Spring (2)	1.484	0.177
Spring (3)	1.616	0.332
Spring (4)	−0.111	−0.070
Spring (5)	0.209	0.114
Spring (6)	0.844	0.223
Summer (1)	12.635	1.003
Summer (2)	4.764	0.812
Summer (3)	5.142	0.920
Summer (4)	0.668	0.593
Summer (5)	−0.813	−0.542
Summer (6)	0.906	0.379
Fall (1)	−10.836	−0.861
Fall (2)	−2.143	−0.365
Fall (3)	0.806	0.144
Fall (4)	−0.100	−0.090
Fall (5)	0.981	0.624
Fall (6)	0.498	0.209

to 1978 and have found that the real opportunity cost of allocative inefficiency trended upward during the prederegulatory period.

Notes

1. The profit function is discussed in Diewert (1973) and McFadden (1978). As Diewert has pointed out, if T satisfies only T.1 and T.2, the derived function π still satisfies $\{\pi.1-\pi.4\}$. In this case π is dual to the convex free disposal hull T^* of T. Thus if technology is characterized by regions of increasing returns to scale, or only weak disposability, these properties will not show up in the derived profit function. Only when all parts of {T.1–T.4} hold does π completely characterize T.

2. The reason for this is basically empirical. The method employed by Lovell and Sickles (1983) specifies the profit function as a "full" rather than a "stochastic" frontier. The problem with the full frontier approach is that the average inefficiency estimates are based on the order statistics of the estimated residuals. Because of the rather heterogeneous data utilized in this study, these residuals were often quite large and the corresponding inefficiency es-

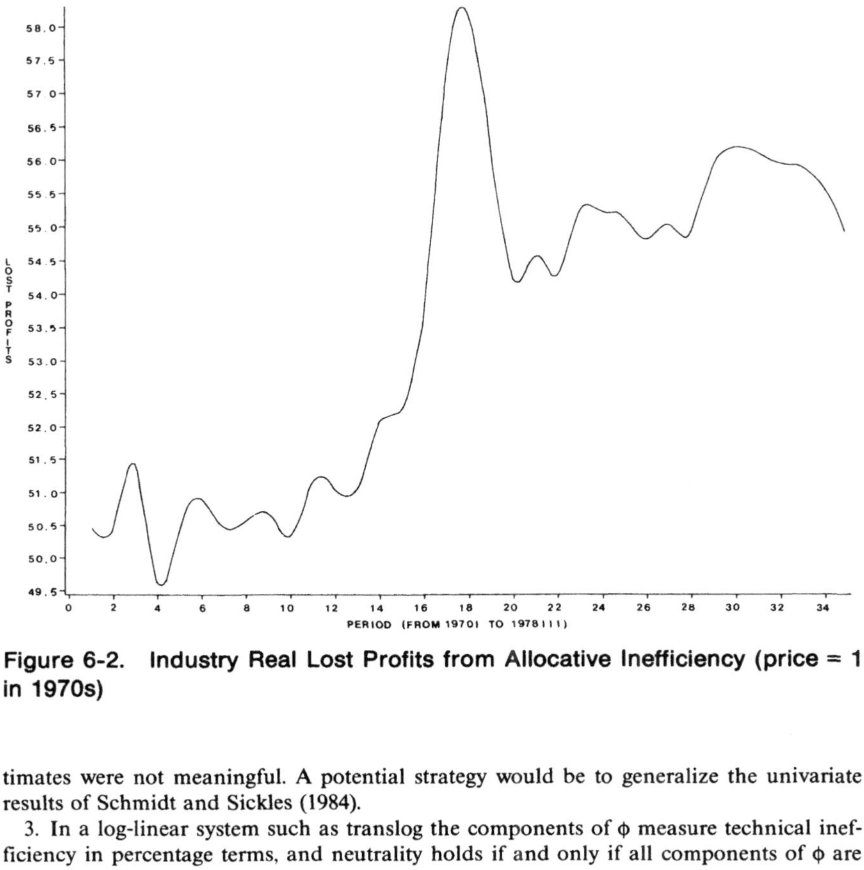

Figure 6-2. Industry Real Lost Profits from Allocative Inefficiency (price = 1 in 1970s)

timates were not meaningful. A potential strategy would be to generalize the univariate results of Schmidt and Sickles (1984).

3. In a log-linear system such as translog the components of ϕ measure technical inefficiency in percentage terms, and neutrality holds if and only if all components of ϕ are equal.

References

Aigner, Dennis J., and S. F. Chu. 1968. "On Estimating the Industry Production Function." *American Economic Review* 58 (September): 826–837.

Atkinson, Scott E., and Robert Halvorsen. 1980. "A Test of Relative and Absolute Price Efficiency in Regulated Utilities." *Review of Economics and Statistics* 62 (February): 81–88.

Caves, D. W., L. R. Christensen, and M. W. Tretheway. 1981. "U.S. Trunk Air Carriers, 1972–1977: A Multilateral Comparison of Total Factor Productivity." In Thomas G. Cowing and Rodney E. Stevenson (eds.), *Productivity Measurement in Regulated Industries.* New York: Academic Press.

Debreu, Gerard. 1951. "The Coefficient of Resource Utilization." *Econometrica* 19 (July): 273-292.

Diewert, W. Erwin. 1971. "An Application of the Shephard Duality Theorem: A Generalized Leontief Production Function." *Journal of Political Economy* 79 (May/June): 481-507.

Diewert, W. Erwin. 1973. "Functional Forms for Profit and Transformation Functions." *Journal of Economic Theory* 6 (June): 284-316.

Farrell, M. J. 1957. "The Measurement of Productive Efficiency." *Journal of the Royal Statistical Society,* ser. A, general, 120, pt. III, 253-278.

Gallant, Ronald A. 1975. "Seemingly Unrelated Nonlinear Regressions." *Journal of Econometrics* 3 (February): 35-50.

Greene, William H. 1980. "Maximum Likelihood Estimation of Econometric Frontier Functions." *Journal of Econometrics* 13 (May): 27-56.

Lovell, C. A. K., and Robin C. Sickles. 1983. "Testing Efficiency Hypotheses in Joint Production: A Parametric Approach." *Review of Economics and Statistics* 65:51-58.

McFadden, Daniel. 1978. "Cost, Revenue, and Profit Functions." In M. Fuss and D. McFadden (eds.), *Production Economics: A Dual Approach to Theory and Applications,* vol. 1. Amsterdam: North-Holland Publishing.

Schmidt, P., and C. A. K. Lovell. 1979. "Estimating Technical and Allocative Inefficiency Relative to Stochastic Production and Cost Frontiers." *Journal of Econometrics* 9:343-366.

Schmidt, Peter, and Robin C. Sickles. 1984. "Production Frontiers and Panel Data." *Journal of Business and Economic Statistics* 2:367-374.

Sickles, Robin C. 1985. "A Nonlinear Multivariate Error-Components Analysis of Technology and Specific Factor Productivity Growth with an Application to the U.S. Airlines." *Journal of Econometrics* 27:61-78.

Toda, Yasushi. 1976. "Estimation of a Cost Function When the Cost Is Not Minimum: The Case Soviet Manufacturing Industries, 1958-1971." *Review of Economics and Statistics* 58 (August): 259-268.

7 CAPACITY UTILIZATION AND PRODUCTIVITY MEASUREMENT: AN APPLICATION TO THE U.S. AUTOMOBILE INDUSTRY*

Catherine J. Morrison

7.1. Introduction

Capacity utilization measures have traditionally been constructed as indexes of output for a firm, industry, or economy, as compared to "potential" output. The determination of "potential" or "capacity" output has, however, rarely been based on an explicit theoretical economic foundation. Recently various studies, including Berndt and Morrison (1981) and Morrison (1982, 1985, 1986), have provided theoretical and empirical analysis in the tradition of Cassels (1937), Klein (1960), and Hickman (1964) on economic capacity utilization measures within an optimization framework. Capacity output, Y^*, is characterized by the steady-state level of production given the existing level of stocks and exogenous prices of inputs and determined as the tangency point between the short- and long-run average cost curves. The capacity utilization (CU) ratio is then constructed as the ratio between this and the realized level of output Y, $CU = (Y/Y^*)$.

*Research Support from the National Science Foundation is gratefully acknowledged. I am also indebted to J. R. Norsworthy, U.S. Bureau of the Census, and Joyce Yanchar, Data Resources Incorporated, for providing data.

Theoretical models based on restricted-cost functions provide the required structure within which to characterize and analyze these measures. These measures allow capacity output to be characterized as an optimal, as contrasted to maximal, output level given input stocks. They also allow for economic interpretation; they provide explicit inference about how changes in exogenous variables will affect Y^* and the CU ratio.

These quantity indexes are useful but it is also important to recognize that additional information can be obtained by analyzing deviations from potential or capacity production—the *disequilibrium gap.* This information is the implied *cost* of the gap, which will depend on the shape of the cost curves. This concept of costs is a very specific one; it reflects the costs of operating at an output level other than the steady-state output level given capital (or, in the more general case, with more quasi-fixed factors, given capacity defined as an aggregate of all quasi-fixed factors). This contrasts with the idea of costs of disequilibrium, costs of being at a level of capital (K) that is not the long-run equilibrium level given output demand. This distinction is critical; the definition and interpretation of utilization of capacity relies on the concept of optimal (steady-state) use of existing capacity, not on the adaptation of that capacity to existing demand conditions.

Note that this producer-side cost measure is a positive rather than normative concept. Specifically, the excess costs of producing a given output level in disequilibrium as reflected in the shadow valuation of the existing capital stock are costs of adjustment or costs of rigidity for the firm rather than necessarily costs to society. In addition, this measure is valid given many different market structures, for example, for a monopolist producing at a point of nonconstant returns to scale. At an output level Y greater than the capacity level Y^*, the shadow value of capital at the margin will exceed the market price, indicating nonoptimal or excess cost use of capacity, even when the average cost curve is downward sloping at the tangency point defining Y^*. Finally, these measures are consistent with representations of CU in terms of capital utilization—by a multiplicative index on capital—if this index is based on the shadow price of capital services. This is, in a sense, a variation on Tobin's q, which indicates over- or underutilization of the existing capital in terms of its valuation. The approach taken here may, however, be used to model q's for fixed factors in addition to capital, by assessing the deviation of their shadow values from market prices or utilization levels.

The contributions of this chapter include the development and analysis of the positive cost-side measure of utilization of existing capacity, the theoretical implementation of this and the corresponding quantity-side measure within an imperfectly competitive framework, and an illustration of the empirical validity and application of these measures. This research suggests that cost-CU measures with a rich potential for both interpretation and application can be defined within a dynamic optimization model of the firm. These cost measures are useful to supplement quantity-side CU measures based on a more traditional concept of CU, and facilitate reconciliation and interpretation of various conceptual indicators of deviations from capacity output, and thus from potential productivity.

Section 7.2 presents a theoretical framework for CU and outlines previous work on quantity-side measures of CU, emphasizing the application to an imperfect competition model with nonconstant returns to scale (NCRTS) from Morrison (1982). The concept of dual cost-side measures is then developed for both a perfectly competitive cost-minimizing firm facing CRTS and an imperfectly competitive firm producing at a point of nonconstant returns to scale. This latter case provides a framework for analysis of many implications of this cost indicator. Section 7.3 provides an empirical illustration of the interpretation and use of estimated quantity and cost-side measures for the U.S. automobile industry from 1959–1980.

7.2. Specification of Economic CU and "Dual" Cost CU Measures

7.2.1. Quantity CU Indicators and Constant Returns to Scale

Economic measures of CU depend fundamentally on the existence of input stocks, which cause short-run behavior—temporary equilibrium—to differ from long-run equilibrium behavior. One representation of short-run disequilibrium is a measure of CU calculated as a comparison of capacity output (Y^*) and the observed output level (Y), Y/Y^*. This measure can be defined within the framework of a dynamic factor demand model which explicitly characterizes short-run decision making, when quasi-fixed inputs are at their given level, as contrasted to the long run when they are adjusted.

This structure has been developed by Berndt and Morrison (1981) and Morrison (1982) on the basis of earlier work carried out by Hickman (1964) and others. Berndt and Morrison use a model based on dynamic optimization of the firm. The model is based on costs of adjustment for quasi-fixed inputs that induce slow adjustment by firms to "optimal" or "desired" levels of the quasi-fixed inputs, represented by x^*, or K^* with capital as the only quasi-fixed factor, an assumption I will retain throughout this study for expositional purposes. The model is structured so that one can explicitly derive a system of short-run demand equations for variable inputs (utilization equations) and accumulation equation(s) for quasi-fixed input(s) based on an endogenous "flexible accelerator" or partial adjustment process. Thus, one can characterize what the firm's optimal behavior would be in the short run (with quasi-fixed inputs fixed), long-run (once quasi-fixed inputs have reached their long-run level), and along the optimal adjustment path between these states.

Short-, intermediate-, and long-run cost curves can be defined analogously. One can derive the firm's short-run average total cost (SRAC) curve defined by the given capital stock, a different SRAC curve defined by the optimal capital stock K^*, and the long-run average total cost (LRAC) envelope. Knowledge of these cost curves can be used to characterize the adjustment behavior of the firm, or to determine why the firm's capacity output Y^* differs from observed output Y. Hence, one can explicitly determine an endogenous measure of capacity utilization, $CU = Y/Y^*$. Specifically, the tangency point between SRAC and LRAC can be directly characterized and the corresponding output Y^* derived using parametric methods. The resulting CU measure is therefore an explicit function of the exogenous variables and parameters of the cost function and can easily be estimated.

This framework allows one to determine how Y^* would be affected by changes in input prices or other exogenous variables. Assume capital (K) is the only quasi-fixed input, and specify a variable cost function with internal costs of adjustment as $G(K,\dot{K},Y,P_j,t)$, where P_j is a vector of j prices of variable inputs, and t represents the state of technology. Total costs therefore are represented by $C = G + P_k \cdot K$, where P_k is the rental price of capital. To determine Y^*, one differentiates average total costs with respect to Y and solves for Y^* at the minimum point on this curve resulting in

$$Y^* = Y^*(K,\dot{K},P_j,P_k,t) \qquad (7.1)$$

If a specific functional form is postulated for the variable cost function G, the resulting expression for Y^* indicates very clearly how the exogenous factors determine short-run capacity output. If G is constant-returns-to-scale quadratic, say, as in Morrison-Berndt (1981), and capital is the only quasi-fixed input, with three variable inputs, labor (L), energy (E), and materials (M), G can be expressed as

$$\begin{aligned}
G &= L + P_E E + P_M M \\
&= Y[\alpha_0 + \alpha_{0t} + \alpha_E P_E + \alpha_M P_M + 0.5(\gamma_{EE} P_E^2 + \gamma_{MM} P_M^2) \\
&\quad + \gamma_{EM} P_E P_M + \alpha_{Et} P_E t + \alpha_{Mt} P_M t + \alpha_K K \\
&\quad + 0.5(\gamma_{KK}(K^2/Y) + \gamma_{\dot{K}\dot{K}}(\dot{K}^2/Y)] \\
&\quad + \gamma_{EK} P_E K + \gamma_{MK} P_M K + \alpha_{Tk} K t
\end{aligned} \tag{7.2}$$

The explicit solution for Y^* can be shown to be

$$Y^* = -\left(\frac{\gamma_{KK}K^2 + \gamma_{\dot{K}\dot{K}}\dot{K}^2}{\alpha_K K + \alpha_{Kt} Kt + \gamma_{EK} P_E K + \gamma_{MK} P_M K + P_k K}\right) \tag{7.3}$$

which results in the capacity utilization measure

$$CU = \frac{Y(\alpha_K K + \alpha_{Kt} Kt + \gamma_{EK} P_E K + \gamma_{MK} P_M K + P_k K)}{\gamma_{KK}K^2 + \gamma_{\dot{K}\dot{K}}\dot{K}^2} \tag{7.4}$$

This CU measure is derived and estimated in Berndt, Morrison, and Watkins (1981) for their dynamic model, and has also been estimated by Berndt (1980).

Using equation (7.3), one can determine how the CU measure varies with changes in exogenous variables. For example, an increase in the price of a variable input such as energy will increase Y^* if the variable input and capital are long-run complements and decrease Y^* if they are substitutes. Intuitively, if capital and energy are complementary inputs in the long run, when the price of energy increases at a given output level, the optimal capital stock decreases. Thus, the existing capital stock is consistent with a higher Y^*. Traditional CU measures may not reflect this type of phenomenon for such measures tend to be calculated mechanically; their theoretical economic underpinnings are unspecified.

Note that the concept of calculating Y^* given $\bar{K}$ is conversely related to calculating the steady-state K^* given $\bar{Y}$; they both depend on all remaining exogenous variables. The development above also implies that factor proportions can be changed; different levels of output can be produced even given $\bar{K}$, since different levels of the variable inputs can be applied to the fixed-capital stock. In this sense this is a putty-putty framework even in the short run since capital can be utilized to different extents even before the long run is reached.

7.2.2. Quantity CU Indexes and Nonconstant Returns to Scale—Incorporating Monopoly Behavior

This measure has been generalized, theoretically and empirically, by Morrison (1982) to incorporate nonconstant returns to scale and monopoly behavior. A formulation was developed which depends on the notion, proposed in Berndt and Fuss (1981), of the firm's shadow cost function, which expands on the notion of capacity output as the steady-state output corresponding to given values of all the exogenous variables, including the fixed input stocks. The steady-state equilibrium is imposed by equating the shadow and total cost functions, or, equivalently, the market and shadow value of capital, with one quasi-fixed input, and finding the implied output level, Y^*. More specifically, given $G(Y,P_j,t,K,\dot{K})$, the shadow cost function can be characterized by

$$G(Y,P_j,t,K,\dot{K}) + Z_k \cdot K \tag{7.5}$$

where K is the current level of capital and Z_k is the corresponding shadow value.[1] As shown in Lau (1978), this shadow value can be specified as $-\partial G/\partial K = -G_k$. Thus (7.5) becomes

$$G(Y,P_j,t,K,\dot{K}) - G_k \cdot K \tag{7.6}$$

The shadow cost function and the corresponding equilibrium condition can be interpreted most easily using the assumption of constant returns to scale (CRTS). With CRTS, the firm is always producing at the minimum of the average shadow cost function, for this point represents long-run equilibrium given the shadow value of capital Z_k as the effective "price" of K. Thus, if the shadow cost function is set equal to the total cost function, the point where these two minimum points coincide is determined; there will be no incentive for the firm to move from this point. The equilibrium condition for the firm can then be stated as

$$G(\cdot) - G_k K = G(\cdot) + P_k K \quad \text{or} \quad -G_k = P_k \tag{7.7}$$

This characterizes the situation where the actual values of K and Y are consistent with long-run optimization. Thus, by the definition of equilibrium, this equation characterizes either the optimal K^* level given Y, or the optimal Y^* level given K. In the context of CU measurement, the latter characterization is appropriate. More specifically, the shadow cost function revalues the capital stock so that the current K is the optimal level of capital given Y; it shifts the cost curve by its revaluation of the quasi-fixed inputs. As K approaches its optimal long-run value, or output demand is deflated to the steady-state level corresponding to actual K, the shadow value approaches P_k. Imposition of an equilibrium condition in terms of equating the shadow cost function with the total cost function in effect forces this equality.

The CU measure resulting from this shadow-function equilibrium condition can readily be shown to be equivalent to the tangency specification for the more general nonconstant-returns-to-scale (NCRTS) case. The LRMC and SRMC curves must intersect at the value representing the point of tangency of LRAC and SRAC. One can therefore calculate Y^* by imposing SRMC = LRMC. To derive SRMC, by definition, only variable inputs are freely adjustable in the short run, so

$$SRMC = \left.\frac{dG(Y,t,P_j,K,\dot{K})}{dY}\right|_{K=\bar{K}} = \frac{\partial G}{\partial Y} \tag{7.8}$$

Derivation of the LRMC is slightly more complex. Since total cost equals $G + P_k \cdot K$, the LRMC curve can be specified as[2]

$$\begin{aligned} \frac{d\,LRTC}{dY} &= \frac{dG(Y,t,P_j,K,\dot{K})}{dY} + P_k \cdot \left(\frac{dK}{dY}\right) \\ &= \frac{\partial G}{\partial Y} + \left(\frac{\partial G}{\partial K}\right)\left(\frac{dK}{dY}\right) + P_k \cdot \left(\frac{dK}{dY}\right) \end{aligned} \tag{7.9}$$

Equating SRMC and LRMC, one obtains

$$\frac{\partial G}{\partial Y} = \frac{\partial G}{\partial Y} + \frac{\partial G}{\partial K}\frac{dK}{dY} + P_k\left(\frac{dK}{dY}\right) \tag{7.10a}$$

or

$$\left(\frac{\partial G}{\partial K} + P_k\right)\left(\frac{dK}{dY}\right) = 0$$

so

$$-\frac{\partial G}{\partial K} = P_k \tag{7.10b}$$

To apply this approach in general, the stock-oriented shadow value of capital must be adjusted to include amortized adjustment costs represented by $r(\partial G/\partial \dot{K}) = rG_{\dot{k}}$, where r represents the discount rate. Such a modification relies on explicit characterization of the *flow* as contrasted to the *stock* aspects of the full dynamic optimization problem of the firm. The existence of $rG_{\dot{k}}$ reflects the essential dynamic nature of the problem even in equilibrium, as suggested by the general equilibrium condition from Morrison (1982) and earlier studies:

$$-(G_k + rG_{\dot{k}}) = P_k \tag{7.11}$$

In a model allowing only for costs of adjustment of net investment, $G_{\dot{k}}(0) = 0$. If the analysis were static and therefore K and $\dot{K}$ were given, the $G_{\dot{k}}$ term would still drop out of the equilibrium characterization. However, in a full dynamic model, in disequilibrium $\dot{K} \neq 0$ so $G_{\dot{k}}(\dot{K}) \neq 0$ in general; and it should be taken into account in derivation of "disequilibrium" indicators such as CU. The compensating adjustment $rG_{\dot{k}}$ can be viewed as a wedge resulting from costs of adjustment and the corresponding dynamic adjustment process.[3]

Since an imperfectly competitive firm will in general produce at a point of increasing returns, it is also necessary to respecify G to allow NCRTS. A quadratic cost function including NCRTS can be represented by

$$\begin{aligned} G &= L + P_E E + P_M M \\ &= Y[\alpha_0 + \alpha_{0t} t + \alpha_E P_E + \alpha_M P_M + \alpha_y Y + \gamma_{EM} P_E P_M \\ &\quad + 0.5(\gamma_{EE} P_E^2 + \gamma_{MM} P_M^2) + \gamma_{EY} P_E Y \\ &\quad + \gamma_{MY} P_M Y + \alpha_{Et} P_E t + \alpha_{Mt} P_M t] \\ &\quad + \alpha_K K + 0.5(\gamma_{KK} K^2 + \gamma_{\dot{K}\dot{K}} \dot{K}^2) \\ &\quad + \gamma_{EK} P_E K + \gamma_{MK} P_M K + \gamma_{Kt} K t + \gamma_{YK} Y K \end{aligned} \tag{7.12}$$

Using this function one can calculate capacity output Y^* as

$$Y^* = -(\alpha_K + \gamma_{KK} K + \gamma_{EK} P_E + \gamma_{MK} P_M + \alpha_{Kt} t + r\gamma_{\dot{K}\dot{K}} \dot{K} + P_K)/\gamma_{YK} \tag{7.13}$$

In this case, the tangency of the SRAC and LRAC curves, represented by Y^*, will in general no longer be at the minimum point of SRAC; at such an output level, the firm would be able to reach a lower cost point by expanding its capital stock if increasing returns could be exploited. The quantity CU measure is again defined as Y/Y^*.

7.2.3. Dual Cost Measures of CU—Derivation and Interpretation with CRTS

To develop the concepts necessary to define a cost-side dual measure, it is useful initially to present the fundamentals graphically. To accomplish this, CRTS will first be assumed; the crucial concepts can be more clearly exposed in the simpler framework. This restriction is relaxed in the next subsection.

The graphical determination of Y^* in this case is presented in figure 7-1. Given the long-run average-cost curve $LRAC_0$, say that the firm is at a disequilibrium position with short-run increasing unit costs characterized by $SRAC_0(K_0,\dot{K}_0,P_k)$ and Y'. Perhaps as a consequence of a previous unexpected increase in exogenous output demand, Y' is larger than the production level corresponding to the minimum point on the current $SRAC_0$ curve defined by K_0.[4] Respecifying the total cost curve in terms of shadow prices or shadow values for the given K, $\dot{K}$, and Y levels defines $SRAC_{sh}$ with the minimum point at Y'. The shadow value of capital exceeds the existing market price at Y' so unit costs are higher; capital is a binding constraint to optimization and more capital is desired to move to $SRAC^*(K^*)$.

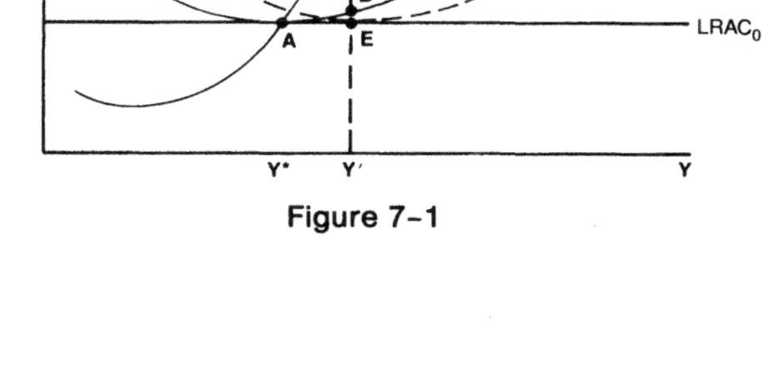

Figure 7-1

If one imposes equilibrium by equating the shadow and market values of the quasi-fixed input(s), and if this is not consistent with the exogenously given K_0, Y', the level of either K or Y must "give" for the equality to hold. If K were allowed to adjust to the implied level consistent with a steady state, K^* would be determined as the capital stock defined such that the SRAC_{sh} curve drops down to a tangency with LRAC_0 at Y'; this defines $\mathrm{SRAC}^*(K^*)$. If, however, K were held fixed and output were adjusted to accommodate to the remaining current exogenous variables, the firm's implied production would reach a level corresponding to point A from D by "sliding" back along the SRMC_0 curve to a tangency with LRAC_0. This defines the stationary point Y^*.

Given this basis, the cost-side dual characterization(s) of the CU quantity measure can be derived. A cost-oriented CU measures the costs of being in disequilibrium, or at Y' instead of Y^*. The problem is how uniquely to represent such a measure, given the various cost points represented on the diagram.

To facilitate interpretation of alternative possible cost measures, it is helpful to determine what the various points in figure 7-1 represent. First, intuitively, the costs of being at Y' instead of Y^* should correspond to comparison of one of the points D, B, or E with point A. Since E is the long-run equilibrium point given full adjustment of the capital stock to the given demand level, it does not represent a good short-run comparison point, and, in fact, equals A with CRTS. It is not as easy to determine which of the two measures, B or D, representing, respectively, short-run average total costs and shadow costs at Y', should be used.

It appears at first that since the CU derivation is based on the comparison of total and shadow costs, the most valid measure may be that which represents the shadow costs at Y' and K_0, which is D. The comparison of this point with point A can be expressed in ratio form by $\mathrm{SHCOST}(Y')/\mathrm{TCOST}(Y^*)$ or $SRAC(Y',Z_k,K_0)/SRAC(Y^*,P_k,K_0)$. This formula poses an interesting question, however, It appears that one may be double-counting the disequilibrium cost measure by altering both Y and the value of capital, as the shadow value of capital depends on the given Y, and therefore embodies the existing disequilibrium.

Conceptually, Y^* is distinguished from Y' by explicitly representing the deviation between P_k and Z_k in quantity terms. Thus, a more appropriate characterization of the disequilibrium would result from adjusting the valuation of K or the output quantity measure but not both. These deviations correspond to the difference between D and B or B and A, respectively. Since D represents the shadow cost function at Y', the measure implied by the comparison of D and B, or $SHCOST(Y')/TCOST(Y')$ will be called the shadow valuation cost-CU measure. The comparison of B to A

or $TCOST(Y')/TCOST(Y^*)$, which depends on assessment of implied market costs at different output levels, will be called the average cost-CU measure. With CRTS, these appear to be the two main conceptual cost characterizations of the disequilibrium; either one may be considered dual. As I shall now show, however, in general these measures are equivalent, resulting in a unique cost-side representation.

The shadow valuation measure is a direct representation of the approach used for deriving the quantity-CU measures, since it depends on the shadow and total cost functions at Y'. To represent the quantity-CU measure, the deviation between shadow and total costs was solved for in terms of the implied output level. In the cost case, the same deviation is expressed by the implied costs of being away from output level Y^* represented by the revaluation of the given capital stock. The average cost measure instead represents the realized—as contrasted to the implicit—costs of being at Y', given K_0, as compared to Y^* which is consistent with K_0 as a steady state. These two approaches are useful characterizations of a dual cost measure for different purposes, but contain the same information—they are structurally equivalent.

One basis from which to start to explore more completely the analytical distinctions—or lack of such—between them is the graphical characterization of the difference between D and B. This can be represented by the difference between the average shadow and total costs or between the points on the short-run marginal and average cost curves at Y'. This difference between marginal cost, MC, and average cost, AC, can be represented analytically as

$$MC = AC + Y \cdot c'(Y) \tag{7.14}$$

where total cost is $C = AC \cdot Y = c(Y) \cdot Y = G + P_k K$, average cost is $c = C/Y$, and marginal cost is $\partial C/\partial Y = c(Y) + Y \cdot c'(Y)$. Expressed in proportional terms, the difference between MC and AC becomes $Yc'(Y)/c(Y)$ or $(Y^2/C)c'(Y)$. Note, however, that this is equivalent to the elasticity of average costs with respect to output:

$$\frac{\partial \ln c(Y)}{\partial \ln Y} = \frac{\partial c}{\partial Y}\frac{Y^2}{C} = \frac{\partial \ln C}{\partial \ln Y} - 1 = \varepsilon_{cy} - 1 \tag{7.15}$$

where ε_{cy} is the elasticity of total costs with respect to a change in output. In addition, by definition

$$\frac{d \ln C}{d \ln Y} = \frac{\partial C}{\partial Y}\frac{Y}{C} + \frac{\partial C}{\partial K}\frac{dK}{dY}\frac{Y}{C} \tag{7.16}$$

$$= \frac{\partial \ln C}{\partial \ln Y} + \frac{\partial \ln C}{\partial \ln K} = \varepsilon_{cy} + \varepsilon_{ck} = 1$$

where $dK/dY = K/Y$ since $(dK/dY)(Y/K)$ must equal unity with CRTS, ε_{ck} is the elasticity of total cost with respect to the capital stock, $\partial \ln C/\partial \ln K$, and $d \ln C/d \ln Y$ must be unity with long-run constant returns to scale.

The cost elasticity with respect to output in the short run, or equivalently the inverse of short-run returns to scale (returns to all variable inputs) (SRTS) can be defined as $\varepsilon_{cy} = 1 - \varepsilon_{ck}$. In the long run, $\varepsilon_{ck} = 0$ since $\partial C/\partial K = \partial G/\partial K + P_k = P_k - Z_k$, so $\varepsilon_{cy} = 1$—the inverse of long-run returns to scale (LRTS). In this case, all inputs are essentially variable so an increase in output causes a proportional increase in costs. The general representation

$$\frac{\partial \ln C}{\partial \ln Y} - \frac{\partial \ln C}{\partial \ln K} = \varepsilon_{cy} - \varepsilon_{ck} = 1$$

captures the proportional adjustment of fixed inputs to the long run to represent CRTS in all inputs, and reflects the distinction in the short run between the cost effects that result from movements along the given SRAC curve—ε_{cy}—and the cost effects that would result from a relaxation of the exogenous K constraint or a shift in the SRAC curve—ε_{ck}.

A crucial result linking the cost-CU measures described above is derived from combining (7.15) and (7.16):

$$\frac{MC - c(Y)}{c(Y)} = \frac{d \ln c(Y)}{d \ln Y} = -\varepsilon_{ck} = \frac{-\partial C}{\partial K}\frac{K}{C} = (Z_k - P_k)\frac{K}{C} \tag{7.17}$$

Thus (1) the proportional difference between MC and AC represented by the shadow valuation cost-CU measure or (2) the proportional change in AC with a change in the level of output represented by the average cost-CU measure is defined uniquely by the differences between Z_k and P_k (which equals zero in long-run equilibrium). When the capital stock is inadequate relative to demand, actual output Y' is to the right of the minimum point of the SRAC curve where MC exceeds AC and Z_k is greater than P_k. The valuation of an incremental unit of capital stock is in this case very high, or conversely, the cost of having too low a capital stock is very high. By contrast, with a capital stock that exceeds the optimal level relative to output demanded, MC is less than AC and Z_k falls short of P_k; the marginal unit of capital has a very low valuation relative to its market cost. This is an implied or opportunity cost of having too high a level of capital.

This equivalence of the cost-CU measures can be further pursued by decomposing the shadow valuation measure to obtain

$$SHCOST(Y')/TCOST(Y') = (C - P_k \cdot K + Z_k \cdot K)/C$$

$$= \left(1 + \frac{K(Z_k - P_k)}{C}\right) \Big/ 1 \qquad (7.18)$$

$$= \frac{1 - \varepsilon_{ck}}{1} = 1 - \varepsilon_{ck}$$

where

$$\frac{K}{C}(Z_k - P_k) \equiv \frac{-K}{C}\frac{\partial C}{\partial K} \equiv -\varepsilon_{ck}$$

The expression derived in equation (7.18) facilitates interpretation of the interrelationships between the scale- and cost-CU concepts alluded to above. Note that the short-run cost elasticity with respect to output divided by the long-run cost elasticity with respect to output is equal to:

$$SRTS/LRTS = \frac{\partial C}{\partial Y}\frac{Y}{C} \Big/ \left(\frac{\partial C}{\partial Y}\frac{Y}{C} + \frac{\partial C}{\partial K}\frac{dK}{dY}\frac{Y}{C}\right)$$

$$= \frac{\varepsilon_{cy}}{\varepsilon_{cy} + \varepsilon_{ck}} \quad \text{or} \quad \frac{1 - \varepsilon_{ck}}{1} = 1 - \varepsilon_{ck} \qquad (7.19)$$

since $dK/dY = Y/K$ with CRTS. In addition

$$MC/AC = \frac{\partial C}{\partial Y} \Big/ \frac{C}{Y} = \frac{\partial C}{\partial Y}\frac{Y}{C} = \varepsilon_{cy} = 1 - \varepsilon_{ck} \qquad (7.20)$$

The disequilibrium costs implied by this measure are therefore represented by the magnitude of the deviation from unity, not by the amount the indicator exceeds unity, since it is expressed in proportions. The index will exceed unity when output exceeds capacity output and will fall short of unity when the converse holds. This does not imply that costs are lower as output falls, however, but that total costs are decreasing, and decreasing less than proportionately, corresponding to an increase in average costs. This measure therefore reflects the cost of an undervalued as well as an overvalued capital stock captured by nonproportional changes in total cost given output changes in the short run; the cost results from the deviation of MC from AC.

The above analysis indicates the close relationship or duality between output and cost-CU measures. When output exceeds capacity output, the existing K is overutilized, and thus is valued highly on the margin; Z_k exceeds P_k and $1 - \varepsilon_{ck}$ is greater than one. This can be interpreted as a short-run scale effect; costs in the short run increase more than proportionately with output, although they increase proportionately in the long run. The reverse holds when capacity is underutilized; costs change less than proportionately with output.

This interpretation can be pursued one step further to consider the relationship between the cost-CU measure and Tobin's q. Tobin's q characterizes the ratio of the securities market value of firms relative to the replacement value of physical plant and equipment. This has been reinterpreted by Abel (1979) and Yoshikawa (1980), among others, as an implicit market valuation measure represented by Z_k/P_k. With only one quasi-fixed input, the shadow valuation cost-CU measure is isomorphic with q, since it also represents simply the difference between Z_k and P_k. With more than one quasi-fixed input, however, the cost-CU measure provides an overall q indicator; weighting of the individual quasi-fixed inputs occurs naturally. Thus, the shadow valuation measure is a useful characterization of the overall potential of the firm, for it includes all implied costs and explicitly characterizes whether overall the firm is at a point of undervaluation (underutilization) or overvaluation (overutilization) of its stocks.

7.2.4. Cost CU Measures with NCRTS

Consider the firm represented by figure 7-2. One fundamental difference from figure 7-1 is that point B is no longer necessarily at a higher cost level than point A since the optimal production level is not represented by the minimum point of the SRAC curve. This is inherent in the NCRTS specification but has the seemingly perverse implication that the firm may incur lower average costs in temporary equilibrium than with equilibrium at capacity output. Thus, the cost-CU measure must distinguish a decrease in costs because of NCRTS in the short run from the implicit excess of costs over that consistent with steady-state output.

An additional and closely related difference with NCRTS is that points E and A no longer coincide in terms of cost level. However, representation of the utilization of given capacity depends on a comparison of the costs at

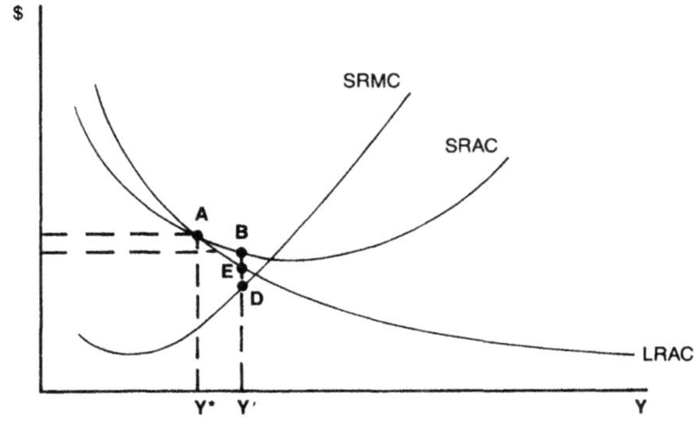

Figure 7-2

Y' and Y^* given K, rather than at K and K^* given Y'. The cost level associated with point E in effect specifies the disequilibrium in terms of the cost savings from adjustment of K to K^* given output demand. Therefore, point E is not a relevant comparison point; capacity utilization measures are not designed to capture movement to long-run equilibrium because that reflects increasing capacity, not changes in the use of existing capacity.

Thus, to define the dual cost measure of CU, the shadow cost valuation measure is still valid since it captures short-run excessive or inadequate utilization of the existing stock of capital.

The difference between the cost-CU measure and long-run potential cost savings can be depicted in terms of the difference between short- and long-run returns to scale. With CRTS the difference between AC and MC is strictly short run; it is dependent on the shadow value of K, which determines short-run returns to scale. With NCRTS there is a difference between AC and MC even in the long run which depends on long-run returns to scale. The cost deviation must therefore be partitioned into the short-run difference determined by the shadow value and the effect of long-run returns to scale.

More specifically, as in the previous subsection, the total proportionate cost change with a change in output from Y^* to Y' can be represented by

$$\frac{d \ln C}{d \ln Y} = \frac{\partial C}{\partial Y}\frac{Y}{C} + \frac{\partial C}{\partial K}\frac{dK}{dY}\frac{Y}{C} \tag{7.21}$$

In the NCRTS case, with homotheticity so that the scale impact of all inputs is the same, $dK/dY(Y/K) = 1/LRTS = \eta \neq 1$. Thus, $dK/dY = (K/Y)\eta$, and equation (7.21) collapses to

$$d \ln C/d \ln Y = \eta = \varepsilon_{cy} + \varepsilon_{ck}\eta \quad \text{or} \quad \varepsilon_{cy} = \eta(1 - \varepsilon_{ck}) \qquad (7.22)$$

Thus returns to scale observed in the short run are decomposed into two parts, a pure disequilibrium component $(1 - \varepsilon_{ck})$ and a long-run returns-to-scale component η, since $LRTS = 1/\eta$.

The information that the cost-CU measure should depict, however, is strictly the cost impact of misutilizing existing fixed capacity, not LRTS. This is represented by the observed cost change relative to the effects of NCRTS, $\eta(1 - \varepsilon_{ck})/\eta = 1 - \varepsilon_{ck}$. Such a cost-CU measure can be justified by showing its equivalence to the various representations of the measures discussed above:

$$SRTS/LRTS = \varepsilon_{cy} \bigg/ \left(\varepsilon_{cy} + \frac{\partial C}{\partial K} \frac{dK}{dY} \frac{Y}{C} \right)$$

$$= \frac{\varepsilon_{cy}}{\varepsilon_{cy} + \eta\varepsilon_{ck}} \quad \text{or} \quad \frac{\eta(1 - \varepsilon_{ck})}{\eta} = 1 - \varepsilon_{ck} \qquad (7.23)$$

$$SHCOST/TCOST = \frac{C - P_k K + Z_k K}{C} = 1 - \varepsilon_{ck} \qquad (7.24)$$

as before, and

$$MC/AC = \varepsilon_{cy} = \eta(1 - \varepsilon_{ck}) \qquad (7.25)$$

Purging the pure LRTS effects to calculate the short-run difference between MC and AC—dividing by η—results in a measure equivalent to the shadow value measure.

Note that for comparison it may be useful also to calculate the measure $\eta(1 - \varepsilon_{ck})$ or $\eta SHCOST/TCOST$. Multiplying $(1 - \varepsilon_{ck})$ by η is equivalent to adding *A–E* to the other measures—it incorporates the pure scale effect, η, by incorporating the movement along the LRAC curve to *E* from *A*. Thus, this adjustment provides additional information; it reflects the cost savings at a given Y (Y') from increasing K to a steady-state level.

An important implication of the effects of NCRTS can be derived from this specification. As in the CRTS case, at any output level greater than Y^*,

K is overutilized and Z_k is greater than P_k because it would pay the firm to increase its capital stock at that output level. However, assume increasing returns exist at Y^*. In the region between Y^* and the minimum point of the SRAC curve, the impact of potential LRTS, represented by η, counteracts the effects of overutilized K and there are potential cost savings. Past that point η and $(1 - \varepsilon_{ck})$ reinforce each other and costs increase more than proportionately. Thus, the full effect $\eta(1 - \varepsilon_{ck})$ will result in a cost-CU measure of less than unity to the minimum SRAC point, although $(1 - \varepsilon_{ck})$ will reflect only the overutilization of K and the implicit costs and therefore will exceed unity at any output level greater than Y^*.[5]

Finally, it is important to pursue adaptations to this framework necessary to incorporate a nonhomothetic production function. Varying returns to different inputs, although intuitively plausible, causes problems since the scale factor can, in this case, be different for the fixed factor from other inputs, and therefore does not cancel. The capital constraint thus has an effect not only in terms of its disequilibrium effect on demand for other inputs but also because of its possible differential scale effect.

To see this, note that under nonhomotheticity

$$\eta = \frac{\partial C}{\partial Y}\frac{Y}{C} + \frac{\partial C}{\partial K}\frac{dK}{dY}\frac{Y}{C} = \varepsilon_{cy} + \eta_k \varepsilon_{ck} \tag{7.26}$$

where $d \ln K/d \ln Y = \eta_k$, since returns to capital now differ from the overall scale effect. Therefore,

$$\varepsilon_{cy} = \eta - \eta_k \varepsilon_{ck} = \eta[1 - (\eta_k/\eta)]\varepsilon_{ck} \tag{7.27}$$

or

$$CU = \eta[1 - (\eta_k/\eta)\varepsilon_{ck}]/\eta = 1 - (\eta_k/\eta)\varepsilon_{ck}$$

So, if the elasticity of demand for K with respect to output, $d \ln K/d \ln Y$ is larger than other demand elasticities with respect to output, the value of having more capital is even larger than if the scale effect on all inputs were the same. It is straightforward to calculate the RTS and MC/AC measures to show that they yield this measure in the nonhomothetic case. However, the shadow cost measure does not take this impact into account; it simply reflects the pure disequilibrium effect.

Since the full effect of the difference between the optimal and actual output given a fixed K stock should be reflected by a cost-CU measure, the shadow cost measure should be "augmented" to be consistent with the marginal cost ratio. MC now represents costs evaluated at the augmented shadow value Z_k', compared to AC as costs evaluated at P_k. Since

$$1 - (\eta_k/\eta)\varepsilon_{ck} = C + (\eta_k/\eta)K \cdot (Z_k - P_k)/C \tag{7.28}$$

this implies that

$$\text{shadow cost} = G + [1 - (\eta_k/\eta)]P_kK + (\eta_k/\eta)Z_kK \tag{7.29}$$

or

$$Z_k' = [1 - (\eta_k/\eta)]P_k + (\eta_k/\eta)Z_k \tag{7.30}$$

This reflects the fact that part of the deviation between MC and AC in the nonhomothetic case is purely the effect of differential returns. When purged of this effect, the ratio is smaller if η_k is less than η and larger if η_k is greater than η. If η_k/η exceeds unity, Z_k is weighted more highly than without scale effects, which emphasizes the effects of disequilibrium—the cost of nonoptimal CU is greater as reflected by a cost-CU measure further from one.

The effects of NCRTS on cost-CU measurement may be complex to analyze. They are, however, particularly important to capture for characterization of an imperfectly competitive firm which, by definition, faces a downward sloping demand curve and thus typically produces at a point at the left-hand side of the minimum point of the LRAC curve. However, for a firm with market power in the output market, it must be recognized that Y' is endogenous, and thus is not the output level to which K must adjust to reach a steady state. This does not cause a problem directly with representation of CU, since CU is a short-run concept and Y' remains the valid short-run output level for purposes of comparison. However, the interpretation of point E in figure 7-2 is different. Movement to E still reflects adjustment of capital along the LRAC curve to a stationary point given Y'. However, in the long run for the monopolist, there will be further output increases to a point such as Y'' which results in lower costs, where Y'' is defined as the output level where $LRMR = LRMC$.

An implication of this analysis is that disequilibrium and foregone output for an imperfectly competitive firm result from lack of capacity given demand, rather than underutilization of existing capacity, which is what the CU framework reflects. Although this does not affect the characterization of short-run behavior and thus CU indicators, it does have important implications for interpretation of disequilibrium behavior of the monopolist. The concept of foregone output is commonly discussed along with capacity utilization, but is actually a very different notion. Within the monopolistic framework, costs of foregone output from disequilibrium can be represented by the costs of producing at Y', the short-run profit-maximizing point, instead of Y''. This concept differs substantially from the idea of comparing costs at Y as compared to Y^*, the latter representing the optimal utilization of existing K.[6]

7.2.5. Application of Cost CU Measures to Productivity Measurement

The cost-CU measures outlined in the previous two subsections have many potential applications for representing the deviation between short- and long-run behavior of the firm. One important application is to productivity measurement. For example, Morrison (1983) has shown that partitioning of observed productivity changes into potential or long-run productivity growth and the effects of short-run disequilibrium can be obtained simply by dividing the observed productivity change by the cost-CU measure.

More specifically, say that productivity growth over time measured as a dual cost indicator can be represented by $\partial \ln C/\partial t = \varepsilon_{ct}$. With all inputs variable and CRTS, this can be written as

$$\partial \ln C/\partial t = \varepsilon_{ct} = \frac{\dot{Y}}{Y} - \sum_j \frac{P_j v_j}{C} \frac{\dot{v}_j}{v_j} \tag{7.31}$$

where P_j is the price of the variable factor v_j. However, with one quasi-fixed factor, K, this becomes

$$\varepsilon_{ct} = (1 - \varepsilon_{ck}) \frac{\dot{Y}}{Y} - \frac{Z_k K}{C} \frac{\dot{K}}{K} - \sum_j \frac{P_j v_j}{C} \frac{\dot{v}_j}{v_j} \tag{7.32}$$

This is the observed measure of productivity given short-run disequilibrium. If, instead, one wishes to determine potential productivity, or true productivity with the effects of disequilibrium purged, it is necessary to calculate

$$\varepsilon'_{ct} = \frac{\varepsilon_{ct}}{1 - \varepsilon_{ck}} = \frac{\dot{Y}}{Y} - \frac{Z_k K}{C^*} \frac{\dot{K}}{K} - \sum_j \frac{P_j v_j}{C^*} \frac{\dot{v}_j}{v_j} \tag{7.33}$$

where C^* represents shadow costs. Thus, to determine true productivity growth, it is sufficient to divide the observed productivity change by $(1 - \varepsilon_{ck})$. This can also be extended along the lines of the previous subsection to incorporate NCRTS by dividing by $\eta(1 - \varepsilon_{ck})$. This is a very attractive and important result.

The above discussion has provided indications of the uses of the cost-CU measure. Since the cost-CU indicator is specified within an economic model, many theoretical applications are possible. The empirical potential of the measure is also very substantial, since all of the measures derived here are easily implementable empirically. The next section explores some of this potential.

7.3. Empirical Results

7.3.1. CU Measures

This section applies the analysis of cost-CU indexes to calculation of (1) primal and dual cost-CU measures, and (2) the impact of the implied disequilibrium on observed growth in total factor productivity, for the U.S. automobile industry, 1959–1980. The CU indexes are based on estimation of a dynamic model incorporating imperfectly competitive behavior outlined in Morrison (1983). The variant of the model used is based on increasing marginal internal costs of adjustment on net accumulation of capital. Capital is the only quasi-fixed factor, and the variable inputs include labor (L), energy (E), and nonenergy intermediate materials (M).[7]

The econometric estimating procedure is based on the normalized variable cost equation presented in (7.12). Similarly to Morrison and Berndt (1981), a system of variable input demand equations and quasi-fixed input accumulation equations can be specified for estimation. The variable input equations are derived from Shephard's lemma—$v_i = \partial G/\partial P_i$. The capital accumulation equation is a flexible accelerator equation $\dot{K} = \lambda(K^* - \bar{K})$ where K^* is determined by solving for K^* from the steady-state expression $Z_k = P_k$ and λ is an endogenous adjustment coefficient calculated as in Morrison and Berndt. For the purposes of this paper, which is based on an industry where imperfectly competitive elements are likely to be important, a price-determination equation was also included, following Appelbaum (1979). This simply requires incorporating the (short-run) $MC = MR$ behavioral assumption $\partial G/\partial Y = f(Y) + f'(Y) \cdot Y$, where $P = f(Y)$ is the inverse demand equation for the firm's output price P, and solving for P to obtain $P = \partial G/\partial Y - f'(Y) \cdot Y$. The resulting system of the variable input demand, capital accumulation, and output price equations was then estimated by maximum likelihood to obtain parameter estimates of the coefficients of G. These coefficient estimates were then used to calculate the indicators developed in section 7.2. This empirical treatment is illustrative; clearly the concepts developed in the previous section can be applied to numerous models and sectors to provide useful information.

At the outset, it is useful to emphasize that economic CU measures will span both sides of unity. For the quantity indicator, CU values above unity indicate a shortage of capacity relative to demand, while values below unity indicate excess capacity relative to demand. The magnitude of the deviation from unity, rather than the shortfall from unity, indicates the extent of misutilization of capacity. For the cost measures, a value above unity indicates a more than proportional increase in costs from Y^* to Y', or a high valuation of the capital stock on the margin (in terms of potential decreased costs with an increase in the capital stock). By contrast, a value of the cost-CU measure that is less than one implies a less than proportional decrease in total costs of production, or a low valuation of the capital stock on the margin relative to its market price; its cost is larger than its worth in terms of production.

The first index to consider is the quantity-CU indicator. Indexes are presented in table 7-1 for both the full-adjustment dynamic model including $rG_{\dot{k}}$ and the static optimization model without $rG_{\dot{k}}$. Analogous traditional CU measures, the Federal Reserve Board (FRB), and Wharton measures for both the manufacturing and automobile industries (where available), are reported in Table 7-2 for purposes of comparison.[8]

One way to consider the usefulness of the representation of CU based on economic theory is to determine how closely these quantity-CU measures relate to existing CU measures. Although the economic indexes exhibit a low correlation with the manufacturing CU indexes—a simple correlation coefficient of between 0.455 and 0.459 for the FRB measure and 0.243–0.319 for Wharton—the correlation is quite close for the auto-specific indexes—0.861–0.872 for the FRB and 0.722–0.771 for Wharton. More useful information may be obtained by considering the year-to-year patterns in the indexes. The quantity-CU measures appear to represent the phenomena captured by conventional measures effectively; for example, they reflect the recessionary drops in 1961, 1967, 1970, 1975, and 1980, and the peaks in 1960, 1965, and 1973, although the 1978 peak is picked up in 1979.

Even though cycles in the indicators are characterized quite well with this model, the levels are different, particularly in the first half of the sam-

Table 7-1. Economic CU Indexes—Quantity and Cost Imperfect Competition Model of the U.S. Automobile Industry

	Quantity CU Indexes		*Shadow Valuation Measures*	
Year	*Without $rG_{\dot{k}}$ ("static")*	*Including $rG_{\dot{k}}$ (full dynamic)*	*CRTS*	*(with scale) NCRTS*
1959	1.051	1.060	1.017	1.005
1960	1.102	1.098	1.029	1.010
1961	0.883	0.910	0.968	0.990
1962	1.062	1.081	1.028	1.010
1963	1.096	1.120	1.043	1.018
1964	1.175	1.180	1.063	1.027
1965	1.313	1.272	1.098	1.051
1966	1.035	1.035	1.017	1.009
1967	0.786	0.828	0.895	0.952
1968	1.044	1.039	1.019	1.011
1969	0.948	0.950	0.971	0.984
1970	0.704	0.726	0.806	0.907
1971	0.832	0.846	0.888	0.933
1972	0.842	0.850	0.885	0.927
1973	0.932	0.921	0.940	0.955
1974	0.838	0.817	0.865	0.910
1975	0.794	0.778	0.828	0.892
1976	0.936	0.898	0.923	0.938
1977	1.033	0.969	0.977	0.977
1978	0.965	0.916	0.930	0.926
1979	0.809	0.785	0.804	0.814
1980	0.545	0.548	0.526	0.643
Simple correlations:				
FRB	0.459	0.455	0.418	0.350
Wharton	0.243	0.319	0.278	0.309
FRB-Auto	0.861	0.872	0.817	0.700
Wharton-Auto	0.771	0.722	0.791	0.644

ple in which the economic measures generally exceed unity, indicating a tendency toward a shortage of capacity except in recent "slow" years. They do not, however, always exceed unity as found in earlier modeling efforts; incorporating the imperfect competition structure appears to counteract the impression of "chronic" shortage of capacity found in, for example, Berndt and Morrison (1981).

Table 7-2. Traditional CU Measures
Manufacturing Industry and Automobile Industry

Year	*Federal Reserve (Manuf.)*	*Wharton (Manuf.)*	*Federal Reserve (Auto)*	*Wharton (Auto)*
1959	0.819	0.789		0.886
1960	0.802	0.768		1.0
1961	0.774	0.737		0.780
1962	0.816	0.765		0.901
1963	0.835	0.776		0.916
1964	0.856	0.795		0.874
1965	0.896	0.842		1.0
1966	0.911	0.882		0.948
1967	0.869	0.869	0.789	0.805
1968	0.871	0.891	0.918	0.921
1969	0.862	0.900	0.863	0.897
1970	0.793	0.838	0.655	0.697
1971	0.784	0.823	0.815	0.868
1972	0.835	0.875	0.907	0.893
1973	0.876	0.926	0.950	1.0
1974	0.838	0.898	0.792	0.814
1975	0.729	0.789	0.668	0.710
1976	0.795	0.849	0.829	0.882
1977	0.819	0.874	0.892	0.988
1978	0.844	0.901	0.894	1.0
1979	0.857	0.917	0.816	0.891
1980	0.791	0.858	0.602	0.625

Additional information is evident from the dual cost-CU measures presented in table 7-1, where a distinction is made between the basic cost-CU measure and the "augmented" measure adjusted for NCRTS.

The cost-CU indicators exhibit a good approximation to the traditional CU measures, although not as closely as the quantity indicators. By column from left to right, the simple correlations of the cost-CU indexes with the FRB manufacturing index are 0.418 and 0.350, and for the auto-specific industry indexes are 0.817 and 0.700. The analogous correlations with Wharton are 0.278, 0.309, 0.791, and 0.644, slightly smaller than for the FRB measure. The general patterns reflected by these measures also appear consistent with a priori knowledge; as with the quantity-based measures, the recessionary downturns captured in the traditional measures are clearly evident.

Although cost measures follow the same trends as the quantity indexes, they tend to be closer to unity, indicating that small deviations from capacity output as reflected in the quantity-CU indicators do not impose substantial costs on auto firms. The scale-adjusted measure is even closer to unity than the simple measure, implying that the SRAC curves tend to be quite flat and that firms take advantage of differential scale effects. Note, however, that for an equivalent shortfall in demand, the cost appears to become slightly higher over time. This can be seen, for example, by considering the years 1961, 1973, and 1978, all of which have similar quantity-CU indicators but which exhibit adjusted cost ratios of 0.990, 0.995, and 0.926, respectively.

These numbers also suggest that the cost impact on auto firms of overutilization of capacity differs from that of underutilizing capacity. The 27% overutilization of capacity in 1965 appears to have only increased costs 5% more than proportionately; whereas the drop in costs in 1970, corresponding to a decrease in capacity utilization of a similar magnitude, dropped 9% more than proportionately. Although this effect is not obvious, this asymmetry is pervasive; it appears to be more costly to err in terms of extra capacity than in terms of insufficient capacity. This implies that in recent years, the auto industry has not adjusted well to changing economic circumstances, since the industry has had substantial extra capacity. For example, the excessive capacity available in 1980 was extremely costly to the auto industry and may have been a result of errors in expectations as well as constraints on adjustment.

Although the economic CU indicators tend to follow the patterns represented by the traditional indexes, and thus capture much of the same information, they are more useful in terms of interpretation; one can trace what causes the fluctuations. For example, the substantial decrease in cost-CU found in 1980 can be attributed to specific impacts; sharply increasing prices of labor along with a decrease in output demand appear to have greatly diminished the value of capacity (capital) on the margin.

More specifically, because of the underlying theoretical framework, the 34.6% drop in CU between 1979 and 1980—from 0.804 to 0.526—can explicitly be partitioned into its components. The impact of the increase in the price of labor to the auto industry alone would have caused CU to drop between 1979 and 1980 by 4.3%, or 12.4% of the total drop. The most dramatic impact on CU was from the decrease in output demand that would have caused a decrease in CU of 20.4%, or 59% of the total drop, holding all else constant. Thus, over 60% of the total decrease in CU can be attributed to these two impacts. By contrast, the increase in the price of energy would have increased the CU ratio by 0.8%, indicating that K and E are substitutable inputs in the auto industry because the implied decrease in energy use would have augmented the value of the capital stock on the margin. This type of information on the components of capacity utilization changes cannot be determined from traditional indexes, and highlights the usefulness of CU indexes based on economic theory.[9]

In summary, these economic-theoretic quantity- and cost-CU indicators can be used to represent CU consistently with the traditional indexes but also are amenable to interpretation, evaluation, and reconciliation of alternative indicators of disequilibrium—i.e., quantity- and cost-based indexes such as CU and Tobin's q. It is evident that this approach is rich in terms of economic application.

7.3.2. Application to Productivity Measurement

One important application of these indexes is to productivity measurement. The auto industry has experienced very large total factor productivity increases over the entire time period represented by the sample, as indicated by the average annual growth rate figures reported in table 7-3. The first column reports the unadjusted average yearly productivity growth estimates for a breakdown common in the literature on productivity growth, 1960–1965, 1965–1973, and 1973–present. Prior to discussing these estimates, two points are worth noting.

First, the averages appear very different depending on the end date used, 1979 or 1980. This occurs because 1980 exhibited a precipitous productivity drop of 15%. Since this is so far out of the range of the other

Table 7-3. Productivity Growth Rates
Average Annual Observed Rates, ε_{ct}, and Adjusted for SRTS and LRTS

Year	ε_{ct}	$\varepsilon_{ct}/(1-\varepsilon_{ck})$	$\varepsilon_{ct}/[\eta(1-\varepsilon_{ck})]$
1960–79	−0.0230	−0.0224	−0.0242
1960–65	−0.0299	−0.0283	−0.0274
1965–73	−0.0243	−0.0235	−0.0263
1973–79	−0.0238	−0.0244	−0.0286
1960–80	−0.0146	−0.0072	−0.0081
1973–80	−0.0015	0.0157	0.0144

yearly measures, it distorts the pattern of growth-rate average for purposes of assessment and comparison. I have therefore presented averages to both 1979 and 1980.

The second point is that the numbers exhibit very large and steady productivity increases when compared to the manufacturing sector as a whole. It is generally asserted that productivity growth in the manufacturing industry has proceeded at an average of approximately 0.7% per annum during this time period, with large growth rates during the first part of the sample, possible declines during the 1965–1973 period (depending on measurement procedures), and further, more dramatic, decreases after 1973. This pattern is not nearly as dramatic for the automobile industry. The overall observed productivity growth rate is about 2.3% per year, dropping slightly over time from a high of about 3% during 1960–1965 to about 2.4% thereafter (the overlapping years cause the overall average to differ from the average of the subperiods). The exception to this is the 1973–1980 subperiod for which the productivity drop in 1980 decreases the average to only 0.15% per year. The large and sustained total factor productivity growth rate to 1979 appears to stem from substantial growth in labor productivity of almost 4% per year; during this time period, the aggregate labor input remained approximately constant (production labor hours decreased somewhat and nonproduction hours increased proportionally) while real output doubled.

I now consider the effect of adjustment to these measures to account for the distorting effects of short-run disequilibrium and long-run scale economies on observed year-to-year productivity changes. These adjustments are represented, respectively, by dividing the yearly productivity growth rate, ε_{ct}, by CU $(1 - \varepsilon_{ck})$ and CU adjusted for the affect of long-run returns to scale $[\eta(1 - \varepsilon_{ck})]$, respectively. The impacts of these adjustments are summarized in the second and third columns of table 7-3.

Consider first the averages to 1979. Note that although the impact of these adjustments is not large—the growth rate in productivity remains very constant over time and the overall average increases only slightly—the pattern over the subperiods changes. It appears after the short-run utilization adjustment that larger productivity increases were observed due to short-run disequilibrium before 1973 than should be credited to pure total factor productivity effects, whereas smaller increases were observed post-1973 than actually occurred. In addition, when potential scale economies are also purged from the observed cost-diminution effect to isolate true productivity growth, the first period—in which the scale of operations of auto firms was increasing at the highest rate and therefore had the most potential for scale economies—appears even worse, and the last period exhibits large enough increases to become the period of largest pure productivity growth.

Including 1980 twists the picture dramatically. The large drop in observed productivity growth in 1980 appears to be only an indication of larger decreases in the long run; as a result of extremely small capacity utilization in 1980, the average productivity change for 1973–1980 adjusted for disequilibrium becomes negative, −1.5%. This can be interpreted in light of the large impact of labor productivity on total factor productivity. In 1980, the drop in output was met by a corresponding large decrease in labor use—the only smaller levels of use were seen in 1975 (almost identical) and 1961. Thus, labor productivity declined but not by as much as it might have if this output–labor combination had been inflated to be consistent with the given level of capacity. Note also that the scale impact for 1980 appears positive; auto firms decreased their scale of operations and therefore were not able to take advantage of potential scale economies, so adjustment for NCRTS attenuates slightly the negative CU adjustment.

Even from this brief illustration of interpretation and use of cost-CU indicators, it is evident that the economic theoretical framework underlying the indexes provides a rich basis for use of these indicators for both theoretical and empirical economic application.

7.4. Concluding Remarks

The major purpose of this chapter has been to demonstrate the importance of economic foundations for economic indicators, both in terms of interpretation and for rationalizing their various uses. I have attempted to accomplish this by linking economic primal and dual capacity utilization measures to each other and to other economic notions such as the shadow value of capital, all within an integrated framework of economic optimization.

The development of cost-CU measures is particularly important; it reconciles various representations of costs and highlights linkages among common indicators such as CU and Tobin's q. For example, the difference between the shadow value and the market value of K, which provides the basis for the deviation of primal or dual cost-CU measures from unity, also is the basis for Tobin's q. Thus, these measures incorporate the same information in different forms. Moreover, the cost-CU measure can be interpreted as a generalized Tobin's q which allows for multiple quasi-fixed inputs.

Since the economic CU measures are based on economic theory, their empirical content is extensive. It can be determined, for example, why a decrease in conventionally measured CU may be a correct response to an increasing price of energy, whether this deviation from capacity output imposes substantial costs on the firm or on industry, and how these costs change depending on input configuration. Conversely, the framework can be used for predicting the impact of, say, an increase in the price of energy; this provides potential for policy analysis and planning. At the same time, the limits to the information provided by CU measures are clear. Without supplementary information, these indicators do not indicate the costs imposed on the economy as a whole; they are positive rather than normative measures.

Knowledge of the behavioral model underlying specification of these measures can also be used to rationalize applications of CU measures. We illustrated the application of CU measures to productivity measurement in order to purge cyclical responses from productivity measures. In addition, the CU measures could also be used, for example, (a) in investment equations, as a determinants of investment behavior, and (b) as causal factors of inflationary forces. Specifically, for (a), the calculation of capacity output as an explicit function of the deviation of the rental and shadow value of capital results in a functional form internally consistent with investment incentives, as it reflects the information contained in Tobin's q. For (b), the impact of deviations in output on inflation have often been specified in terms of a short-run Phillips curve. Although the linkage here is not as clear, explicit adjustment for disequilibrium is important, and disequilibrium inflationary forces may therefore be represented by CU, or, more directly, as the impact of the cost of being away from long-run equilibrium, represented by the dual cost-CU measure.

Note, finally, that many additional applications can be pursued simply by using the techniques discussed here with other data and models. The empirical analysis in this study has been based on the auto industry; in other studies quantity-CU measures have been calculated for the manufacturing sector as a whole. Analysis of alternative bodies of data may be even more informative—analysis of the capital-intensive electric utility industry, for example.

I conclude, therefore, that the interpretation of cyclical economic phenomena is facilitated by the formal derivation of economic indicators such as primal and dual measures of CU within a dynamic optimization framework. Moreover, the various implications and conceptual extensions generated by such an exercise provide a useful basis for further theoretical and empirical work on analyzing economic fluctuations.

Notes

1. Although I retain the assumption of one quasi-fixed input, capital, note that this analysis can easily be extended to multiple quasi-fixed inputs.

2. Note that here $\partial G/\partial K$ with $I = \dot{K} + dK$ (gross investment) substituted is equivalent to $\partial G/\partial K + \partial G/\partial I(\partial I/\partial K)$ in the specification in terms of K and I instead of K and $\dot{K}$. Hence (2.10) is equivalent to

$$\frac{dG(Y,t,P_i,K,\dot{K})}{dY} = \left(\frac{\partial G}{\partial K}\right)\left(\frac{dK}{dY}\right) + \left(\frac{\partial G}{\partial I}\right)\left(\frac{dI}{dY}\right)$$

3. This allowance for the inherent dynamic nature of the problem has not properly been taken into account in previous work (e.g., see Berndt, Morrison, and Watkins (1981) for CU measures and Berndt (1980) for q measures in the CRTS cost function case). Typically, even though the framework is dynamic, the measures have been interpreted as short-run static concepts. Note also that the measures here are based on internal costs of adjustment. External costs of adjustment have also been specified in Morrison (1982) and appeared relatively unimportant empirically. If these costs were included, the shadow value of K would also become more complex.

An additional adjustment is necessary if the analysis is to be based on the monopoly framework developed in Morrison (1982), for which adjustment costs on gross investment are characterized. In this case, the conventional equilibrium expression $-(G_k + rG_{\dot{k}}) = P_k$ is still valid. To show this, note that the calculus of the variations problem for determining the optimal path of the capital stock is expressed in terms of K and $\dot{K}$ instead of K and I, where I is gross investment. Thus, if G is written by substituting $I = \dot{K} + dK$ and it is recognized that the replacement component of gross investment, dK, will still be nonzero in long-run equilibrium, it is easy to derive the above equilibrium expression as equivalent to

$$-(G_k + (r + d)G_i) = P_k$$

the investment path equilibrium equality in terms of I instead of $\dot{K}$. This corresponds more closely to intuition as it resembles the equilibrium expressions from traditional neoclassical theory. Along the optimal investment path, the rental price of capital can therefore be interpreted as the marginal capital stock evaluation including the required replacement investment ($-G_k$) plus the marginal adjustment costs of new investment, that is, $-rG_{\dot{k}}$ or $-(r + d)G_i$—reflecting the impact of depreciation and adjustment costs, the marginal adjustment cost of installing the annual replacement investment required to maintain the desired capital stock.

4. Note that the original cost point corresponding to Y' on the SRAC curve must therefore be defined inclusive of costs of currently existing K and $\dot{K}$, as K defines the current disequilibrium situation.

5. This analysis also suggests that RTS determines how large $|\varepsilon_{ck}|$ must be to counteract the effects of RTS and show up as increasing costs—how large this disequilibrium effect must be to counteract the scale effects.

6. The theoretical analysis to this point has been based on the idea of a one-shot increase in demand. Other examples of exogenous shocks can, of course, by analyzed analogously, but this example serves to point out the interpretation difficulties with NCRTS and monopolistic behavior, and the important distinction between the ideas of nonoptimal utilization of

capacity and foregone output. Useful information may be gathered by pursuing the cost and output effects of eliminating rigidities and thus facilitating adjustment to long-run equilibrium, but this is conceptually different from CU.

7. The data, originally developed and used by Robert Levy and James Jondrow at the Public Research Institute, were kindly provided by J. R. Norsworthy, U.S. Bureau of the Census.

8. The auto industry CU indexes were graciously provided by Joyce Yanchar at Data Resources Incorporated, Lexington, MA.

9. These impacts can be determined, for example, for the price of labor, by substituting the 1980 value of P_L into the model for 1979, holding everything else constant, and calculating what the effect would have been on both the SHCOST and TCOST values.

References

Abel, A. B. 1979. *Investment and the Value of Capital.* New York: Garland Publishing.

Appelbaum, E. 1979. "Testing Price-Taking Behavior." *Journal of Econometrics* 9(February): 283–294.

Berndt, E. R. 1980. "Energy Price Increases and the Productivity Slowdown in U.S. Manufacturing." In *The Decline in Productivity Growth,* Proceedings of the Federal Reserve Bank of Boston Conference on Productivity, June, Conference Series No. 22, Federal Reserve Bank of Boston.

Berndt, E. R., and Melvyn Fuss. 1981. "Productivity Measurement Using Capital Asset Valuation to Adjust for Variations in Utilization." Paper presented at the Econometric Society Summer Meetings, San Diego, California, June 24–27.

Berndt, E. R., and C. Morrison. 1981. "Capacity Utilization: Underlying Economic Theory and an Alternative Approach." *American Economic Review* 71(May): 48–52.

Berndt, E. R., C. Morrison, and G. C. Watkins. 1981. "Dynamic Models of Energy Demand: An Assessment and Comparison." In E. R. Berndt and B. C. Fields (eds.), *Modeling and Measuring National Resource Substitution.* Cambridge, MA.: M.I.T. Press.

Cassels, J. M. 1937. "Excess Capacity and Monopolistic Competition." *Quarterly Journal of Economics* 51(May): 426–443.

Hickman, B. G. 1964. "On a New Method of Capacity Estimation." *Journal of the American Statistical Association* 59(June): 529–549.

Klein, L. R. 1960. "Some Theoretical Issues in the Measurement of Capacity." *Econometrica* 28(April): 272–286.

Lau, L. J. 1978. "Applications of Profit Functions." In D. McFadden and M. Fuss, *Production Economics: A Dual Approach to Theory and Applications.* Amsterdam: North Holland Publishing.

Morrison, C. J. 1982. "Three Essays on the Dynamic Analysis of Demand for Factors of Production." Ph.D. thesis, University of British Columbia, September.

Morrison, C. J. 1983. "Dynamic Factor Demands, Market Power, and the Shape of the Adjustment Cost Function." Unpublished manuscript, January.

Morrison, C. J. 1985. "On the Economic Interpretation and Measurement of Optimal Capacity Utilization with Anticipatory Expectations." *Review of Economic Studies* vol LII(2), no. 169:295–310.

Morrison, C. J. 1986. "A Structural Model of Dynamic Factor Demands with Nonstatic Expectations: An Empirical Assessment of Alternative Expectations Specifications," *International Economic Review,* Vol. 27, No. 2, June, pp. 365–386.

Morrison, C. J., and E. R. Berndt. 1981. "Short-Run Labor Productivity in a Dynamic Model." *Journal of Econometrics* 16(November): 339–365.

Yoshikawa, H. 1980. "On the "q" Theory of Investment." *American Economic Review* 70(4): 739–743.

8 THE EFFECT OF SHIFTS IN THE COMPOSITION OF EMPLOYMENT ON LABOR PRODUCTIVITY GROWTH: CANADA 1971–1979*

Peter Chinloy

8.1. Introduction

Analysis of the contribution of labor input to the growth of output or output per hour has typically been concerned with broadly defined characteristics such as education or age-sex composition. In this chapter, the contribution of separate levels of schooling, individual age groups, and each sex is measured. In the case of changes in the sex composition of employment, upper and lower bounds for the effects on labor productivity are derived, depending on whether all observed wage differentials can be ascribed to marginal productivity or to other factors such as discrimination.

It is possible to calculate the productivity benefits attributable to each educational level, as well as the effect of changes in relative earnings.[1] Regarding age and sex, the effects of relative increases in youth employment and the employment of women can be similarly examined.

In section 8.2, the structure of labor productivity growth accounting is

*University of Santa Clara. I am grateful to Bill Deacon for research assistance and two referees for their constructive comments. The Social Sciences and Humanities Research Council of Canada provided research support.

described, and the effect of labor market factors detailed. The data on the labor market, discussed in section 8.3, are for employment and earnings in Canada by sex, age, and education, biennially for the period 1971–1979. Estimates of the contribution of each sex, six age and five education groups to the growth of labor productivity are in section 8.4. The growth of labor productivity is then decomposed into sources for labor quality, as derived from employment shifts, capital intensity, and total factor productivity.

The empirical results indicate that up to the mid-1970s, education contributes to increasing labor productivity growth at rates similar to long-term estimates of 0.3% annually.[2] By the late 1970s, the education effect almost disappears. The largest changes in effect on labor productivity growth occur among the most highly educated: those with university education, and those with postsecondary certificates. Estimates of contributions to productivity growth by educational level for biennial periods exhibit fluctuations, suggesting that there may be errors in interpolation of measured effects, for example between Census years, or from extrapolation forward.

For age categories, the individual contributions to labor productivity growth are virtually zero, other than a negative effect for teenagers. The sex effect on productivity is small, even when all wage differentials are assumed to reflect differences in marginal product. The slowdown in the growth of labor productivity after 1973 does not appear to be associated with changing age–sex composition.

The growth of labor productivity declines by 1.7 percentage points between the pre- to post-1973 subperiods, and averages almost zero in the latter. Labor market factors have contributed little to this decline.

If 1973 is regarded as a watershed year, both labor and total factor productivity growth decline substantially after this year; but accompanying reductions in labor quality are delayed until 1975. The effects of age–sex composition shifts toward youth and women are small and exhibit little change over the period. Education, by contrast, has contributed less to productivity growth, particularly since 1975.

8.2. Aggregation of Labor Inputs and Productivity Measurement

The first step in the measurement of shifts in employment composition is the construction of an index of labor inputs. Included in the index is employment classified by such factors as age, sex, and education. In previous studies of the effect of labor inputs on labor productivity, the principal assumptions have been:

i. There exists an index of labor input, separable from all other services used in production, inputs, and outputs.
ii. All input factors, once disaggregated by characteristic, are paid the value of their marginal product.

In addition, the following assumptions have been used in empirical application.

iii. Within groups, part-time and full-time workers have the same marginal product per hour, and it is possible to construct hourly wages for all workers.
iv. Relative earnings exhibit little variation over long periods, so if data are missing, interpolation can be applied.
v. Contributions can be measured as aggregates, such as "education."
vi. Observed wages can be used to measure the benefits from educational investments, even though these accrue over the long term rather than the short term.

In this chapter, assumption (i), that there is a labor input index, is retained.[3] In the case of wage differentials by sex, assumption (ii), on payment of marginal product by characteristic, is not retained. Factors such as discrimination can affect absolute and relative wage levels. If all wage differentials by sex are assumed to reflect productivity, and this does not apply, the productivity gap between men and women is overstated.

If earnings are reported as received over an entire year, on an annual basis, these must be assigned to multiplicative components for the wage per hour worked and the number of hours worked per year. For both Canada and the United States, the question on the household surveys is for hours worked per week paid, and weeks paid per year. The product of these two is annual weeks paid and not annual weeks worked. The marginal product of part-time workers is assumed to be the same as for full-time workers, where the two categories are not separately identified. Assumption (iii), that full-time and part-time workers have the same marginal product, is not maintained. Separate series are constructed for full-time and part-time workers, and part-time workers converted to full-time equivalents.

Assumption (iv) on relative earnings is examined directly by the use of a biennial survey, instead of the decennial survey of the Census. The data indicate that relative earnings by educational and age category are not constant, but exhibit fluctuations. Productivity contributions are weighted by relative earnings by each two-year period.

The effects of individual shifts in employment composition, for assumption (v), are measured by level of schooling and by age group. It can be determined, for example, how much high school education has contributed to labor productivity growth. This is required in calculating the benefits of educational investments.

Assumption (vi) is used by Jorgenson and Griliches (1967) and Christensen, Cummings, and Jorgenson (1980) in measuring the effect of labor market factors on productivity growth. This assumption is applied here, but an extension of the model would be to construct capitalized values of educational investments, or to use wages reflecting annuity values of human capital.[4] In the former case, with human capital accounts, a user cost is required for the services; and utilization depends on hours worked and intensity of work per hour.

The variables used in the model are as follows:

T = transformation function between inputs and outputs, for a given technology
Y_i = quantity levels of output services, $i = 1, \ldots, M$
X_i = quantity levels of input services, the first L being labor, $i = 1, \ldots, N$
P_i = prices per unit of output services, $i = 1, \ldots, M$
W_i = prices per unit of input services, $i = 1, \ldots, N$
E = total employment, sum of first L input quantities
e = growth rate of total employment
C = total labor compensation, sum of first L products W_iX_i
s_i = compensation share W_iX_i/C of ith labor input, $i = 1, \ldots, L$
b_i = employment share E_i/E of ith labor input, $i = 1, \ldots, L$
q_i = quality share, $s_i - b_i$ of ith labor input, $i = 1, \ldots, L$
v_i = compensation share $W_iX_i/\Sigma_{i=L+1}^{N} W_iX_i$ of ith nonlabor input, $i = L + 1, \ldots, N$
x_i = growth rate of ith input quantity, $i = 1, \ldots, N$
D = index of labor input, of X_i, $i = 1, \ldots, L$
d = growth rate, of labor input index
D^* = index of labor quality D/E
d^* = growth rate, index of labor quality
A = index of total factor productivity
a = growth rate, index of total factor productivity

Let the production possibility set be represented by the transformation function $T(Y,X,A) = 0$, where $Y = (Y_1, \ldots, Y_M)$, and $X = (X_1, \ldots, X_N)$, at total factor productivity level A. Levels of variables are denoted in upper case, and growth rates in lower case. The labor input index is $D = D(X_1, \ldots, X_L)$.

Total employment is

$$E = \sum_{i=1}^{L} X_i$$

and total labor compensation is

$$C = \sum_{i=1}^{L} W_i X_i$$

In equilibrium, the elasticity of D with respect to X_i is equal to the share in labor compensation s_i, where $s_i = W_i X_i / C$. The growth rate of the labor input index is

$$d = \sum_{i=1}^{L} s_i x_i \tag{8.1}$$

This is a weighted average of growth rates, the weights being shares in total compensation, with $\Sigma_{i=1}^{L} s_i = 1$.

If the labor input index is linearly homogeneous

$$\begin{aligned} D &= ED^*(X_1/E, \ldots, X_L/E) \\ &= ED^*(b_1, \ldots, b_L) \end{aligned} \tag{8.2}$$

where D^* is an efficiency or quality index of labor. The employment share of group i is $b_i = X_i/E$, and is also the elasticity of E with respect to X_i, where $\Sigma_{i=1}^{L} b_i = 1$. The labor quality index D^* acts as a shift factor for total employment E. If D^* is unity, labor input is identical to total employment. The growth rate of total employment is

$$e = \sum_{i=1}^{L} b_i x_i \tag{8.3}$$

This is another weighted average of growth rates by category, but with shares of employment rather than compensation as weights. Labor quality grows at rate

$$\begin{aligned} d^* &= \sum_{i=1}^{L} (s_i - b_i) x_i \\ &= \sum_{i=1}^{L} q_i x_i \end{aligned} \tag{8.4}$$

This is the sum of the products of growth in employment x_i and quality weights $q_i = s_i - b_i$, $i = 1, \ldots, L$, the differences between the shares in labor compensation and those in employment. The quality weights q_i sum to zero, and if $q_i > 0$, a positive contribution to labor input arises from a factor whose employment is increasing. Where $q_i < 0$, a positive contribution may arise where employment is decreasing.

The quality weight is positive when the wage for group i exceeds the average wage for all workers. The product $q_i x_i$ is the contribution to labor quality growth of group i. The sign of $q_i x_i$ can be positive for any type of worker. Although the share in total compensation for those with no schooling is likely to be less than the share of total employment, with q_i negative, programs which cause a negative x_i, by reducing the number of hours worked in this category, imply $q_i x_i$ is positive, increasing the growth of labor quality d^*. If education does not increase the wage, there is no productivity gain, but this will be reflected in the observed data. Education may not increase the wage immediately, but the wage can be increased in the long run. Consequently, it is desirable to construct the present value of the future increases in earnings arising from current investments in education.

Among college graduates, the wage typically exceeds the average, so s_i is greater than b_i and q_i is positive. Provided q_i remains positive, even if decreasing, an increase in employment of such graduates implies $q_i x_i$ is positive. The increase in d^* from highly educated workers continues even if their relative wage decreases, provided there is an above average increase in their employment. Hence any educational group can contribute positively to labor quality growth. If a worker increases educational attainment without a change in wage, there is no effect of the increased education.

Suppose there is an output index $Y(Y_1, \ldots, Y_M)$. The transformation function becomes $T(Y, D, X_{L+1}, \ldots, X_N, A) = 0$, which can be expressed in terms of one of its arguments. Selecting output, $Y = F(D, X_{L+1}, \ldots, X_N, A)$, and the growth of output is

$$y = s_d\left(e + \sum_{i=1}^{L} q_i x_i\right) + \sum_{i=L+1}^{N} v_i x_i + a \qquad (8.5)$$

where s_d is the share of labor in the value of output and v_i, $i = L + 1, \ldots, N$ are the corresponding shares of each nonlabor input. Output growth is the sum of three components. The first is labor input growth weighted by the compensation share of labor. Labor input growth is the sum of growth rates in total employment, equation (8.3) and labor quality, equation (8.4). The second is the growth of nonlabor inputs, weighted by respective compensation shares. The third is the growth of total factor productivity. Subtracting employment growth from that for output

$$y - e = s_d \sum_{i=1}^{L} q_i x_i + \sum_{i=L+1}^{N} v_i(x_i - e) + a \tag{8.6}$$

since

$$1 - s_d = \sum_{i=L+1}^{N} v_i$$

The growth in labor productivity is the sum of three components.[5] These are respectively the growth of labor quality $\Sigma_{i=1}^{L} q_i x_i$ multiplied by the compensation share of labor, the growth of intensity of usage of nonlabor inputs weighted by compensation shares, and the growth of total factor productivity. The components to be measured are those in $s_d \Sigma_{i=1}^{L} q_i x_i$.

The growth accounting form (8.6) is altered if wage differentials reflect factors other than productivity, such as discrimination. This is potentially the case between men and women. Let there be separate indexes of labor input $D_1(X_{11}, \ldots, X_{1R})$ and $D_2(X_{21}, \ldots, X_{2R})$ for men and women respectively, where $R = L/2$ is the number of employment categories other than sex. Output is

$$Y = G[D_1(X_{11}, \ldots, X_{1R}), D_2(X_{21}, \ldots, X_{2R}), X_{L+1}, \ldots, X_N, A]$$

The growth of labor input by sex is $d_i = e_i + d_i^*$, $i = 1,2$, the sum of growth rates for employment e_i and labor quality d_i^*. Further,

$$d_i^* = \sum_{j=1}^{M} q_{ij} x_{ij}$$

are products of quality weights and employment growth rates by sex, analogous to (8.4). In the application, the remaining characteristics of employment are age and education, with respective levels J and H, or $R = JH$. For each sex

$$X_{ij.} = \sum_{h=1}^{H} X_{ijh}, \qquad j = 1, \ldots, J \tag{8.7}$$

and

$$X_{i.h} = \sum_{j=1}^{J} X_{ijh}, \qquad h = 1, \ldots, H \tag{8.8}$$

are the employment levels by age and education. In (8.7), employment by sex and age, respectively i and j, is summed over educational levels. In (8.8), employment by sex and education is summed over age groups.

Corresponding wages are defined by

$$W_{ij.} = \sum_{h=1}^{H} W_{ijh}X_{ijh}/X_{ijh}, \qquad j = 1, \ldots, J \tag{8.9}$$

and

$$W_{i.h} = \sum_{j=1}^{J} W_{ijh}X_{ijh}/X_{ijh}, \qquad h = 1, \ldots, H \tag{8.10}$$

The growth rates of employment by age and education are $x_{ij.}$ and $x_{i.h}$ respectively from (8.7) and (8.8). The quality weights $q_{ij.}$ and $q_{i.h}$ are constructed analogously to those in (8.4), as the difference between compensation and employment shares.

The contribution of a given age group to the growth in labor quality is, for sex i

$$z_{ij.} = q_{ij.}x_{ij.}, \qquad j = i, \ldots, J \tag{8.11}$$

and for each education group

$$n_{i.h} = q_{i.h}x_{i.h}, \qquad h = 1, \ldots, H \tag{8.12}$$

These are the products of quality weights and the growth of employment. The growth of labor quality by sex is

$$d_i^* = \sum_{j=1}^{J} z_{ij.} + \sum_{h=1}^{H} n_{i.h}, \qquad i = 1,2 \tag{8.13}$$

The d_i^* are weighted by sex to produce a growth rate for labor input. Two alternative weighting methods involve shares of each sex in either labor compensation or employment, summed over age and education, respectively $s_{i..}$, $i = 1,2$ and $b_{i..}$, $i = 1,2$. Using compensation shares to aggregate growth rates by sex, all wage differentials reflect productivity. Using employment shares, all workers have the same unit productivity. Labor productivity growth is, using compensation shares,

$$y - e = s_d \sum_{i=1}^{2} s_{i..} \left[\sum_{j=1}^{J} z_{ij.} + \sum_{h=1}^{H} n_{i.h} \right] + \sum_{i=L+1}^{N} v_i(x_i - e) + a \quad (8.14)$$

where $b_{i..}$ replaces $s_{i..}$ if employment shares are applied. Total factor productivity growth is

$$a = (y - e) - s_d \sum_{i=1}^{2} s_{i..} \left[\sum_{j=1}^{J} z_{ij.} + \sum_{h=1}^{H} n_{i.h} \right] - \sum_{i=L+1}^{N} v_i(x_i - e) \quad (8.15)$$

The age and education effects are calculated using equations (8.7) through (8.12), for the components of labor quality growth and two sex weight specifications. Nonlabor inputs are aggregated into a capital index. Labor productivity growth $y - e$ is measured as the growth of real value added per full-time equivalent worker employed. Total factor productivity growth a is obtained from the growth accounting equation (8.15) as a residual.

8.3. Data and Empirical Results

8.3.1. Specification and Employment Data

The data are biennial observations on employment and earnings by sex, age, and education for 1971–1979 for Canada. The levels of the three characteristics of employment are indicated in table 8-1. The growth rate

Table 8-1. Classification of Labor Input

Sex	*Age (years)*	*Education*
1. Male	1. 15–19	1. 0–8 years of schooling
2. Female	2. 20–29	2. some or completed high school
	3. 30–39	3. some post secondary
	4. 40–49	4. post secondary certificate or diploma
	5. 50–64	5. university degree
	6. 65 or older	

of employment over a two-year period is $\Delta \ln x_{i,t} = \ln x_{i,t} - \ln x_{i,t-1}$, for $i = 1, \ldots, L$, at successive dates $t - 1$ and t. For the quality weights, the specification $q^*_{i,t} = (q_{i,t} + q_{i,t-1})/2, i = 1, \ldots, L$ is applied. The quality effects by age and education for each sex are the products of analogously specified quality weights and employment growth rates, using equations (8.11) and (8.12).

The principal source of the employment data is the *Survey of Consumer Finances* which accompanies the monthly Labour Force Survey of Canada each alternate April. Employed persons are employees, own-account workers in the public and private sectors, and unpaid family workers who did any work for pay or profit in the survey week. Employed persons are divided between full-time and part-time status. The former includes those who worked, mostly full time, for 50 to 52 weeks in the reference year. A person who worked less than 50 weeks during the reference year is a part-time worker. Total earnings include wages and salaries and net income from self-employment. Since the latter includes a return to capital in the noncorporate sector, a subtraction of this is required.

Previous estimates of the contribution of characteristics to labor input and productivity growth in Canada have been presented by Walters (1968, 1970) and May and Denny (1979). The latter distinguish labor input by sex and occupation. The former calculates the effects of sex, age, and education on labor input, using data from the Census of Canada. The Canadian data are on quantities only, with the earnings based on corresponding United States series. The Walters results are therefore not strictly comparable to other estimates, and if relative earnings differ between the two countries, there is a source of error.

Walters constructs the following labor quality index by education for Canada

1950	100.0	1955	102.0
1960	103.8	1962	104.3

with the average contribution increasing by 0.35% annually, about half that for the United States over the same period.[6] The estimates derived by Norsworthy, Harper, and Kunze (1979) for the United States 1973–1978 are larger, with education contributing 1.05% annually to the growth of labor input. Other estimates obtained there are for sex, −0.23, age, −0.23, and occupation, 0.25% annually, for the private business sector.

Education is the only factor used by Christensen, Cummings, and Jorgenson (1980) in a study of productivity growth in Canada. Their index of educational attainment is

1947	0.923
1961	1.000
1973	1.059

For 1950–1962, they obtain an annual growth rate of 0.47%, and 0.52% over 1947–1973.[7] Weighted earnings by education are used. The same estimates on the contribution of education in Canada are used by Hulten and Nishimizu (1980). These are below those for the United States over the comparable period. The earnings relatives used are based on Census of Canada data, and do not account for shifts in relative earnings between Census years.

Previous results for Canada suggest lower contributions of education to the growth of labor input than for the United States, but the difference is small. Daly (1980, 239) argues that this is because management training in Canada lags behind the U.S. No empirical evidence is offered in support of this argument, but it can be examined with the structure developed, since the contribution of each educational level is measured.

The results here are based on procedures that differ from those previous in three ways. First, the data are separately disaggregated by sex. If there are wage and earning differentials unrelated to productivity by sex, a distortion arises. Estimates of the rate of return to educational investment are frequently confined to samples of men. This is because the wages of women can reflect discrimination or large portions of time spent out of employment in home production. Second, relative earnings for each year are used, instead of interpolation between two years, or using constant earnings of a base year. Third, the data are for full-time workers employed 50–52 weeks per year, reducing error in estimating effort or utilization.

8.3.2. *Education*

The quality effects $n_{i,h}$ are in table 8-2 for sex i and education $h = 1, \ldots, 5$. The quality effects are larger for those with more education. The total effect of education appears to be zero subsequent to 1975, in contrast with estimates prior to the early 1970s.

The annual contribution to labor input growth for all males exhibits little variation over the period, between 0.01 and 0.12%, but the quality effects for those with higher education indicate substantial decreases after 1975. This is notably the case for those with a university degree. The effect among all males declines from an average of 0.69% annually for 1971–1975 to 0.16% for 1975–1979. The results are similar if the sample is con-

Table 8-2. Quality Effects of Education, $z_{ij.}$, 1971–1979 (annual percent, product of quality weight, and employment growth)

	Category	Men All	Men Full-Time	Women All	Women Full-Time
1971–1973	0–8 years	0.01	−0.4	−0.05	−0.05
	some/completed high school	−0.16	−0.13	−0.46	−0.30
	some postsecondary	−0.04	0.04	−0.05	0.11
	postsecondary certificate	0.22	0.16	0.63	0.41
	university degree	0.26	0.35	0.47	0.37
	Total	0.29	0.38	0.54	0.54
1973–1975	0–8 years	0.12	0.37	−0.15	−0.17
	some/completed high school	0.14	0.20	−0.05	0.00
	some postsecondary	−0.12	0.02	−0.07	0.14
	postsecondary certificate	0.33	0.13	0.66	0.37
	university degree	1.12	0.99	1.37	1.26
	Total	1.59	1.71	1.76	1.60
1975–1977	0–8 years	0.06	−0.03	−0.02	0.03
	some/completed high school	−0.16	−0.19	−0.40	−0.48
	some postsecondary	−0.02	0.00	−0.06	0.01
	postsecondary certificate	−0.02	0.01	−0.03	−0.06
	university degree	0.12	0.20	0.36	0.47
	Total	−0.02	−0.01	−0.15	−0.03
1977–1979	0–8 years	0.04	0.10	0.02	−0.01
	some/completed high school	−0.23	−0.15	−0.36	−0.31
	some postsecondary	0.07	−0.01	0.05	−0.01
	postsecondary certificate	−0.01	0.00	0.13	0.05
	university degree	0.21	0.18	0.38	0.28
	Total	0.08	0.12	0.22	0.00

fined to full-time employed males, where the corresponding estimates are 0.67% and 0.19%. There has been a decline in the relative contribution of the educated, although university graduates remain the schooling group with the largest contribution to labor input growth.

There is also virtually no contribution in total, by age, sex, and education to labor input growth after 1975. For full-time workers, the average annual effect is 0.05% for 1975–1979 for men, and 0.015% for women, in comparison with 1.05% and 1.07% respectively in the pre-1975 period.

The results for women are contained in the third and fourth columns of table 8-2. Comparing full-time employed men and women in each of the four two-year subperiods, the contribution of educated women to growth in labor input is similar to that for men. For full-time workers only, there is almost no contribution of education to labor input growth for 1975–1979.

Among women, the slowdown is most pronounced among those holding a postsecondary certificate. In this category, the annual growth rates of contribution to labor input are 0.63% for 1971–1972 and 0.67% for 1973–1975 respectively, but the average annual growth rate for 1975–1979 is 0.05%. These remain substantially below previous estimates in the range of 0.35 to 0.52% annually. Over the whole period, the estimates of 0.53% for men and 0.57% for women, but this is largely because of the rapid growth from 1971 to 1975.

The difference between the estimates in the two columns for all employed and those employed full-time has two components. The first is the increase in labor input provided by the quantity of part-time workers.[8] The second is the relative shift between full-time and part-time status. If wage rates differ between the two, labor quality is affected. The difference between labor quality estimates for all employed workers and those employed full time has both a quantity effect, in the number of workers at reduced annual hours on part-time status, and a quality effect, if part-time and full-time workers differ in productivity per hour.

In the shifting contributions by education, there are three basic conclusions. First, educational effects are similar between women and men throughout the period. The contribution of education to labor input for men is almost identical to that for women. Second, for both sexes, particularly among full-time workers, quality effects by education are almost zero after 1975. Third, while university graduates continue to contribute positively, there is a decline in the effect from this group after 1975. The group containing those with postsecondary certificates exhibits similar declines. The decline in the educational market occurs almost entirely among the relatively educated, and does not occur among those with no postsecondary education.

8.3.3. Age

Walters (1968) reports on labor quality change in Canada by both age and sex. The labor quality index by age and sex is

1950	100.0	1955	99.9
1960	98.7	1962	98.3.

The decline in quality over the 12-year period averages 0.14% annually.

The quality effects by age group $z_{ij.}$, for sex i and age j, with six groups as in table 8-1, are in table 8-3. Among men, the overall contribution to labor input is negative over 1971–1979. In all subperiods, the effects for those aged 15–19 years are negative. There is a reduction in the negative age effect over the period. Among teenagers, it declines from −1.01% over 1971–1973 to −0.40% for 1977–1979. For full-time workers, these estimates are smaller, but remain negative. With demographic predictions of reductions in the relative number of teen-aged workers employed, the negative effect from this group is likely to be reduced over time.

There is little effect among any other age group. For women, the categories of 20–29 and 30–39 contribute positively. Among men, the corresponding effects are close to zero. Considering full-time workers, the average man contributes lower quality by age throughout the period. The reduction averages −0.15% annually, with the largest effect arising from male teenage employment.

The age effects are uniformly larger for women than for men. The overall age effect is positive for the whole period, and negative only in one subperiod, among full-time employed women. For full-time workers 1971–1979, the age effect increases labor quality by 0.24% annually for women, and −0.12% for men. For 1975–1979, the corresponding estimates are −0.19% for men and −0.03% for women.

8.3.4. Effect on Productivity

It remains to examine the effect of shifts in the quality of labor input on the growth of labor and total factor productivity, in equations (8.14) and (8.15). If the growth accounting is rearranged, as in (8.15), total factor productivity is explained. Labor compensation data are from the *National Income and Expenditure Accounts, (NIEA), 1966–1980,* Statistics Canada, Catalogue 13-206.

The aggregate labor compensation share s_d must be assigned between

Table 8-3. Quality Effects by Age, $n_{i.k}$, 1971-1979
(annual percent, product of quality weight and employment growth)

	Category (years)	*Men*		*Women*	
		All	*Full-Time*	*All*	*Full-Time*
1971-1973	15-19	−1.01	−0.32	−0.79	−0.20
	20-29	0.13	−0.03	0.46	0.26
	30-39	0.11	0.12	0.12	0.09
	40-49	0.63	0.41	0.14	0.02
	50-64	0.02	−0.01	0.09	0.01
	65 or older	−0.01	−0.02	−0.04	−0.02
	Total	−0.67	−0.21	−0.01	0.16
1973-1975	15-19	−0.15	0.04	−0.31	−0.06
	20-29	0.17	−0.02	0.54	0.24
	30-39	0.00	−0.08	0.22	0.12
	40-49	−0.02	−0.04	0.08	0.04
	50-64	−0.02	0.02	0.02	−0.01
	65 or older	0.03	0.06	−0.03	−0.02
	Total	0.01	−0.02	0.52	0.31
1975-1977	15-19	−0.22	−0.21	−0.37	−0.22
	20-29	0.07	−0.04	0.20	0.14
	30-39	0.00	0.06	0.13	0.07
	40-49	0.12	0.11	0.14	0.04
	50-64	0.03	−0.01	0.04	−0.17
	65 or older	0.04	0.01	−0.06	0.00
	Total	0.04	−0.08	0.08	−0.14
1977-1979	15-19	−0.40	−0.28	−0.31	−0.08
	20-29	0.05	0.00	0.18	0.08
	30-39	0.13	0.07	0.18	0.09
	40-49	−0.06	−0.06	0.03	0.00
	50-64	0.02	0.00	0.05	0.00
	65 or older	−0.04	−0.03	−0.01	0.00
	Total	−0.03	−0.30	0.12	0.09

men and women. Two procedures are used. First, the share is allocated by proportion of total compensation. This includes the relative weight in each age and education cell. All wage differentials are assumed to reflect differences in marginal productivity. Second, the share is allocated on the basis of proportions of total full-time equivalent employment. This assumes that the average person employed full time has the same base productivity level.[9] The first procedure establishes an upper bound for the effect of sex composition on labor productivity growth. The second procedure sets a lower bound.

Total output, in constant and current dollars, is from the NIEA. The gross national product series is used, and converted to constant dollars by the gross national expenditure deflator.[10] Total employment, both full-time and part-time, is from *Historical Labour Force Statistics,* Statistics Canada, Catalogue 71-201, Annual.

The computation of labor income and the share of labor is contained in table 8-4. This is the sum of wages, salaries, and supplementary labor income from entrepreneurial activity. This latter is contained in net income of nonfarm unincorporated business, including rent, and the accrued net income of farm operators from farm production.

Table 8-4. Labor Income and Compensation Shares
(compensation in millions of current dollars, shares as fractions)

	(1) Wages, Salaries, and Supplementary Labor Income	*(2) Net Income Nonfarm, Noncorporate*	*(3) Net Income Farm, Noncorporate*	*(4) Noncorporate Income*
1971	51,528	5,928	1,576	7,504
1972	57,570	6,170	1,662	7,832
1973	66,757	6,656	3,009	9,665
1974	80,086	6,901	3,859	10,760
1975	93,289	7,669	3,944	11,613
1976	107,922	8,438	3,317	11,755
1977	118,992	9,113	2,831	11,944
1978	129,848	9,644	3,585	13,229
1979	145,091	10,503	3,983	14,486

Sources: Columns (1) to (3), Statistics Canada, Catalogue 13-201, table 1. Column (4) is colur (2) plus (3). Column (6) is column (1) divided by column (5). Column (7) is column (6) times (column plus column (2)). Column (8) is column (1) plus column (7).

This noncorporate income contains returns from both capital and labor. Column (3) of table 8-4 contains gross national product excluding noncorporate labor income. The labor share is the ratio of wages, salaries, and supplementary labor income to gross national product exclusive of noncorporate income. This share is multiplied by noncorporate income, and the sum of this noncorporate labor income and wages, salaries, and supplementary labor income represents total labor income.

Employment is constructed on a full-time equivalent basis. In table 8-5, average compensation per full-time worker is reported separately for men and women. Total compensation by sex, as obtained from the *Labour Force Survey,* is divided by average full-time compensation to obtain the number of full-time equivalent employees. The share of men in employment on a full-time equivalent basis is in table 8-5. The share of men in total compensation is also indicated.

These two share procedures form the upper and lower bounds for the estimation of the effect of shifting sex composition on productivity growth. Restricting the compensation to full-time and equivalents prevents differences in average hours and week worked from affecting estimates. The shares used are two-period moving averages of those in table 8-5.

Table 8-4. *(Continued)*

(5) Gross National Product Excluding Noncorporate Income	*(6) Share of Wages and Salaries in (5)*	*(7) Value of Noncorporate Labor Compensation*	*(8) Labor Income*
86,946	0.593	4,450	55,978
97,402	0.591	4,629	62,199
113,895	0.586	5,664	72,421
136,768	0.586	6,305	86,391
153,730	0.607	7,049	100,338
179,276	0.602	7,077	114,999
196,924	0.604	7,214	126,206
217,124	0.598	7,911	137,759
247,475	0.586	8,489	154,480

Table 8-5. Full-Time Equivalent Employment, Labor Compensation, and Labor Share

	Average Compensation Full-Time Workers (million dollars)		*Employment Full-Time Equivalent ('000)*		*Total Employment ('000)*	*Relative Shares, Men*	
	Men	*Women*	*Men*	*Women*		*Compensation*	*Employment*
1971	8,769	5,231	4,864	2,024	6,888	0.8012	0.7062
1973	10,434	6,182	5,268	2,322	7,590	0.7929	0.6941
1975	13,673	8,231	5,324	2,630	7,954	0.7708	0.6693
1977	15,776	9,791	5,605	3,028	8,633	0.7489	0.6493
1979	18,537	11,742	5,837	3,261	9,098	0.7386	0.6416

In table 8-6 are estimates of the contribution to growth in labor productivity of each of the separate age and education groups, by sex. These are the respective quality effects $z_{ij.}$ and $n_{i.h}$ for sex i, age $j = 1, \ldots, 6$ and education $h = 1, \ldots, 5$ multiplied by compensation shares $s_{i..}$ and by the share of labor in value added s_d. The largest component is among those with a university degree, with the effect on productivity growth reduced after 1975.

The total of all effects annually, the last entry in the table, indicates that labor quality change is negative after 1975. This arises entirely from the reduction in the contribution of education, particularly among men. In 1973–1975, educated men increase labor productivity growth by 0.798% annually, but this declines to 0.054% annually in 1977–1979. Over half of this decline arises in the category of those with university education. For women, the decline over the comparable period is from 0.164% to 0.043% annually among university graduates, again accounting for over half the decline in the effect of educated workers.

Table 8-7 is similar to table 8-6, but with men and women assumed equally productive. The entries are the products of the $z_{ij.}$ or $n_{i.h}$, the $b_{i..}$, full-time equivalent employment shares by sex, and the labor share in value added s_d. There is a reduction in the differential between men and women in effects.

The suppression of a wage-related sex effect increases the contribution of labor quality to labor productivity growth. The differences are small, indicating that the sex effect, while negative, is not substantial. The sex effects are, in annual percent, −0.005 for 1971–1973, −0.017 for 1973–1975, −0.005 for 1975–1977 and −0.011 for 1977–1979, for an average of −0.010. Using the results of table 8-6, the average over age effects is −0.059, so age-sex composition shifts reduce labor productivity growth by −0.069% in the period, where these are upper-bound estimates, given the sex effects. Further, there is no rapid deterioration in age-sex composition after 1973.

8.4. Accounting for the Growth in Labor Productivity

In table 8-8 is indicated the decomposition of labor productivity growth, as in equation (8.14). Capital data are from *Fixed Capital Flows and Stocks,* Statistics Canada, Catalogue 13-368. Capital stocks are constructed using the perpetual inventory method. The net capital stock series are used. The series are constant dollar estimates for capital 1971–1979. Data on capital intensity are obtained by division of current dollar capital stock by the

Table 8-6. Contributions to Labor Productivity Growth, 1971-1979 (annual percent)

	1971-1973	*1973-1975*	*1975-1977*	*1977-1979*
Men				
Age				
15-19	−0.150	0.019	−0.097	−0.124
20-29	−0.014	−0.009	−0.018	0.000
30-39	0.056	−0.037	0.028	0.031
40-49	0.023	−0.019	0.051	−0.027
50-64	−0.005	0.009	−0.005	0.000
65 or above	−0.009	0.028	0.005	−0.013
	−0.099	−0.009	−0.036	−0.133
Education				
0-8 years	−0.012	0.173	−0.014	0.044
some/completed high school	−0.061	0.093	−0.087	−0.066
some postsecondary	0.019	0.009	0.000	−0.004
postsecondary certificate	0.075	0.061	0.005	0.000
university degree	0.164	0.462	0.092	0.080
	0.185	0.798	−0.004	0.054
Women				
Age				
15-19	−0.024	−0.008	−0.032	−0.012
20-29	0.031	0.031	0.020	0.012
30-39	0.011	0.012	0.010	0.014
40-49	0.002	0.005	0.006	0.000
50-64	0.001	−0.001	−0.025	0.000
65 or above	−0.002	−0.002	0.000	0.000
	0.019	0.037	−0.021	0.014

Table 8-6. *(Continued)*

	1971–1973	*1973–1975*	*1975–1977*	*1977–1979*
Education				
0–8 years	−0.006	−0.022	0.004	−0.001
some/completed high school	−0.036	0.000	−0.070	−0.047
some postsecondary	0.013	0.018	0.001	−0.001
postsecondary certificae	0.049	0.048	−0.009	0.006
university degree	0.044	0.164	0.069	0.043
	0.064	0.208	−0.005	0.000
Total	0.169	1.034	−0.066	−0.061

Note: Productivity by sex measured by wages. Entries in table are product of $z_{ij.}$ or $n_{i.k}$ and $s_{i..}$ and s_{d} or quality effects for education and age, sex shares in labor compensation, and labor share in gross national product.

level of full-time equivalent employment. The growth of this capital intensity is multiplied by the share of capital. Capital intensity annual percentage growth rates are −0.166 for 1971–1973, 2.830 for 1973–1975, 0.520 for 1975–1977, and 1.260 for 1977–1979.

The growth in output per full-time equivalent employed person declines from 1.766% in 1971–1973 to 0.691% in 1977–1979. As indicated in the disaggregated measures, there is no quality change in labor input after 1975. Total factor productivity growth declines after 1973. The disappearance of this residual factor in the United States has also been noted.[11]

The lower part of table 8-8 presents the labor quality estimates if there is no productivity-based wage differential by sex. If men and women have equal unit productivity, and all wage differentials arise from discrimination or other factors, the labor quality growth rate is increased, and total factor productivity growth rates altered. The substantive conclusions remain, that there has been reduced or negative growth of the residual in the 1970s.

Labor productivity growth in Canada declines sharply after 1973. The 1971–1973 growth rate in labor productivity is 1.766% annually, but this falls to 0.075% averaging over 1973–1979. The decline in the growth of

Table 8-7. Contributions to Labor Productivity Growth, 1971-1979 (annual percent)

	1971-1973	*1973-1975*	*1975-1977*	*1977-1979*
Men				
Age				
15-19	−0.132	0.016	−0.084	−0.108
20-29	−0.012	−0.008	−0.016	0.000
30-39	0.049	−0.033	0.024	0.027
40-49	0.021	−0.016	0.044	−0.023
50-64	−0.004	0.008	−0.004	0.000
64 or above	−0.008	0.024	0.004	−0.012
	−0.086	−0.009	−0.032	−0.116
Education				
0-8 years	−0.016	0.151	−0.012	0.038
some/completed high school	−0.054	0.081	−0.076	−0.058
some postsecondary	0.016	0.008	0.000	−0.004
postsecondary certificate	0.066	0.053	0.004	0.000
university degree	0.144	0.403	0.080	0.069
	0.156	0.696	−0.004	0.045
Women				
Age				
15-19	−0.035	−0.011	−0.045	−0.017
20-29	0.046	0.046	0.029	0.017
30-39	0.016	0.023	0.014	0.019
40-49	0.004	0.008	0.008	0.000
50-64	0.002	−0.002	−0.035	0.000
65 or older	−0.004	−0.004	0.000	0.000
	0.029	0.060	−0.029	0.019

Table 8-7. *(Continued)*

	1971–1973	*1973–1975*	*1975–1977*	*1977–1979*
Education				
0–8 years	−0.009	−0.032	0.006	−0.002
some/completed high school	−0.053	0.000	−0.099	−0.065
some postsecondary	0.019	0.027	0.002	−0.002
postsecondary certificate	0.073	0.070	−0.012	0.010
university degree	0.065	0.239	0.097	0.059
	0.095	0.304	−0.006	0.000
Total	0.174	1.051	−0.071	−0.052

Note: Men and women are assumed to have equal unit productivity. Entries in table are product of $z_{ij.}$ or $n_{i.k}$ quality effects by education or age, sex shares in employment $b_{i..}$ and s_d, labor share in gross national product.

Table 8-8. Sources of Growth in Labor Productivity, 1971–1979 (annual percent)

	1971–1973	*1973–1975*	*1975–1977*	*1977–1979*
A. Wage weighted productivity, men and women				
Labor productivity	1.766	−0.107	−0.358	0.691
= labor quality (weighted by labor share)	0.169	1.034	−0.076	−0.063
+ capital intensity (weighted by capital share)	−0.068	1.140	0.205	0.510
+ total factor productivity	1.665	−2.281	−0.479	0.244
B. Equal unit productivity, men and women				
Labor quality (weighted by labor share)	0.174	1.051	−0.071	−0.052
Total factor productivity	1.660	−2.298	−0.484	0.233

labor productivity occurs simultaneously with that for total factor productivity. For the 1971–1973 period, total factor productivity growth averages 1.660%, but this declines to −0.425% for 1973–1979, although there is a recovery in the later part of the decade. Almost the entire decrease in labor productivity growth arises through a decline in total factor productivity growth. Labor quality is a contributor to the productivity slowdown after 1975. In terms of attributing the decline in labor productivity growth to sources, labor quality and capital intensity effects have fallen after 1975, but the precipitous decline in labor productivity occurs in the 1973–1975 period.

8.5. Concluding Remarks

The structure has developed the contribution to labor input and ultimately labor productivity growth of men and women, and of education and age, using Canadian data for 1971–1979. A range for the effect of shifts in sex composition on productivity growth is established. The bounds are determined by whether all factor payments are equal to marginal products, whereupon shares in total compensation are used. If all wage differentials between men and women are unrelated to productivity, then employment shares are applied.

For each sex, the contribution of education to productivity growth declines during the period. This applies at all schooling levels, but is acute in the postsecondary sector. The contribution of those with university education to labor productivity growth declines to less than 0.1% after 1975, from 0.3% prior to 1975. Only among teenagers is there a nonnegligible effect on productivity by age, and this is negative. The declines are more pronounced among men than women.

In education, there remains the issue of the relationship between education and training. If workers are increasing their tendency to accept postschool jobs intensive in training, initial wages exceed marginal products. One possibility for measuring the effect of schooling is to construct annuity wages for each level of education. These wages would capture the long-term benefits from educational investments. There are also arguments that the wage profile is steeper than that for marginal products.[12] The estimates of the productivity effects of education are not all the benefits. Education also can be viewed as partly consumption.

The decline in labor productivity appears to occur after 1973. Not all measured effects move in tandem. The decline in labor quality occurs after 1975, and this partly accounts for why labor markets do not explain a large proportion of the labor productivity slowdown. With a more disaggregated structure using gross production rather than value added, energy and materials are explanatory factors. No assignment of capital between productivity- and nonproductivity-enhancing categories is possible. Pollution control equipment may be included in the capital stock, but not add to measured value added, though this is a problem more with the definition of output.

The results indicate that there is a reduced effect of education during the 1970s. The age–sex composition of employment has shifted toward youth and women, but this has had little impact on labor productivity growth. There is a reduction in the estimates of labor quality change and its contribution to labor productivity growth.

Notes

1. The potential crisis in education is indicated in the Carnegie Foundation (1983) report on high schools. Freeman (1976) notes the declining rate of return to education and reduction of the relative earnings level of those with higher education.

2. Estimates of the contribution of education to labor input growth have typically been measured at 0.5% annually up to the 1970s. If labor compensation is 60% of value added, education increases labor productivity growth by 0.3% annually. Estimates of this magnitude have been presented by Jorgenson and Griliches (1967) and Chinloy (1981) for the United States and Christensen, Cummings, and Jorgenson (1980) for Canada.

3. In a more general context, the existence of a labor subaggregate could be tested.

4. There are data and measurement problems associated with this procedure. The rate of discount must be determined, and the expected future stream of earnings.

5. This structure is developed in Christensen, Cummings, and Jorgenson (1980).

6. Walters (1968,65, table 40).

7. Christensen, Cummings, and Jorgenson (1980), table II.A, 3C, no pagination.

8. Since in the sample all those working less than 50 weeks per year are included as part-time, this group is relatively heterogeneous.

9. The mix of workers across skill categories such as age and education can vary. However, some weighting structure is required on the various categories.

10. Output can alternatively be defined in value-added form, for capital and labor only, or in gross form, also including intermediate inputs.

11. Examples are in Denison (1979) and Norsworthy, Harper, and Kunze (1979). The latter perform a similar analysis of the growth of labor productivity for the United States 1948–1978. The period is divided into three subperiods. In the last subperiod 1973–1978, a deceleration in capital intensity is a large contributor to reduced productivity growth.

12. The model of mandatory retirement of Lazear (1979) exemplifies this.

References

Carnegie Foundation for the Advancement of Teaching. 1983. *High School: A Report on Secondary Education in America.* New York: Harper & Row.

Chinloy, P. 1981. *Labor Productivity*. Cambridge: MA: Abt Books.

Christensen, L. R., E. D. Cummings, and D. W. Jorgenson. 1980. "Relative Productivity Levels, 1947-1973: An International Comparison." *European Economic Review* 16:61-94.

Daly, D. 1980. "Remedies for Increasing Productivity Levels in Canada." In S. Maital and N. Meltz (eds.), *Lagging Productivity Growth*. Cambridge, MA: Ballinger, 223-239.

Denison, E. F. 1979. *Accounting for Slower Economic Growth*. Washington, D.C.: Brookings Institution.

Freeman, R. 1976. *The Overeducated American*. New York: Academic Press.

Hulten, C. R., and M. Nishimizu. 1980. "The Importance of Productivity Change in the Economic Growth of Nine Industrialized Countries." In S. Maital and N. Meltz (eds.), *Lagging Productivity Growth*. Cambridge, MA: Ballinger, 85-105.

Jorgenson, D. W., and Z. Griliches. 1967. "The Explanation of Productivity Change." *Review of Economics and Statistics* 34:249-283.

Lazear, E. P. 1979. "Why Is There Mandatory Retirement?" *Journal of Political Economy* 87:1261-1284.

May, J. D., and M. Denny. 1979. "Post-War Productivity Change in Canadian Manufacturing." *Canadian Journal of Economics* 12:29-41.

Norsworthy, J. R., M. J. Harper, and K. Kunze. 1979. "The Slowdown in Productivity Growth: Analysis of Some Contributing Factors." *Brookings Papers on Economic Activity* 7:387-421.

Statistics Canada. *National Income and Expenditure Accounts*, Ottawa, Ontario, Statistics Canada, Catalogue 13-201, various issues.

Statistics Canada. *Fixed Capital Stocks and Flows, 1926-1978*. Ottawa, Ontario: Statistics Canada, Catalogue 13-568.

Statistics Canada. *Fixed Capital Stocks and Flows, Annual*. Ottawa, Ontario: Statistics Canada, Catalogue 13-211, various issues.

Statistics Canada. *The Labour Force*. Ottawa Canada: Statistics Canada, Catalogue 71-001, various issues.

Walters, D. 1968. *Canadian Income Levels and Growth: An International Comparison*. Economic Council of Canada Staff Study 23. Ottawa, Ontario: Economic Council of Canada.

Walters, D. 1970. *Canadian Growth Revisited, 1950-1967*. Economic Council of Canada Staff Study 28. Ottawa, Ontario: Economic Council of Canada.

PART THREE

9 MEASURING SHADOW PRICE EFFICIENCY

Rolf Färe and Shawna Grosskopf

9.1. Introduction

In this chapter we develop nonparametric (linear programming) methods for calculating efficiency in the dual (price) space. The immediate purpose is to augment the existing efficiency literature by introducing an alternative method of measuring efficiency, namely a method based on dual information. A by-product of this research is a framework that can be adapted to serve as nonparametric tests of indirect production and utility functions along the lines of Afriat (1972).[1]

The notion that a technology can be modeled in either the factor space (primal) or price space (dual) was first introduced by Shephard (1953). Since then, duality theory has been widely applied (see Diewert 1982). These applications extend to the literature on the measurement of efficiency. In particular, Kopp and Diewert (1982) and Zieschang (1983) introduce a dual approach to measuring primal efficiency in a parametric framework. The nonparametric approach used here is a natural complement to this work. The focus here is to develop shadow price efficiency

We are sincerely grateful for comments by Professor Bob Russell.

measures in the dual or price framework rather than using duality theory to derive information to be used in the primal.

In this framework, we are comparing observed cost-normalized factor prices to their optimal shadow prices; that is, the prices rather than quantities are the variables of choice. This framework could prove useful for centralized planning models. Another potential application is the case of transfer pricing, where a vertically integrated firm seeks efficiency "shadow" prices for intermediate inputs. More generally, when markets are imperfect, resulting in a divergence between market and shadow prices, this method could be used to determine shadow prices and to calculate losses due to the market imperfection. An obvious example is the case of regulated firms.

In terms of organization, section 9.2 develops the reference input price technologies as monotone hulls of polytopes. Section 9.3 is devoted to specifying the various efficiency measures in a linear programming framework.

9.2. The Input Price Correspondence

The dual (price) technology transforming cost deflated input prices $p \in R^n_+$ into net output $u \in R_+ := \{v \in R: v \geqslant 0\}$ is here modeled by an input price correspondence[2]

$$L: R_+ \to L(u) \subseteq R^n_+ \tag{9.1}$$

where $L(u)$ denotes the set of all deflated input prices yielding a minimal total cost for u more than or equal to one. Here, we require L to satisfy certain axioms, namely:

L.1 $L(0) = \emptyset;\ 0 \notin L(u),\ u > 0$

L.2 $p \geqslant q \in L(u) \Rightarrow p \in L(u)$

L.3 $L(u)$ is convex

L.4 $L(u)$ is closed

L.5 $u \geqslant v \Rightarrow L(v) \subseteq L(u)$

The axioms (L.1–L.5) are weaker than those suggested by Shephard (1970),[3] but stronger than those suggested by Lehmijoki (1981).[4] The axioms are self-explanatory. For an exposition of how they can be deduced from the cost function, see Shephard (1970).

We wish to formalize a reference technology that can be used in determining dual efficiency using nonparametric methods. Thus, assume that there are k observations. Each observation, i, consists of a positive output u_i, an input price vector $p^i \in R^n_+$, $p^i > 0$,[5] and a positive total cost c_i, $i = 1,2,\ldots,k$. Denote the ith cost deflated price vector by $\hat{p}_i = p^i/c_i = (p^i_1/c_i, p^i_2/c_i, \ldots, p^i_n/c_i)$, $i = 1,2,\ldots,k$, and denote the matrix of observed cost deflated prices by $\mathbf{N}$, where $\mathbf{N}$ is of order $(k \times n)$, k observations and n prices. We assume that each column as well as each row has a positive element. Denote the vector of inverse outputs by $\mathbf{M}$; that is, $\mathbf{M} = (1/u_1, 1/u_2, \ldots, 1/u_k)^T$. Now, define

$$L^H(u) := \{\hat{p} \in R^n_+ : 1 \leqslant z\mathbf{M}u, z\mathbf{N} \leqslant \hat{p}, z \in R^k_+\} \tag{9.2}$$

where $z = (z_1, z_2, \ldots, z_k)$ denotes the intensity vector.[6] These serve as the "weights" for each process; that is, they show the level at which each activity $i(u_i, \hat{p}^i)$ is utilized. The z's are determined in the solution to the linear programming problems discussed in section 9.3.

9.2.1. Proposition: The input price correspondence $L^H(u)$ satisfies axioms L.1–L.5.

Proof: If $u = 0$, there does not exist a $z \in R^k_+$ such that $1 \leqslant z\mathbf{M}\,(0)$, thus $L^H(0) = \emptyset$. If $u > 0$, then z is semipositive, thus $p \geqslant z\mathbf{N} \geqslant 0$ from the assumption on $\mathbf{N}$.

Property L.2 follows directly from the conditions that $z\mathbf{N} \leqslant \hat{p}$ and $\hat{p} \in R^n_+$.

To prove property L.3, let $\hat{p}, \bar{\hat{p}} \in L^H(u)$, then there exist activity vectors z and $\bar{z}$ such that

$$1 \leqslant z\mathbf{M}u, \quad z\mathbf{N} \leqslant \hat{p} \qquad \text{and} \qquad 1 \leqslant \bar{z}\mathbf{M}u, \quad \bar{z}\mathbf{N} \leqslant \bar{\hat{p}}$$

Thus,

$$1 \leqslant [\lambda z + (1-\lambda)\bar{z}]\mathbf{M}u$$

and

$$[\lambda z + (1-\lambda)\bar{z}]\mathbf{N} \leqslant \lambda\hat{p} + (1-\lambda)\bar{\hat{p}}$$

for $0 \leqslant \lambda \leqslant 1$. Now since $(\lambda z + (1-\lambda)\bar{z}) \in R_+^k$, the convex combination $(\lambda \hat{p} + (1-\lambda)\bar{\hat{p}}) \in L^H(u)$.

Next, let $\hat{p}^l$ be a sequence in $L^H(u), \hat{p}^l \to \hat{p}^0$. Then there exists a sequence z^l such that

$$1 \leqslant z^l \mathbf{M} u, \quad z^l \mathbf{N} \leqslant \hat{p}^l$$

for all l. Since $\hat{p}^l$ is convergent, the sequence is bounded and therefore there exists a $\bar{\hat{p}}$ such that $\bar{\hat{p}} > \hat{p}^l$ for all l. Now consider the set

$$\{z \in R_+^k \colon\ 1 \leqslant z\mathbf{M}u, z\mathbf{N} \leqslant \bar{\hat{p}}\}$$

This set is compact, thus there exists a subsequence z^{l_k} such that $z^{l_k} \to z^0$ and

$$1 \leqslant z^{l_k}\mathbf{M}U, \quad z^{l_k}\mathbf{N} \leqslant \hat{p}^{l_k}, \qquad \text{for all } l_k$$

Finally, since $z\mathbf{N}$ and $z\mathbf{M}$ are continuous functions,

$$1 \leqslant z^0\mathbf{M}u, \quad z^0\mathbf{N} \leqslant \hat{p}^0$$

proving property L.4.

Property L.5 follows from $\{z \in R_+^k\colon\ 1 \leqslant z\mathbf{M}u\} \supseteq \{z \in R_+^k\colon\ 1 \leqslant z\mathbf{M}v\}$ for $u \geqslant v$.

Q.E.D.

Proposition 9.2.1 verifies that $L^H(u)$ is an input price correspondence. In addition to properties L.1–L.5, $L^H(u)$ satisfies a homogeneity property, namely:

9.2.2. Proposition

$$L^H(\theta u) = 1/\theta L^H(u), \qquad \theta > 0$$

Proof:

$$L^H(\theta u) = \{\hat{p} \in R_+^n\colon\ 1 \leqslant z\mathbf{M}(\theta u), z\mathbf{N} \leqslant \hat{p}, z \in R_+^k\}$$

$$= \{\hat{p} \in R_+^n\colon\ 1 \leqslant (\theta z)\mathbf{M}u, (\theta z)\mathbf{N} \leqslant \theta\hat{p}, z \in R_+^k\}$$

$$= 1/\theta\{\hat{p}^0 \in R^n_+ : 1 \leqslant z^0\mathbf{N} \leqslant \hat{p}^0, z^0 \in R^k_+\}$$

$$= 1/\theta L^H(u)$$

where $\hat{p}^0 := \theta\hat{p} \in R^n_+$ and $z^0 := \theta z \in R^k_+$.

Q.E.D.

Eventually we will be interested in dual cost minimization. Then we will not assume that each observed input price vector has all components positive. Thus to ensure the existence of a minimum, we need to show that the efficiency subset of $L^H(u)$ is bounded and nonempty whenever $L^H(u)$ is nonempty. To pursue this, introduce:

9.2.3. Definition: The efficient subset of $L^H(u)$ is defined to be

$$\text{Eff}\, L^H(u) = \{\hat{p} \in R^n_+ : \hat{p} \in L^H(u), \hat{q} < \hat{p} \Rightarrow \hat{q} \notin L^H(u)\}$$

Proposition 9.2.3

Eff $L^H(u)$ is bounded for each observed output.

Proof: If $L^H(u) = \emptyset$, we are done, thus assume $L^H(u) \neq \emptyset$. Next consider all $\hat{p}^i, i = 1,2, \ldots ,k$. Choose the largest components of these vectors. Denote the vector of those components by p^m. Then for each observed output, $[L^H(u_i) \cap \{\hat{p}: \hat{p} \leqslant p^m\}]$ contains its efficiency subset. To verify this, assume that $\hat{p} \in \text{Eff}\, L^H(u_i)$, some i, then $\hat{p}$ is the convex combination of some observed $\hat{p}_i$, $1 \leqslant i \leqslant k$. But $\hat{p}^m \geqslant \hat{p}_i$, $i = 1,2, \ldots ,k$. Thus $\hat{p} \in (L^H(u_i) \cap \{\hat{p}: \hat{p} \leqslant \hat{p}^m\}$. Thus the efficient subset is bounded.

Q.E.D.

Since $\hat{p}^i \in L^H(u_i)$, for each i, $L^H(u_i)$ is nonempty. Following arguments similar to those in Shephard (1970, 16) or Färe (1980, 15) it is evident that Eff $L^H(u_i)$ is nonempty. Finally, since $L^H(u)$ is closed, Eff $L^H(u_i) \subseteq L^H(u_i)$ and Eff $L^H(u_i)$ is compact. Eff $L^H(u_i)$ denotes the closure of Eff $L^H(u_i)$. Therefore, dual cost minimization can be done without requiring that all inputs be positive.

To determine scale efficiency, that is, deviations from the long run optimal constant returns to scale technology, we next introduce two additional technologies.[7]

$$L^N(u):\ = \{\hat{p} \in R^n_+:\ 1 \leqslant z\mathbf{M}u, z\mathbf{N} \leqslant \hat{p}, \sum z_i \leqslant 1, z \in R^k_+\} \quad (9.3)$$

$$L^A(u):\ = \{\hat{p} \in R^n_+:\ 1 \leqslant z\mathbf{M}u, z\mathbf{N} \leqslant \hat{p}, \sum z_i = 1, z \in R^k_+\} \quad (9.4)$$

In comparing these to L^H, we note that L^N restricts the intensity variables to $\Sigma z_i \leqslant 1$, while L^A is even more restrictive; that is, the sum of the z_i's equals unity.[8] It is also clear that L^N and L^A satisfy (L.1–L.5) and have bounded efficient subsets for each observation. We note, however, that neither L^N nor L^A is homogeneous of degree -1. Regarding L^N, we have:

9.2.4. Proposition

$$L^N(\theta u) \supseteq 1/\theta L^N(u), \qquad \theta \geqslant 1$$

Proof:

$$\begin{aligned} L^N(\theta u) &= \{\hat{p} \in R^n_+:\ 1 \leqslant z\mathbf{M}\theta u, z\mathbf{N} \leqslant \hat{p}, \textstyle\sum z_i \leqslant 1, z \in R^k_+\} \\ &= \{\hat{p} \in R^n_+:\ 1 \leqslant \theta z\mathbf{M}u, \theta z\mathbf{N} \leqslant \theta\hat{p}, \textstyle\sum z_i \leqslant 1, z \in R^k_+\} \\ &= 1/\theta\{\hat{q} \in R^n_+:\ 1 \leqslant \mu\mathbf{M}u, \mu\mathbf{N} \leqslant \hat{q}, \textstyle\sum \mu_i \leqslant \theta, \mu \in R^k_+\} \\ &\supseteq 1/\theta\{\hat{q} \in R^n_+:\ 1 \leqslant \mu\mathbf{M}u, \mu\mathbf{N} \leqslant \hat{q}, \textstyle\sum \mu_i \leqslant 1, \mu \in R^k_+\} \\ &= 1/\theta L^N(u) \end{aligned}$$

since $\theta \geqslant 1$, and $\hat{q}:\ = \theta\hat{p}$, $\mu = \theta z$.

Q.E.D.

Next, we introduce the isoquant set of $L(u)$. This subset of $L(u)$ serves two purposes: (1) it is needed to define returns to scale and (2) it is used as a reference set for some of the efficiency measures developed in section 9.3.

Definition 2: The isoquant of $L(u)$ is defined by

$$IL(u):\ = \{\hat{p} \in R^n_+:\ \hat{p} \in L(u), \lambda\hat{p} \notin L(u), \lambda < 1\}, u > 0$$

We observe first that Eff $L(u)$ is nonempty, thus $IL(u)$ is nonempty whenever $L(u)$ is nonempty.

Definition 3: The input price correspondence $L(u)$ exhibits

i. Increasing returns to scale (IRS) at u if $L(\theta u) \subseteq 1/\theta L(u)$, $\theta \leqslant 1$, and $IL(\theta u) \cap IL/\theta L(u) = \emptyset$, $\theta \neq 1$
ii. Constant returns to scale (CRS) at u if $L(\theta u) = 1/\theta L(u)$, $\theta \geqslant 1$
iii. Decreasing returns to scale (DRS) at u if $L(\theta u) \supseteq 1/\theta L(u)$, $\theta \geqslant 1$ and $IL(\theta u) \cap IL/\theta L(u) = \emptyset$, $\theta \neq 1$

We note that if $IL^N(\theta u) \cap IL/\theta L^N(u) = \emptyset$ for $\theta \neq 1$, L^N exhibits DRS and that L^H exhibits CRS.

9.3. Dual Efficiency Measures

Dual measures of efficiency, in the spirit of Farrell (1957), have been independently introduced by Muro (1982) and Färe (1984), where Muro measures dual technical efficiency and Färe measures shadow price efficiency. In this section, we develop the linear programming techniques for calculation of the shadow price.

Let $(u^0,\hat{p}^0)$ be an observed output level and an observed cost-deflated price vector. The dual (Farrell) measure of technical efficiency is calculated as

$$F(u^0,\hat{p}^0): = \min \lambda \tag{9.5}$$

$$\text{s.t. } 1 \leqslant z\mathbf{M}u^0$$

$$z\mathbf{M} \leqslant \hat{p}^0\lambda$$

$$z \in R^k_+$$

that is, $F(u^0,\hat{p}^0): = \min \{\lambda: \lambda\hat{p}^0 \in L^H(u)\}$. Thus this measure calculates the minimal ray-distance from $\hat{p}^0$ to $\lambda\hat{p}^0$, under the condition that $\lambda\hat{p}^0$ belongs to $L^H(u)$. It is clear that $F(u^0,\hat{p}^0) = 1$ if and only if $\hat{p}^0$ belongs to the isoquant of $L^H(u)$ and thus, $F(u^0,p^0) = c^0$.

Assume next that the input vectors $x^i \in R^n_+, x^i \geqslant 0, i = 1,2,\ldots,k,$ one for each observation, are given. The dual cost minimum is then defined by[9]

$$Q(u^0,x^0): = \min \{\hat{p}x^0: \hat{p} \in L^H(u^0)\} \tag{9.6}$$

The dual cost minimum is calculated as

$$Q(u^0,x^0): \; = \min \hat{p}x^0 \tag{9.7}$$

$$\text{s.t } 1 \leqslant z\mathbf{M}u^0$$

$$z\mathbf{N} \leqslant \hat{p}$$

$$z \in R^n_+$$

Given the dual cost minimum $Q(u^0,x^0)$, dual overall productive efficiency is obtained from

$$O(u^0,x^0,\hat{p}^0): \; = Q(u^0,x^0)/\hat{p}^0x^0 \tag{9.8}$$

We note that since $\hat{p}^0 = p^0/c^0 = p^0/p^0x^0$, $O(u^0,x^0,\hat{p}^0) = Q(u^0,x^0)$.[10] Based on these two measures, the dual allocative efficiency measure can be defined as

$$A(u^0,x^0,\hat{p}^0): \; = O(u^0,x^0,\hat{p}^0)/F(u^0,\hat{p}^0) \tag{9.10}$$

From this definition we obtain

$$O(u^0,x^0,\hat{p}^0) = A(u^0,x^0,\hat{p}^0) \cdot F(u^0,\hat{p}^0) \tag{9.11}$$

that is, the dual overall productive efficiency measure has a decomposition property similar to Farrell's measures in the primal (factor) space.

To decompose the dual overall productive efficiency measure further, we will next introduce the dual scale efficiency measure and the dual purely technical efficiency measure.[11] Thus, consider

$$T(u^0,\hat{p}^0): \; = \min \lambda \tag{9.12}$$

$$\text{s.t. } 1 \leqslant z\mathbf{M}u^0$$

$$z\mathbf{N} \leqslant \hat{p}^0\lambda$$

$$\textstyle\sum z_i = 1, z \in R^k_+$$

We call this measure the dual purely technical efficiency measure. Clearly, $T(u^0,\hat{p}^0)$: $= \min \{\lambda\hat{p}^0 \in L^A(u^0)\}$; that is, it measures the minimum ray-distance relative to the $L^A(u)$ input price set. It is also clear that $T(u^0,\hat{p}^0) = 1$ if and only if $\hat{p}^0$ belongs to the isoquant of $L^A(u)$. Moreover, $T(u^0,\hat{p}^0) \geqslant F(u^0,\hat{p}^0)$ and the ratio $F(u^0,\hat{p}^0)/T(u^0,\hat{p}^0)$ measures inefficiency due to deviations from the constant returns to scale technology. Thus, scale efficiency in the dual is measured by

$$S(u^0,\hat{p}^0) = F(u^0,\hat{p}^0)/T(u^0,\hat{p}^0) \tag{9.13}$$

From (9.11), (9.12), and (9.13) we now have the following decomposition of the dual overall productive efficiency measure:

$$O(u^0,x^0,\hat{p}^0) = A(u^0,x^0,\hat{p}^0) \cdot S(u^0,\hat{p}^0) \cdot T(u^0,\hat{p}^0) \tag{9.14}$$

Finally, given that there exists scale inefficiency—that is, that $S(u^0,\hat{p}^0) \neq 1$—it is of interest to determine if it is due to increasing or decreasing returns to scale. To pursue this, consider

$$D(u^0,\hat{p}^0) := \min \{\lambda: \lambda\hat{p}^0 \in L^N(u^0)\} \tag{9.15}$$

that is, the ray-minimal distance relative to the $L^N(u^0)$ input price set. $D(u^0,\hat{p}^0)$ is calculated by

$$D(u^0,\hat{p}^0) = \min \lambda \tag{9.16}$$

$$\text{s.t. } 1 \leqslant z\mathbf{M}u^0$$

$$z\mathbf{N} \leqslant \hat{p}^0\lambda$$

$$\sum z_i \leqslant 1, z \in R^k_+$$

If $S(u^0,\hat{p}^0) \neq 1$ and $D(u^0,\hat{p}^0) = F(u^0,\hat{p}^0)$, scale inefficiency is due to increasing returns to scale.

These measures can be easily illustrated in a fairly simple diagram. Consider figure 9-1, where $\hat{p}_1$ and $\hat{p}_2$ represent the cost-deflated input prices of input x_1 and x_2, respectively. *XX* represents the (given) input plane, and $L^H(u)$ and $L^A(u)$ are as defined above. Thus, point *R* represents the input price combination in $L^H(u)$ given *XX* which is overall efficient. Suppose, on the other hand, that we observe the input price combination at point *P* with output level *u*. That combination is clearly not overall efficient. Our method follows that developed by Farrell by measuring $O(u^0x^0,\hat{p}^0)$ radially. Thus, $O(u^0x^0,\hat{p}^0)$ for point *P* is equivalent to *OS*/*OP*.

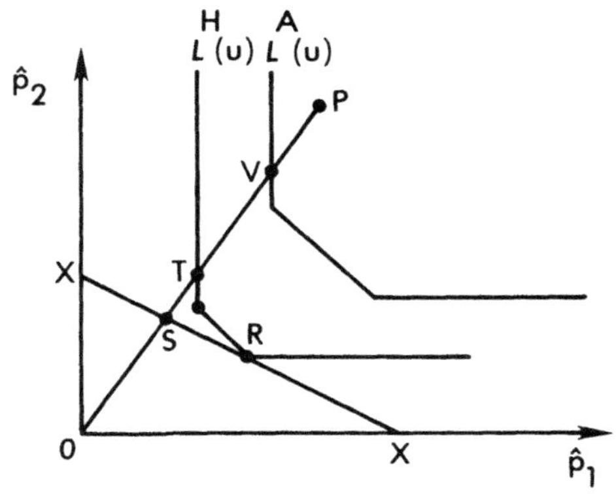

Figure 9-1

As mentioned above, overall efficiency can be decomposed into allocative, scale, and purely technical efficiency. In our figure, the allocative efficiency of point P is captured as OS/OT. Scale efficiency is measured by OT/OV; that is, the minimal ray distance between $L^H(u)$ and $L^A(u)$. Purely technical efficiency is captured as OV/OP, the minimal ray distance to the reference technology $L^A(u)$. The decomposition from (9.13),

$$O(u^0,x^0,\hat{p}^0) = A(u^0,x^0,\hat{p}^0) \cdot S(u^0,\hat{p}^0) \cdot T(u^0,\hat{p}^0)$$

is confirmed for our example since

$$OS/OP = OS/OT \cdot OT/OV \cdot OV/OP \tag{9.17}$$

By way of summary, we note that these measures should prove useful to researchers who are interested in shadow pricing of inputs, or in cases where one would expect input prices rather than input quantities to be the appropriate choice variables. It is also clear that the reference technologies developed here could prove useful in testing for regularity conditions of the indirect utility and production functions.

Notes

1. See also Diewert and Parkan (1983), Varian (1984) among others.
2. The set $L(u)$ is also called "input price set," Lehmijoki (1981), and the family $\{L(u)\colon u \in R_+\}$ is called the cost structure, Shephard (1970).

3. Shephard treats the input price correspondence $L(u)$ as a derived notion; that is, $L(u) = \{p: Q(u,p) \geqslant 1\}$, where Q is a cost function. Consequently, he obtains additional properties on $L(u)$ from $Q(u,p)$.

4. Lehmijoki, like Shephard, treats $L(u)$ as a derived notion; however she uses weaker assumption on the production technology than Shephard (1970) does. Compared to L.1-L.5, wheshe only requires input prices to be weakly disposable; that is, $p \in L(u) \Rightarrow \lambda p \in L(u)$, $\lambda \geqslant 1$, and she allows for negative prices. Otherwise her properties on $L(u)$ coincide with (L.1-L.5).

5. $p^i > 0$ *means* $p^i \geqslant 0$ but $p^i \neq 0$; that is, at least one price is positive.

6. We note that if $c_i = c$ for all i, then $L^H(u) = c \cdot \bar{L}^H(u)$, where $\bar{L}^H(u)$ is the nondeflated input price correspondence.

7. Our scale efficiency measure is the dual equivalent of that proposed by Färe, Grosskopf, and Lovell (1985). It corresponds to the notion that a neoclassical competitive firm with U-shaped costs will be in long-run equilibrium at minimum costs, corresponding to constant returns to scale. Thus deviations from scale efficiency (i.e., deviations from CRS) do not necessarily imply that the firm is technically inefficient in a private, short-run sense, but rather from the long-run social viewpoint.

8. The N in L^N stands for "non" as in non-increasing returns to scale, while A in L^A stands for Afriat. Afriat (1972, 571) also restricts the intensity variables sum to one.

9. Since Eff $L^H(u^0)$ is compact, the minimum exists.

10. Clearly, $O(u^0,x^0,\hat{p}^0) \leqslant F(u^0,\hat{p}^0) \leqslant 1$, thus if $O(u^0,x^0,\hat{p}^0) = 1$, $F(u^0,\hat{p}^0) = 1$ and thus $F(u^0,p^0) = c^0 = p^0x^0$.

11. This decomposition in the dual space follows the corresponding decomposition in the primal space introduced by Färe, Grosskopf, and Lovell (1983, 1985).

References

Afriat, S. 1972. "Efficiency Estimation of Production Functions." *International Economic Review* 13:568-598.

Diewert, E. 1982. "Duality Approaches to Microeconomic Theory." In K. Arrow and M. Intriligator (eds.), *Handbook of Mathematical Economies,* vol. II. Amsterdam: North-Holland.

Diewert, E., and C. Parkan. 1983. "Linear Programming Tests of Regularity Conditions for Production Functions." In W. Eichhorn, R. Henn, K. Neumann, and R. W. Shephard (eds.), *Quantitative Studies on Production and Prices.* Würzburg-Wien: Physica-Verlag.

Färe, R. 1984. "The Dual Measurement of Productive Efficiency." *Zeitschrift für Nationalökonomie* 44(3), 283-288.

Färe, R. 1980. *Laws of Diminishing Returns.* Lecture Notes in Economics and Mathematical Systems 176. Berlin: Springer-Verlag.

Färe, R., S. Grosskopf, and C. Lovell. 1985. *The Measurement of Efficiency of Production.* Boston: Kluwer-Nijhoff.

Färe, R., S. Grosskopf, and C. Lovell. 1983. "The Structure of Technical Efficiency." *The Scandinavian Journal of Economics* 85:181-190.

Farrell, M. 1957. "The Measurement of Productive Efficiency." *Journal of the Royal Statistical Society,* ser. A 120:253-281.

Kopp, R., and W. Diewert. 1982. "The Decomposition of Frontier Cost Function Deviations into Measures of Technical and Allocative Efficiency." *Journal of Econometrics* 19:319–322.

Lehmijoki, U. 1981. "Production Technology and Dual Theory of Firms." Department of Economics, Universiti of Turku.

Muro, J. 1982. "Dual Farrell Measures of Efficiency." Mimeo.

Shephard, R. 1970. *Cost and Production Functions.* Princeton, NJ: Princeton University Press.

Varian, H. 1984. "The Nonparametric Approach to Production Analysis." *Econometrica* 52:579–597.

Zieschang, K. 1983. "A Note on the Decomposition of Cost Efficiency into Technical and Allocative Components." Washington, D.C.: Bureau of Labor Statistics.

10 GENERAL HOMOTHETIC PRODUCTION CORRESPONDENCES*

King-Tim Mak

10.1. Introduction

Production correspondences exhibiting certain scaling laws have been investigated over the years. Apart from the simple homogeneous technologies, Shephard (1970; 1974) introduced and studied homothetic and semihomogeneous structures and Eichhorn (1970; 1978) developed the class of quasi-homogeneous production correspondences. It was shown by Färe and Shephard (1977) that these various structures are special classes of the family of ray-homothetic structure, which in turn was characterized in terms of linear (proportional) expansion paths. Al-Ayat and Färe (1977) then formulated the class of almost ray-homothetic production structure which includes ray-homotheticity while allowing for nonproportional changes in the inputs (outputs). Nonlinear expansion was also investigated there.

In this chapter, scaling of production factors is formulated abstractly so

*The author gratefully acknowledges the many helpful comments of Professor Ronald W. Shephard, and the encouragement of Professor Rolf Färe.

as to encompass all the aforementioned structures. By doing this, insight into the structure of homotheticity is gained.

The arguments to follow are carried out within the framework of a production technology introduced by Shephard (1974). A mapping $x \to P(x) \in 2^{\mathbf{R}^m_+}$, of input vectors $x \in \mathbf{R}^n_+$ to subset $P(x)$ of all output vectors $u \in \mathbf{R}^m_+$ obtainable by x is called an output correspondence. Inversely, the input correspondence $u \to L(u) := \{x \mid u \in P(x)\}$ determines the set of all input vectors yielding the output vector $u \in \mathbf{R}^m_+$. Both $L(u)$ and $P(x)$ are assumed to satisfy the inversely related set of weak axioms in Shephard (1974). Unless specifically indicated, free disposability of inputs or outputs is not enforced, nor is the convexity of $L(u)$ or $P(x)$.

10.2. Scaling of Production Factors and General Homotheticity

General scaling operation on factor (input or output) space is modeled by

10.2.1. Definition

$$T: \mathbf{R}^1_{++} \times \mathbf{R}^n_+ \to \mathbf{R}^n_+$$

is a *scaling operation* on space $\mathbf{R}^n_+$ if it satisfies the following:

i. for all $(\mu,x) \in \mathbf{R}^1_{++} \times \mathbf{R}^n_+$, $T(\mu;\cdot)$: $\mathbf{R}^n_+ \to \mathbf{R}^n_+$ is 1–1 and onto map, and $T(\cdot\,;x)$: $\mathbf{R}^1_{++} \to \mathbf{R}^n_+$ is 1–1 map if $x \neq 0$
ii. $T(1;x) = x$; $T(\mu;0) = 0$ for all $\mu \in \mathbf{R}^1_{++}$
iii. $T(\mu;x) = y \Leftrightarrow T(1/\mu;y) = x$ for $\mu \in \mathbf{R}^1_{++}$
iv. $T(\lambda \cdot \mu;x) = T[\lambda;T(\mu;x)]$ for all $(\lambda,\mu,x) \in \mathbf{R}^2_{++} \times \mathbf{R}^n_+$

It should be noted that the above set of assumptions is not independent; in particular, ii and iv imply iii: if $\mu > 0$ and $T(\mu;x) = y$, then

$$x = T(1;x) = T(1/\mu \cdot \mu;x) = T[1/\mu;T(\mu;x)] = T(1/\mu;y)$$

10.2.2. Definition

For given scaling operation T on $\mathbf{R}^n_+$, vector y is a *scaled version* of x, denoted $y\boldsymbol{R}x$, if $\exists\lambda \in \mathbf{R}^1_{++}$ with $T(\lambda;x) = y$.

The relation $\boldsymbol{R}$ induced by T clearly satisfies

$$x\boldsymbol{R}x, \quad \text{by definition 10.2.1(ii)}$$

$$y\boldsymbol{R}x \Leftrightarrow x\boldsymbol{R}y, \quad \text{by definition 10.2.1(iii)}$$

$$z\boldsymbol{R}y \text{ and } y\boldsymbol{R}x \Rightarrow z\boldsymbol{R}x, \quad \text{by definition 10.2.1(iv)}$$

Thus, $\boldsymbol{R}$ generates equivalence classes of scaled versions of vectors. Denote the partition of space $\mathbf{R}^n_+$ via such equivalence classes by $\mathscr{T}: = \{C_\alpha\}_{\alpha \in A}$ where A is a collection of representative elements, one from each equivalence class. If $x' \in A$, then $C_{x'}$ is simply $\{x \mid x\boldsymbol{R}x'\}$. The singleton $\{0\}$ belongs to $\mathscr{T}$. All this should be clear from the following example of usual (ray) scaling of vectors:

$$(\mu,x) \in \mathbf{R}^1_{++} \times \mathbf{R}^n_+ \twoheadrightarrow T(\mu;x): = \mu \cdot x$$

$$A: = \{y \mid \|y\| = 1\} \cup \{0\}$$

where $\| \cdot \|$ denotes Euclidean norm; and for $y \in A, C_y: = \{\lambda \cdot y \mid \lambda \in \mathbf{R}^1_{++}\}$.

10.2.3. Definition

An output correspondence $x \twoheadrightarrow P(x)$ with scaling operation T on input space is called *scale-homothetic* if it satisfies a functional equation of the form

$$P[T(\lambda;x)] = \psi(\lambda,x) \cdot P(x)$$

$$\text{for all } (\lambda,x) \in \mathbf{R}^1_{++} \times \mathbf{R}^n_+ \tag{10.1}$$

$$\psi: \mathbf{R}^1_{++} \times \mathbf{R}^n_+ \twoheadrightarrow \mathbf{R}^1_{++}, \qquad \psi(1,x) = \psi(\lambda,0) = 1$$

$$\text{for all } \lambda \in \mathbf{R}^1_{++}, x \in \mathbf{R}^n_+$$

If H is a scaling operation on output space, the scale-homothetic input correspondence is defined analogously.

For simplicity, scaling operation will henceforth be denoted by the symbol $*$ (or $\circledast$), that is, with x,T (u,H) addressing to the input (output) space and $\lambda \in \mathbf{R}^1_{++}$,

$$\lambda * u: \; = T(\lambda; x); \qquad \lambda \circledast u: \; = H(\lambda; u)$$

10.2.4. Proposition

An output correspondence $x \to P(x)$ is scale-homothetic if and only if $\exists F\colon \mathbf{R}^n_+ \to \mathbf{R}^1_+$ such that

$$P(\mu * x) = \frac{F(\mu * x)}{F(x)} \cdot P(x), \; \mu \in \mathbf{R}^1_{++} \tag{10.2}$$

Proof:
Since (10.2) implies (10.1), it is only necessary to prove that (10.1) implies (10.2). For λ, $\mu \in \mathbf{R}^1_{++}$,

$$P[(\lambda \cdot \mu) * x] = \psi(\lambda \cdot \mu, x) \cdot P(x) \qquad \text{by (10.1)}$$

also

$$P[(\lambda \cdot \mu) * x] = P[\lambda * (\mu * x)] \qquad \text{by 10.2.1(iv)}$$

$$= \psi(\lambda, \mu * x) \cdot P(\mu * x) = \psi(\lambda, \mu * x) \cdot \psi(\mu, x) \cdot P(x)$$

This implies that ψ satisfies the functional equation

$$\psi(\lambda \cdot \mu, x) = \psi(\lambda, \mu * x) \cdot \psi(\mu, x) \tag{10.3}$$

To solve this functional equation, an auxiliary function $f\colon \mathbf{R}^n_+ \backslash \{0\} \to \mathbf{R}^1_{++}$ is defined as follows:

a. arbitrarily select a vector $\tilde{x}_\alpha$ from each of the equivalence class C_α, $C_\alpha \neq \{0\}$, where $\{C_\alpha\}_{\alpha \in A}$ is the partition by T;
b. for $y \in C_\alpha$, $f(y)\colon = \mu$ iff $y = \mu * \tilde{x}_\alpha$.

Note that if $y \in C_\alpha$ and $y \neq 0$, we have $f(y) = T^{-1}(y; \tilde{x}_\alpha)$ where $T^{-1}(\cdot\, ; \tilde{x}_\alpha)$ is the inverse to the function $T(\cdot\, ; \tilde{x}_\alpha)\colon \mathbf{R}^1_+ \to \mathbf{R}^n_+$ with $\tilde{x}_\alpha$ fixed.

Suppose $y \in C_\alpha$, $y \neq 0$. Let $\mu = f(y)$. Since $\mu > 0$, $y \in C_\alpha$ implies $\mu * y \in C_\alpha$; and

$$f(\mu * y) = T^{-1}(\mu * y; \tilde{x}_\alpha)$$

$$= T^{-1}(\mu * T(\mu;\tilde{x}_\alpha);\tilde{x}_\alpha)$$

$$= T^{-1}[T(\mu^2;\tilde{x}_\alpha);\tilde{x}_\alpha]$$

$$= \mu^2 = \mu \cdot f(y)$$

That is to say

$$f(\mu * y) = \mu \cdot f(y), \forall(\mu,y) \in \mathbf{R}^1_{++} \times (\mathbf{R}^n_+ \backslash \{0\}) \tag{10.4}$$

If $x = 0$, let $F(\lambda * x) \equiv 1$ in (10.2) for all $\lambda \in \mathbf{R}^1_{++}$, then (10.2) holds. If $x \neq 0$, let $\lambda := 1/f(\mu * x)$, and rewrite (10.3) as

$$\psi[\mu/f(\mu * x),x] = \psi[1/f(\mu * x),\mu * x] \cdot \psi(\mu,x)$$

From (10.4), it follows that

$$\psi(\mu,x) = \frac{\psi[1/f(x),x]}{\psi[1/f(\mu * x),\mu * x]}$$

Defining

$$F(\mu * x) := \{\psi[1/f(\mu * x),\mu * x]\}^{-1} \tag{10.5}$$

and noting that $1 * x = x$, it follows that

$$\psi(\mu,x) = \frac{F(\mu * x)}{F(x)}$$

and (10.2) is established.

Q.E.D.

10.2.5. Examples

i. Ray-homothetic output correspondence:

$$(\lambda,x) \rightarrow T(\lambda;x) := \lambda \cdot x$$

$$P[T(\lambda;x)] = P(\lambda \cdot x) = \psi(\lambda,x) \cdot P(x)$$

ii. Almost ray-homothetic output correspondence:
Given $\alpha_i > 0, i = 1, \ldots, n$

$$(\lambda, x) \rightarrow T(\lambda; x): = (\lambda^{\alpha_1} \cdot x_1, \ldots, \lambda^{\alpha_n} \cdot x_n) = \lambda * x$$

$$P(\lambda * x) = \psi(\lambda, x) \cdot P(x)$$

iii. A scaling operation constructed by transformations:
Let functions G_i: $\mathbf{R}^1_+ \rightarrow \mathbf{R}^1_+$ $(i = 1, \ldots, n)$ satisfy:

(a) $G_i(0) = 0$ and $G_i(\alpha) > 0$ if $\alpha > 0$
(b) G_i nondecreasing and $G_i(\alpha) \rightarrow +\infty$ as $\alpha \rightarrow +\infty$
(c) for $x, y \in \mathbf{R}^n_+, x \neq y$ implies

$$[G_1(x_1), \ldots, G_n(x_n)] \neq [G_1(y_1), \ldots, G_n(y_n)]$$

Furthermore, let G_1 be invertible with inverse function $G_1^{-1}(\cdot)$. Define for $(\theta, x) \in \mathbf{R}^1_{++} \times \mathbf{R}^n_+$

$$T(\theta; x): = \begin{cases} 0, \text{ if } x = 0 \\ \left[\dfrac{G_1(\theta\alpha)}{G_1(\alpha)} \cdot x_1, \ldots, \dfrac{G_n(\theta\alpha)}{G_n(\alpha)} \cdot x_n\right] \\ \qquad \text{where } \alpha = G_1^{-1}(x_1), \text{ if } x_1 \neq 0 \\ \theta \cdot x, \text{ if } x \neq 0, x_1 = 0 \end{cases}$$

That T defines a scaling operation may be easily verified.

Note that if F is *scale-homogeneous of degree* β $(\beta > 0)$, that is,

$$F(\mu * x) = \mu^{\beta} \cdot F(x)$$

then the output correspondence, as given by (10.2) is also *scale-homogeneous of degree* β, that is,

$$P(\mu * x) = \mu^{\beta} \cdot P(x)$$

Another special case of interest is when $\psi(\mu, x)$ in (10.1) has the form

$\psi(\mu,x) = \Delta[\mu,\phi(x)]$ where ϕ is scale homogeneous of degree β. Then (10.3) may be rewritten as

$$\Delta[\lambda \cdot \mu,\phi(x)] = \Delta[\lambda,\mu^{\beta} \cdot \phi(x)] \cdot \Delta[\mu,\phi(x)] \qquad (10.6)$$

which by manipulation—using (10.6) itself—gives

$$\Delta(\mu,\phi) = \frac{\Delta(\lambda\mu,\phi \cdot 1)}{\Delta(\lambda,\mu^{\beta}\phi \cdot 1)} = \frac{\Delta(\lambda\mu \cdot \phi^{1/\beta},1)/\Delta(\phi^{1/\beta},1)}{\Delta(\lambda \cdot \mu\phi^{1/\beta},1)/\Delta(\mu \cdot \phi^{1/\beta},1)}$$

where for simplicity, ϕ denotes $\phi(x)$. With the definition $\tilde{F}(\gamma) = \Delta(\gamma^{1/\beta},1)$, the solution to (10.6) is seen to be

$$\Delta[\mu,\phi(x)] = \frac{\tilde{F}[\mu^{\beta} \cdot \phi(x)]}{\tilde{F}[\phi(x)]}$$

Then the output correspondence has a form similar to the usual ray-homothetic structure (see Färe and Shephard (1977)):

$$P(\mu * x) = \frac{\tilde{F}[\mu^{\beta} \cdot \phi(x)]}{\tilde{F}[\phi(x)]} \cdot P(x)$$

with ϕ scale homogeneous of degree β.

10.3. Inversely Related Scale-Homothetic Structures

In the last section, scale-homothetic structure is defined for the output correspondence. In general, scale-homothetic output structure does not imply the same for the input structure. However, if both the input and output correspondences are in some sense homothetic, special structures arise—as in the case that when both the input and output correspondences are ray-homothetic, they are semihomogeneous (see Eichhorn (1978). Two such special structures are investigated in this section.

10.3.1. Definition

Output correspondence $x \rightarrow P(x)$ with scaling operation T on input space is *semihomogeneous* if for each index α of the partition $\{C_{\alpha}\}_{\alpha \in A}$ induced by T, there exists positive scalar $g(\alpha)$ such that for $x \in C_{\alpha}$, $P(\lambda * x) = \lambda^{g(\alpha)} \cdot P(x)$.

10.3.2. Definition

Scaled disposability of input holds if $P(x) \subset P(\lambda * x)$ for all $\lambda \in [1,+\infty)$.

Similar definition is made for the input correspondence.

10.3.3. Proposition

Let the output correspondence P and the input correspondence L be ray-homothetic and scale-homothetic respectively; that is,

$$P(\lambda \cdot x) = \psi(\lambda,x) \cdot P(x) \quad \text{for all} \quad (\lambda,x) \in \mathbf{R}^1_{++} \times \mathbf{R}^n_{++}$$

$$\psi\colon \mathbf{R}^1_{++} \times \mathbf{R}^n_{+} \to \mathbf{R}^1_{++}, \qquad \psi(1,x) = 1 \quad \text{for all} \quad x \in \mathbf{R}^n_{+}$$

and

$$L(\mu \circledast u) = \chi(\mu,u) \cdot L(u) \quad \text{for all} \quad (\mu,u) \in \mathbf{R}^1_{++} \times \mathbf{R}^m_{++}$$

$$\chi\colon \mathbf{R}^1_{++} \times \mathbf{R}^m_{+} \to \mathbf{R}^1_{++}, \; \chi(1,u) = 1 \quad \text{for all} \quad u \in \mathbf{R}^m_{+}$$

Moreover, for each $x \in \mathbf{R}^n_{++}$, $u \in \mathbf{R}^m_{++}$, let the functions $\psi(\cdot,x)$ and $\chi(\cdot,u)$ have inverses. Then the assumption of weak disposability of the inputs and the scaled outputs implies the semihomogeneity of P and L in the usual sense (see Shephard (1974) for definition of semihomogeneity).

Proof:
It is clear that the following relations are equivalent:

$$x \in L(\mu \circledast u) = \chi(\mu,u)L(u) \tag{10.7}$$

$$\frac{x}{\chi(\mu,u)} \in L(u) \tag{10.8}$$

$$u \in P\left[\frac{x}{\chi(\mu,u)}\right] = \psi\left[\frac{1}{\chi(\mu,u)},x\right]P(x) \tag{10.9}$$

$$x \in L\left\{\frac{u}{\psi[1/\chi(\mu,u),x]}\right\} \tag{10.10}$$

Consequently (10.7) and (10.10) imply

$$L(u) = \frac{1}{\chi(\mu,u)} \cdot L\left\{\frac{u}{\psi[1/\chi(\mu,u),x]}\right\} \tag{10.11}$$

With the assumption of weak disposal of inputs, for $\sigma > 1$, $x \in L(\mu \circledast u)$ implies $\sigma \cdot x \in L(\mu \circledast u)$. By repeating the argument (10.7) to (10.11) using $\sigma \cdot x$ instead of x, it follows that

$$\psi\left[\frac{1}{\chi(\mu,u)},\sigma \cdot x\right] = \psi\left[\frac{1}{\chi(\mu,u)},x\right] \tag{10.12}$$

Now, using similar arguments as that leading to (10.3), the ray-homothecity of output correspondence P gives rise to the following functional equation:

$$\psi(\lambda\sigma,x) = \psi(\lambda,\sigma x) \cdot \psi(\sigma,x) \tag{10.13}$$

In view of (10.12) and the assumption that $\chi(\cdot,u)$ has inverse, the solution to (10.13) is given by (see Eichhorn (1978)).

$$\psi(\lambda,x) = \lambda^{h(x/\|x\|)}, \qquad h(x/\|x\|) > 0 \tag{10.14}$$

Then it follows from (10.11) and (10.14) that

$$L\{[\chi(\mu,u)]^{h(x/\|x\|)} \cdot u\} = \chi(\mu,u) \cdot L(u) \tag{10.15}$$

Note that if the ray $\{\theta y \mid \theta \geqslant 0\} \cap L(\mu \circledast u) \neq \phi$ and $y \neq x$, $h(y/\|y\|)$ must be equal to $h(x/\|x\|)$. Furthermore, the scale-homothecity of input correspondence $u \to L(u)$ implies that the ray $\{\theta x \mid \theta \geqslant 0\} \cap L(\mu \circledast u) \neq \emptyset$ if and only if $\{\theta x \mid \theta \geqslant 0\} \cap L(u) \neq \emptyset$. Thus, the exponent $h(x/\|x\|)$ in (10.15) really depends on the equivalent classes and has the form $h(\alpha)$ if u belongs to the αth equivalence class of the partition induced by the scaling operation H.

Finally, with $\chi(\cdot,u)$ invertible, we conclude from (10.15) that

$$L(\theta \cdot u) = \theta^{1/h(\alpha)} \cdot L(u) \qquad \text{Q.E.D.}$$

Unfortunately, there does not appear to be any simple result if the input and output structures are both scale-homothetic respectively. This is because the formula

$$P(\lambda * x) = \psi(\lambda, x) \cdot P(x)$$

implicitly applies the usual proportional (ray) scaling operation $\cdot$ (see Example 10.2.4(i) with $\alpha = 1$) on the output space, which could be different from $\circledast$. To resolve this difficulty, we redefine the notion of scale homotheticity. We again assume a scaling operation H on the output space, T on the input space as before, and denote them by $\circledast$ and $*$ respectively.

10.3.4. Definition

For all $\lambda \in \mathbf{R}^1_{++}$,

$$\begin{aligned} \lambda \circledast P(x) &:= \{u \in \mathbf{R}^m_{++} \mid u = \lambda \circledast v \quad \text{for some} \quad v \in P(x)\} \\ \lambda * L(u) &:= \{x \in \mathbf{R}^n_{++} \mid x = \lambda * y \quad \text{for some} \quad y \in L(u)\} \end{aligned}$$

10.3.5. Definition

An output correspondence $x \rightarrow P(x)$ has *general scale-homothetic structure* if it satisfies a functional equation

$$\begin{gathered} P(\lambda * x) = \psi(\lambda, x) \circledast P(x), \ \forall (\lambda, x) \in \mathbf{R}^1_{++} \times \mathbf{R}^n_{++}; \\ \psi\colon \mathbf{R}^1_{++} \times \mathbf{R}^n_{+} \rightarrow \mathbf{R}^1_{++}, \ \psi(1, x) = \psi(\lambda, 0) = 1, \ \forall \lambda \in \mathbf{R}^1_{+}, x \in \mathbf{R}^n_{++} \end{gathered} \tag{10.16}$$

10.3.6. Definition

An input structure $u \rightarrow L(u)$ has *general scale homothetic structure* if it satisfies a functional equation

$$\begin{gathered} L(\mu \circledast u) = \chi(\mu, u) * L(u), \ \forall (\mu, u) \in \mathbf{R}^1_{++} \times \mathbf{R}^m_{+}; \\ \chi\colon \mathbf{R}^1_{++} \times \mathbf{R}^m_{+} \rightarrow \mathbf{R}^1_{++}, \ \chi(1, u) = \chi(\mu, 0) = 1, \ \forall \mu \in \mathbf{R}^1_{++}, u \in \mathbf{R}^m_{+} \end{gathered} \tag{10.17}$$

Now, we may follow Eichhorn (1978, theorem 12.5.3) and establish the following

10.3.7. Proposition

Let both the output correspondence P and input correspondence L have general scale-homothetic structure, that is, (10.16) and (10.17) hold. Moreover, let $\psi(\cdot, x)$ and $\chi(\cdot, u)$ both have inverses for each $x \in \mathbf{R}^n_{++}$ and $u \in \mathbf{R}^m_{++}$. Then the assumption of scale disposability (definition 10.3.2) of both inputs and outputs implies the semihomogeneity (definition 10.3.1) of P and L.

Proof:
It is clear that the following relations are equivalent:

$$x \in L(\mu \circledast u) = \chi(\mu,u) * L(u) \tag{10.18}$$

$$(1/\chi(\mu,x)) * x \in L(u), \text{ by definitions 10.3.4 and 10.2.1(iii)} \tag{10.19}$$

$$u \in P[1/\chi(\mu,u) * x] = \psi[1/\chi(\mu,u),x] \circledast P(x) \tag{10.20}$$

$$\frac{1}{\psi[1/\chi(\mu,u),x]} \circledast u \in P(x) \tag{10.21}$$

$$x \in L\left\{\frac{1}{\psi[1/\chi(\mu,u),x]} \circledast u\right\} = \chi\left\{\frac{1}{\psi[1/\chi(\mu,u),x]}, u\right\} * L(u) \tag{10.22}$$

Thus, by (10.18) and (10.22), for all $u \in S$, where

$$S = \{u \mid L(u) \neq \emptyset, \quad L(u) \neq \mathbf{R}^n_+\}$$

we have

$$\chi(\mu,u) = \chi\left\{\frac{1}{\psi[1/\chi(\mu,u),x]}, u\right\} \tag{10.23}$$

Since $\chi(\cdot, u)$ has inverse, identity (10.23) implies

$$\frac{1}{\mu} = \psi\left[\frac{1}{\chi(\mu,u)}, x\right] \tag{10.24}$$

Since $\psi(\cdot, x)$ has inverse $\psi^{-1}(\cdot, x)$, (10.24) may be written as

$$\psi^{-1}\left(\frac{1}{\mu},x\right) \cdot \chi(\mu,u) = 1 \tag{10.25}$$

Using assumption of scale disposability of output, that is,

$$L(u) \subset L(\sigma \circledast u) \quad \text{for} \quad \sigma \in (0,1]$$

we may repeat the argument from (10.18) on and start with $x \in L[\mu \circledast(\sigma \circledast u)]$ instead of $x \in L(\mu \circledast u)$. Then we obtain, analogously to (10.25),

$$\psi^{-1}(1/\mu,x) \cdot \chi(\mu,\sigma \circledast u) = 1, \qquad (\sigma \in (0,1]) \tag{10.26}$$

Equations (10.25) and (10.26) imply

$$\chi(\mu,\sigma \circledast u) = \chi(\mu,u) \tag{10.27}$$

From (10.17) by taking $L(\mu\sigma \circledast u) = L[\mu \circledast(\sigma \circledast u)]$, we obtain the following: for all $u \in S$,

$$L(\mu\sigma \circledast u) = \chi(\mu\sigma,u)*L(u) \tag{10.28}$$

also

$$\begin{aligned} L[\mu \circledast(\sigma \circledast u)] &= \chi(\mu,\sigma \circledast u)*L(\sigma \circledast u) \\ &= \chi(\mu,\sigma \circledast u)*[\chi(\sigma,u)*L(u)] = [\chi(\mu,\sigma \circledast u) \cdot \chi(\sigma,u)]*L(u) \end{aligned} \tag{10.29}$$

Thus, for all $u \in S$, (10.27), (10.28), and (10.29) gives

$$\chi(\mu\sigma,u) = \chi(\mu,u) \cdot \chi(\sigma,u) \tag{10.30}$$

And the solution of (10.30) yields

$$\chi(\mu,u) = \mu^{g(\beta)} \tag{10.31}$$

where $g\colon B \rightarrow \mathbf{R}^1_{++}$ and B is the index set for the partition $\mathscr{H} = \{D_\beta\}_{\beta \in B}$ of output space induced by the scaling operation H (i.e., $\circledast$).

By similar argument applied to P, we obtain

$$\psi(\lambda,x) = \lambda^{h(\alpha)} \tag{10.32}$$

where $h\colon A \to \mathbf{R}^1_{++}$ and A is the index set for the partition $\mathscr{T}\colon = \{C_\alpha\}_{\alpha\in A}$ of input space induced by the scaling operation T (i.e., $*$).

Checking back, we see that χ and ψ as given by (10.31) and (10.32) satisfies

$$h(\alpha) \cdot g(\beta) = 1$$

for all pairs (α,β) for which exists $x \in C_\alpha$, $u \in D_\beta$ and $x \in L(u)$ with $u \in S$ and $x \in W\colon = \{x \mid P(x) \neq \{0\}\}$.

In case $u \notin S$ or $x \notin W$, that is, $L(u) = \emptyset$ or $L(u) = \mathbf{R}^n_+$ or $P(x) = \{0\}$, equations (10.16) and (10.17) still apply via definition 10.2.1(iii), and the proof is completed.

Q.E.D.

10.4. Linear Expansion Paths

A class of expansion paths will be considered in this section. For this purpose, define the cost minimization set $K(u,p)$ for input price $p \geqslant 0$, $u \geqslant 0$ with $L(u)$ not empty, by

$$K(u,p) = \{x \mid x \in L(u), \quad \langle p,x\rangle = Q(u,p)\}$$

where $Q(u,p)$ is the cost function given by

$$Q(u,p) = \min\{\langle p,x\rangle \mid x \in L(u)\}$$

That $Q(u,p)$ is well defined and $K(u,p)$ not empty follows from the axioms of Shephard's technology.

10.4.1. Definition

Given $p \geqslant 0$ and $u \geqslant 0$ with $L(u)$ not empty, the expansion of output according to scaling operation H (denoted $\circledast$) has *linear input expansion path* if there exists a scalar valued function $(\theta,u) \to \chi(\theta,u)$ such that $K(\theta \circledast u,p) = \chi(\theta,u) \cdot K(u,p)$ for $\theta > 0$.

If the input structure $u \to L(u)$ is scale-homothetic, the cost function satisfies

$$Q(\theta \circledast u,p) = \min \{\langle p,x\rangle \mid x \in \chi(\theta,u) \cdot L(u)\}$$
$$= \chi(\theta,u) \cdot Q(u,p)$$

for $\theta > 0$, $p \geqslant 0$, and $u \geqslant 0$ with $L(u)$ not empty. Hence, the cost-minimization set is

$$K(\theta \circledast u,p) = \chi(\theta,u) \cdot K(u,p) \tag{10.33}$$

Thus, the expansion of output according to a scaling operation H for scale-homothetic input structure has a linear input expansion path.

For the converse to hold, further conditions on the input structure L are imposed; namely, convexity and free disposal of inputs—i.e., $x' \geqslant x \in L(u) \Rightarrow x' \in L(u)$. The following lemma proved in Färe and Shephard (1977) is of use.

10.4.2. Lemma

If $L(u)$ is convex for $u \in \mathbf{R}^m_+$ and inputs are freely disposable, then $L(u) = \cup_{p>0} K(u,p) + \mathbf{R}^n_+$.

Now, assume the expansion according to scaling operation H has linear input expansion path—that is, equation (10.33) holds for $\theta > 0$, $u \geqslant 0$ and, $p \geqslant 0$. Since $\chi(\theta,u)$ is independent of p, it follows that

$$\bigcup_{p>0} K(\theta \circledast u,p) = \chi(\theta,u) \cdot \bigcup_{p>0} K(u,p)$$

By adding $\mathbf{R}^n_+$ to both sides of the above expression and invoking lemma 10.4.3, we see that $L(\theta \circledast u) = \chi(\theta,u) \cdot L(u)$.

Thus, we have established the following:

10.4.3. Proposition

If input structure L with scaling operation H (i.e., $\circledast$) is scale-homothetic, then expansion of output according to H has a linear input expansion path. Furthermore, if the input sets $L(u)$ are convex and satisfy free disposability, the converse is also true.

The relationship of scale-homotheticity (on inputs) and linear output expansion paths may be established analogously.

References

Al-Ayat, R., and R. Färe. 1977. "Almost Ray-Homothetic Production Correspondences." *Zeitschrift für Nationalökonomie* 39(1-2):143-152.

Eichhorn, W. 1970. *Theorie der Homogenen Produktions Funktion,* vol. 22. Lecture Notes in Operations Research and Mathematical Systems. Berlin: Springer Verlag.

Eichhorn, W. 1978. *Functional Equations in Economics.* Reading, MA: Addison-Wesley.

Färe, R., and R. W. Shephard. 1977. "Ray-Homothetic Production Functions." *Econometrica* 45(1): 133-146.

Shephard, R. W. 1970. *Theory of Cost and Production Functions.* Princeton, NJ: Princeton University Press.

Shephard, R. W. 1974. "Semi-Homogeneous Production Functions and Scaling of Production." In *Production Theory,* vol. 99, Lecture Notes in Economics and Mathematical Systems. Berlin: Springer-Verlag.

11 EFFICIENCY IN PRODUCTION AND CONSUMPTION*

Sydney N. Afriat

11.1. Introduction

Efficiency is what makes a thing what it is, serving a purpose or realizing a utility; it is a relation between ends and means. Its measure is the extent to which these are matched, so with given ends it would be the choice criterion for the means. It is a pervasive idea, and it would be excessive to regard it as belonging peculiarly to economics.

In a mechanical application, the term represents the ratio of useful work performed to the amount of energy expended. This pertains to cases for which the terms are clearly measurable, and proportional. One can take the ratio and state the efficiency achieved; anyone can know exactly what is meant, and possibly can make some use of the knowledge. Other applications are not so clear; there are qualities to which numbers cannot be attached, or the objective is nebulous, or there is not the proportionality that permits a useful summary by a single number. Economists and engineers are among those concerned with efficiency, and the term is used

*Research supported by a grant from the Social Sciences and Humanities Research Council of Canada.

frequently by both. From engineering we have straightforward examples. However, although the term turns up frequently in economics and does much work in the area, its meaning there can be problematic. The engineering model is also a typical economic model. The efficiency ratio for both is the relationship between input and useful output, and an objective in each is to achieve the greatest possible output from a given input. An engine designer might compare the outputs from various designs with the maximum output that physical principles allow. A design that realizes the known limit might never be achieved, but better designs are continually produced. Other engineers might be concerned more with development and production costs and impose a budget constraint. Alternatively, a required performance could be specified, and the objective then would be to minimize the cost of realizing it.

Where engineers test and measure, economists make use of the production function or the utility function. But the bases for these are less systematic than the engineer's measurements, and this creates problems. The production function is understood to specify the maximum possible output obtainable from any given inputs, with a generally available technology. This is not derived by inspection of technology and calculation, but from data on the activities of firms. Producers as well as engines can be found to be short of efficiency, and so there can be the question of how short. Unlike engines, the possible maximum performance of firms cannot be calculated from a theoretical model provided by the physical sciences. The firms themselves make the standard, and provide the data for it. The concern with production functions, and the productivity of firms, creates a peculiar problem that requires its own methodology.

There are similar problems with the utility function. It is a sort of production function, but its magnitude has no meaning; only the order it gives to bundles of goods is significant. The ordinary theory of the consumer is based on utility—and unquestioned efficiency. Even when the utility is granted, perfect efficiency seems an extravagant requirement. The familiar volatilities of real consumers make such intolerance unsuitable.

What follows is an account of some ways in which an allowance can be made for inefficiency in consumers and producers, in the analysis of observations of their activities. The method is related to von Neumann's activity analysis where, from given feasible activities, other activities are derived on the basis of some model. Here the initial knowledge of feasibilities is a matter of direct observation, and the principle that, if anything has been seen to have been done, then it must have been possible to do it. From observed activities of firms, and the classical model for technology, an activity system can be constructed which gives a limited basis for evaluating the efficiency of activities, in particular the activities of the firms themselves. Construction of the model is the same as von Neumann's, though not necessarily with the additional constant returns to scale assumption used in his original formulation. Also, our concern here is with a production function with a single output, though the approach need not be so limited.

Some feasibilities are revealed from observations, and then others are inferred from them on the basis of a model. It is exactly like the revealed preferences of consumer theory, and the parallel goes further. There are revealed infeasibilities also, for the activities that would have given greater profit but were not employed because—as is supposed or "revealed"—they were technologically infeasible. The absence of contradictions where an activity is revealed simultaneously to be both feasible and infeasible provides a test of the admissibility of the model, just as Houthakker's revealed preference axiom provides a similar test in the case of the consumer.

Models for consumers or producers that accept inefficiency are obtained at first by introduction of a parameter e, between 0 and 1, with the requirement that any activity have an efficiency of at least e. With $e = 1$, there is a return to the usual strict efficiency model. The tests of the data are more relaxed for smaller values of e, and there is an upper limit to the values of e that any given data will accept, which is easily calculated.

In this way there is a determination of upper bounds of efficiencies that should be associated with observed activities and, quite uninformatively, some will be no better than 1. With a further development, efficiency is taken to have a probability distribution on a certain model, whose parameters, and at the same time all the efficiencies, can be estimated by the principle of maximum likelihood. With this there is the more suitable result that all activities become represented as inefficient, in some degree. This approach can be compared with a statistical treatment of the speed v at which people run 100 yards. Records are continually broken, so the upper limit v^*, which could give $e = v/v^*$ as the running efficiency of any individual, has not been observed. But an assumption about the distribution of efficiency being on some model carrying parameters enables both v^* and the distribution parameters to be estimated by maximum likelihood, on the basis of a sample of speeds. In the result, v^* would be larger than any observed v. Correspondingly, a production function f is determined, the counterpart of v^*; and any observed production activity (x,y) would be such that $y < f(x)$, and so represented as inefficient, $f(x)$ being an estimate of the maximum output attainable with inputs x.

This account proceeds along the lines of the finite nonparametric approach to utility construction that has been exploited most especially for demand analysis and index-number theory, and has application also for production analysis. The construction now makes sense as an approximation, and as providing a "frontier" utility function similar to the "frontier production function" familiar in connection with production efficiency measurement.

The approach to inefficiency in consumption and approximate utility (Afriat 1967b, 1972b, 1973) was influenced by a communication with H. Rubin (1967). When we submitted to him the need to accommodate inefficiency by relaxing the inequalities required by perfect efficiency, he proposed the introduction of a single parameter, now identified as a cost efficiency. A similar method (Afriat 1969b, 1971) for production analysis, applied to the special case of constant returns, was observed by Charles Geiss (1969) to be equivalent to the method of Farrell (1957) concerning production efficiency measurement. Geiss (1971a,b) recomputed and extended Farrell's results, using the same data. He developed computer programs for carrying out tests of various production models, defined by restrictive properties, and the corresponding efficiency determinations.

This renewed account has reference mainly to Afriat (1967b, 1973) as concerns consumption, and to Afriat (1971) for production. Only a part of the material is covered; not included, but for the brief mention, is the maximum likelihood estimation method proposed in Afriat (1971), based on a probability model for the distribution of efficiency proposed. This method was applied by Richmond (1974) with the Cobb-Douglas production function model, and then by others. Most interesting is the development of this method where the function is without parameters and is restricted to having only the classical properties of being nondecreasing and concave.

The approach as concerns consumption has received no attention, but a great deal of attention has been devoted to the production side by many writers. Varian (1984) reviews some aspects of the subject and its history. Other related items (within the author's awareness) are to be found in Farrell and Fieldhouse (1962); Aigner and Chu (1968); Hanoch and Rothschild (1972); Charnes, Cooper, and Schinner (1976); Meeusen and van den Broeck (1977); Charnes, Cooper, and Rhodes (1978); Aigner and Schmidt (1980); Charnes, Cooper, Seiford, and Stutz (1981); Färe, Grosskopf, and Lovell (1985); and Afriat (1985). More recent work renders the representation provided by this list, including bibliographies in the articles mentioned, incomplete.

11.2. Consumer Inefficiency

When a utility order R is taken to govern demand, it signifies that demand must meet efficiency requirements that have reference to R. With a demand (x,p), px is the money spent, and an efficiency ordinarily required is that x must have at least the utility of any other bundle y attainable with that expenditure, that is, the condition

$$H' \equiv py \leqslant px \Rightarrow xRy$$

holds. Another efficiency that can be required is that as much utility as is provided by x should not be attainable with any smaller expenditure, that is, it should not be possible to find a y such that yRx and $y < px$, or, what is the same,

$$H'' \equiv yRx \Rightarrow py \geqslant px$$

is required. In general, these requirements are independent, but relations are produced between them if R has special properties, as shown in the last chapter. For instance if R is insatiable, that is, if it is impossible to have xRy while $y < x$, then $H' \Rightarrow H''$. Also, if R is a complete order and the sets xR are closed, then $H'' \Rightarrow H'$. Since R has all these properties if it is representable by a continuous semi-increasing utility function, in which case H' and H'' become equivalent, it would seem that there is no need to deal with more than one of these conditions. However, there is advantage for development in making both explicit, and dealing with both.

The condition H, which is the conjunction of H' and H'' and defines *compatibility* between demand (x,p) and utility R, gives the model for exact efficiency; a model is now sought where efficiency is achieved only in some degree. With production, the comparison of observed output with the maximum possible output with the inputs used, as determined by a production function, provides one type of efficiency measure. It is not a measure that is available with utility, which has only an order representation; but the criterion can have reference instead to cost, and inefficiency can be represented as a measure of wastage there.

Instead of asking that the utility of x be at least as great as any attainable with the expenditure px, we could ask that it be as great as any utility attainable with a fraction epx of the expenditure. In effect, an amount of the budget not exceeding the remainder $(i - e)px$ is allowed to be wasted, since by better programming at least the same utility could have been obtained with an expenditure not exceeding epx.

With this principle, the utility of x should be at least that attainable with any expenditure not exceeding epx, as stated by the condition

$$H'(e) \equiv py \leqslant epx \Rightarrow xRy$$

Also, it should be impossible to achieve the utility of x with any less expenditure than epx, so for no y should we have $py < epx$ and yRx; or,

$$H''(e) \equiv yRx \Rightarrow py \geqslant epx$$

holds. The condition $H(e)$, which is the conjunction of $H'(e)$ and $H''(e)$ for any e between 0 and 1, defines a relation between any demand and utility, *of compatibility at the level of cost efficiency e.*

Evidently, for the case $e = 1$, we have $H(1)$ identical with the earlier compatibility condition H. Also, $H(0)$ holds unconditionally; that is, every demand is compatible with every utility at a level of cost efficiency 0. Generally,

$$H(e) \text{ and } e' \leqslant e \Rightarrow H(e')$$

so any demand and utility that are compatiable at a given level of cost efficiency are compatible also at every lower level. Thus, when e decreases from 1 there is increasing tolerance, with complete tolerance when $e = 0$.

In terms of the utility cost function

$$c(p,x) = \inf [py\colon\ yRx]$$

derived from the utility order R, a restatement of the condition $H''(e)$ is that

$$c(p,x) \geqslant epx$$

When R is restricted to being a complete order for which the sets xR are closed, this implies $H'(e)$, so this condition alone suffices to express the condition $H(e)$. We can define

$$e^* = c(p,x)/px$$

as the *cost efficiency* of the demand (x,p) as determined by the utility order R. Then $H(e)$ becomes equivalent to the requirement $e^* \geqslant e$.

In terms of a normalized demand (x,u), for which $ux = 1$, we have

$$uy \leqslant e \Rightarrow xRy, \qquad yRx \Rightarrow uy \geqslant e$$

as a statement for $H(e)$, and

$$e^* = c(u,x)$$

Since $c(u,x) \leqslant ux$ for all x and u, this always gives $0 \leqslant e^* \leqslant 1$.

11.3. Attainable Efficiencies

The consistency of a given collection of demand observations (x_t,p_t) requires the existence of a utility order with which they are simultaneously compatible. They are *consistent at a level of cost efficiency e* if a utility order exists with which they are simultaneously compatible at that level. Each demand has a cost efficiency $e_t(R)$ determined in respect to any utility R, and their compatibility at the level e requires $e_t(R) \geqslant e$ for all t; equivalently, $e(R) \geqslant e$, where

$$e(R) = \min e_t(R)$$

Consistency in the former sense implies the existence of R such that $e(R) = 1$. If we introduce

$$e^* = \max_R e(R)$$

as the critical cost efficiency for the collection, consistency at level e implies $e \leqslant e^*$; and consistency in the original absolute sense implies $e^* = 1$.

The critical cost-efficiency coefficient e^* for a collection of demands is therefore an index of their consistency absolutely and at every level of cost efficiency. Even if they are not consistent in the strict sense they are at some level $e \leqslant 1$, and, in fact, at any level $e < e^*$. Whether they are consistent at the threshhold level e^* is not generally decided, and also not important. In any case, for any $e < e^*$ it is possible to find a utility order R with which they are compatible at the cost-efficiency level e. The question now is how to determine e^*, and then such an R for any $e < e^*$. Though it might not now be obvious, the determinations are quite straightforward and depend on a simple extension of the theory developed for the exact efficiency case.

Enlarging on the result found for strict consistency, it will appear that whenever there exists any utility order compatible with the demands at some cost-efficiency level, there also exists a utility order which is represented by a classical utility function, and which, moreover, can be constructed on the same finite polyhedral and polytope models used formerly.

One merit of this scheme is that some construction can always be made, whereas inconsistency formerly prevented any construction made on the basis of demand observations. Before, the fit between the utility and the data was required to be exact; now, it can be approximate, with a discrepancy that can be measured in an economically significant way and can be made as small as possible. The result will be an approximate utility function, with discrepancy from fitting all the data exactly stated by $1 - e^*$, so when the data are strictly consistent this discrepancy will be zero.

When a best-fitting utility is constructed in this way, every demand (x_t, p_t) of the collection that is the basis for the construction will have an efficiency e_t determined in respect to it. If these are to be regarded as efficiency estimates, they have a poor distribution, since some will have the unlikely value 1. With a prior probability model for the distribution of efficiency, one might proceed differently, by determining distribution parameters, if any, and efficiencies e_t which given maximum likelihoods under the constraint that there exists a utility R which is compatible with (x_t, p_t) at the level e_t, for all t. Should utility be taken on the model of a utility function carrying parameters, these parameters could be estimated at the same time. Though this method has interest, and is applicable also to production, it will not be taken far. The first described approach, which is also a preparation for the second, is more straightforward, and we shall continue with that.

11.4. Utility Approximation

Consider any numbers e_r such that there exists a utility order R which, for all r, is compatible with the demand (x_r, u_r) at the level of cost efficiency e_r. For such numbers,

$$u_r x \leqslant e_r \Rightarrow x_r R x, \qquad u_r x < 1 \Rightarrow x \bar{R} x_r$$

in particular,

$$u_r x_s \leqslant e_r \Rightarrow x_r R x_s, \qquad u_r x_s < 1 \Rightarrow x_s \bar{R} x_r$$

so with the cross-coefficients $D_{rs} = u_r x_s - 1$ and cost inefficiencies $w_r = 1 - e_r$,

$$D_{rs} + w_r \leqslant 0 \Rightarrow x_r R x_s, \qquad D_{rs} + w_r < 0 \Rightarrow x_s \bar{R} x_r$$

The arguments that applied with $w_r = 0$ apply again now, with $D_{rs} + w_r$ in place of D_{rs}. The conclusions are in the following theorem. Any numbers e_r are *allowable cost efficiencies* for the given demands if there exists a utility order compatible with them at these levels of cost efficiency. Then the $w_r = 1 - e_r$ are allowable cost inefficiencies. These always exist for any given demands, and complete consistency corresponds to the case where taking all $e_r = 1$, or all $w_r = 0$, is allowable. Thus theorem gives a characterization of all allowable cost efficiencies. Also, corresponding to any, it gives a construction of examples of utility functions that fit the data as required.

THEOREM I For any normalized demands (x_r, u_r) $(u_r x_r = 1)$ with cross-coefficients $D_{rs} = u_r x_s - 1$, and any numbers e_r, there exists a utility order which is compatible with (x_r, u_r) at the level of cost efficiency e_r if and only if, with $w_r = 1 - e_r$,

$$D_{rs} + w_r \leqslant 0, \ldots, D_{tr} + w_t \leqslant 0$$

$$\Rightarrow D_{rs} + w_r = 0, \ldots, D_{tr} + w_t = 0$$

and, equivalently, there exist numbers λ_r, φ_r such that

$$\lambda_r > 0, \qquad \lambda_r(D_{rs} + w_r) \geqslant \varphi_s - \varphi_r$$

With any such numbers, the utility functions

$$\varphi^0(x) = \min_r \varphi_r + \lambda_r(u_r x - e_r)$$

and

$$\varphi^i(x) = \max\,[\textstyle\sum \varphi_r t_r\colon \sum x_r t_r \leqslant x,\ \sum t_r = 1, t_r \geqslant 0]$$

fit the data in the way required.

For any allowable e_r there are many such functions, just as there were previously in the case of fully consistent data, with a similar characterization by inner and outer bracket pairs φ_i, φ^0. The questions now concern the allowable cost efficiencies e_r, and the critical cost efficiency e^*.

If e_r are allowable, then so are any $e_r' \leqslant e_r$, and so any $e_r' = \min e_r$. The critical cost efficiency for the collection of demands is the upper limit e^* of e such that $e_r = e$ are allowable. Such e are the values that validate the condition $H(e)$ for the existence of a utility compatible with all the demands within the cost-efficiency level e. A consequence of theorem I is that these are also the values e which, with $w = 1 - e$, validate the condition $K(e)$ given by

$$D_{rs} + w \leqslant 0, \ldots, D_{tr} + w \leqslant 0$$

$$\Rightarrow D_{rs} + w = 0, \ldots, D_{tr} + w = 0$$

We have to find the upper limit of e, and so the lower limit of w, satisfying this condition. It should be noted that $K = K(1)$, corresponding to $e = 1$ and $w = 0$, is the earlier general consistency test, a counterpart of Houthakker's revealed preference condition.

Let

$$d = \min_{ij\ldots k} \max\,[D_{ri}, D_{ij}, \ldots, D_{kr}]$$

Then immediately,

$$d > 0 \Rightarrow K, \qquad d < 0 \Rightarrow \bar{K}$$

while $d = 0$ leaves K undecided. Moreover,

$$d \leqslant 0 \quad .\Rightarrow. \quad d + w > 0 \Leftrightarrow K(e)$$

where it is understood that $w = 1 - e$. With

$$e^* = \sup\,[e\colon\ K(e)]$$

and $w^* = 1 - e^*$, this shows that

$$d \geqslant 0 \Rightarrow w^* = 0, \qquad d < 0 \Rightarrow w^* = -d$$

and hence that $w^* = \max\,[0, -d]$, so proving the following.

THEOREM II For any given demands with cross-coefficients D_{rs}, the upper limit of values of e such that there exists a utility order R compatible with all of them within a level of cost efficiency e is given by

$$e^* = 1 - w^*$$

where

$$w^* = \max [0,-d]$$

and

$$d = \min_{rij\ldots k} \max [D_{ri}, D_{ij}, \ldots, D_{kr}]$$

Given any $e < e^*$, and taking $e_r = e$, utility functions can be constructed as in theorem I. Whether $K(e)$ holds for $e = e^*$ is not generally decided.

11.5. Production Efficiency

If a single activity (x,y) has been observed, where n inputs x have been used to produce a single output y, then it is known that the output y is feasible with the inputs x, by some available means. Without further information it cannot be known whether a greater output would have been possible by any means. Therefore there cannot be any judgement about the efficiency of the activity in producing output from the inputs used. In the concept of a production function f, it determines the maximum output $f(x)$ for any inputs x attainable with the generally available technology. Were it known, it could be used to determine $e = y/f(x)$ as a certain measure of the efficiency of any activity (x,y), where $0 \leqslant e \leqslant 1$ since necessarily $y \leqslant f(x)$. Since other types of efficiency also can be considered, this one is distinguished as *technical efficiency*.

An issue in making such efficiency measurements is the availability of the production funtion. With data of activities (x_r,y_r) $(r = 1,\ldots,m)$ of producers in an industry, econometricians determine a production function f by estimating the parameters in some model. The result is more a statistical predictor of output from given inputs than an assessment of the maximum possible output, and as such is not so suitable for efficiency measurement or comparison. Parametric models of production functions that suit such econometrics are a limited variety, imposing restrictions that reflect no hypothesis about production. But all, or most, such restrictions are on the classical model, where the function is nondecreasing and concave. Using just that aspect, one can proceed differently, in a way that maintains recognition of the production function as a provider of information about maximum possible output instead of likely output, and so also about efficiency.

The von Neumann approach to representing production possibilities is by means of an activity system generated from a collection of activities on the basis of a model, by taking their closure with respect to the model. With the observed activities (x_r, y_t) and the classical production model one would take the *classical closure*

$$F = [(x,y):\ x \geqslant \sum x_r t_r, \sum y_r t_r \geqslant y,\ \sum t_r = 1, t_r \geqslant 0]$$

This is an input-output relation where xFy, or $(x,y) \in F$, means that y is producible from x, or (x,y) is a feasible activity. With the production function

$$f(x) = \max\,[y:\ xFy]$$

determined from the relation, we have

$$xFy \Leftrightarrow y \leqslant f(x)$$

so the relation is also represented by this function. Its construction is automatic in that it is nondecreasing and concave, and so has the classical properties. Also, $y_r \leqslant f(x_r)$ for all r; and if f' is any other classical function such that $y_r \leqslant f'(x_r)$ for all r, then $f(x) \leqslant f'(x)$ for all x.

This function so constructed is therefore the smallest production function on the classical model consistent with the requirement that it provides a bound, if not the maximum, of output attainable with given inputs. With it, therefore, $e_r = y_r/f(x_r)$ is an upper bound for the efficiency of the activity (x_r, y_r). In some cases $e_r = 1$ so there is no "revealed" inefficiency, but in other cases possibly $e_r < 1$.

Prior ideas about the distribution of efficiency give some basis for going further with the concept of a production function as telling the maximum of output, more than just a bound, as here. The parallel with the running efficiency of individuals is described in the introduction to this chapter. The beta distribution is a fair model for the distribution of efficiency, consistent with density approaching zero near 0 and 1 with a peak in between, with two parameters related to location of the peak and the concentration around it. Any production function determines efficiencies e_t, and these have a likelihood based on any distribution. Making this likelihood a maximum under the constraint that the function is classical or, on any model, gives a principle for estimating the distribution parameters and the efficiencies, and possibly function parameters as well. Without further restriction on its form, the function would not generally be unique, except that always $f(x_r) = y_r e_r$. One such function would be that constructed as before, but now, instead, from the activities $(x_r, y_r e_r)$. Should the function be taken on some parametric model, the parameters might be uniquely determined at the same time as the distribution parameters and efficiencies; in which case a unique function would be obtained. In any case, the estimates of efficiencies e_t would all be, realistically, strictly less than 1. Whether or not they have fair sense as absolute measures, they might still give a better basis for efficiency comparisons.

In von Neumann's original formulation, the activity system, while based on the classical model, was also conical; that is, it had constant returns to scale. Following that, the activity system generated by the observations (x_r, y_r) would be

$$F = [(x,y): \ x \geqslant \sum x_r t_r, \sum y_r t_r \geqslant y, t_r \geqslant 0]$$

$$= [(x,y): \ xy^{-1} \geqslant \sum a_r t_r, \sum t_r = 1, t_r \geqslant 0]$$

where $a_r = x_r y_r^{-1}$ are input bundles for a unit of output. Hence the input possibility set for a unit of output is

$$X = [x: \ x \geqslant \sum a_r t_r, \sum t_r = 1, t_r \geqslant 0]$$

This set is simply the orthoconvex closure of the points a_r, described by points which lie above some point of the convex closure. The efficiency e_r of the activity (x_r, y_r) as provided by this system is determined by $a_r e_r^{-1}$ being the point where the ray to a_r cuts the boundary of this region, which is the unit isoquant for the production function f representing the input–output relation F. The efficiencies so determined correspond exactly to those obtained by the method of M. J. Farrell (1957). The connection was pointed out by Charles Geiss (1969).

Technical efficiency is a limited view of efficiency, since it takes the inputs x not to be a choice but as given, and the objective is to make the best of them. If the inputs x are, instead, chosen and have a cost—which becomes the production cost of output—the unit cost of output could be the efficiency criterion. Then an efficiency is also required in the choice of inputs, since in addition to technical efficiency it should be impossible to obtain the same output with some other inputs which cost less. Such *competitive efficiency* reflects the ability to sell the product at a low price. There is also *profit efficiency,* which compares profit gained with the maximum profit achievable with the prevailing prices and technology; these two efficiencies coincide in the constant-returns case.

References

Aczel, J., and W. Eichhorn. 1974. "Systems of functional equations determining price and productivity indices." *Utilitas Mathematica* 5: 213–226.

Afriat, S. N. 1955. "The consistency condition and other concepts in the theory of value and demand." Department of Applied Economics, Cambridge. Mimeo.

Afriat, S. N. 1960. "The system of inequalities $a_{rs} > X_s - X_r$. Research memorandum no. 18 (October), Econometric Research Program, Princeton University. Published in *Proceedings of the Cambridge Philosophical Society* 9(1963): 125–133.

Afriat, S. N. 1961. "Expenditure configurations." Research memorandum no. 21 (February), Econometric Research Program, Princeton University.

Afriat, S. N. 1964. "The construction of utility functions from expenditure data." Cowles Foundation Discussion Paper no. 144 (October), Yale University; presented at the First World Congress of the Econometric Society, Rome, September 1965. Published in *International Economic Review* 8(1) (1967): 67–77.

Afriat, S. N. 1966. "The production function." Summer School in Mathematical Economics, Frascati, Italy, 1966. In *Economia Mathematica,* edited by Bruno de Finetti. Rome: Edizioni Cremonese, 1–64.

Afriat, S. N. 1967b. "The construction of cost-efficiencies and approximate utility functions from inconsistent expenditure data." Department of Economics, Purdue University. New York meeting of the Econometric Society, December 1969.

Afriat, S. N. 1969a. "The construction of separable utility functions from expenditure data." Department of Economics, University of North Carolina at Chapel Hill. Mimeo.

Afriat, S. N. 1969b. "Analytical theory of production." Department of Economics, University of North Carolina at Chapel Hill. Mimeo.

Afriat, S. N. 1971. "Efficiency estimation of production functions." Boulder meetings of the Econometric Society, September 1971. Published in *International Economic Review* 13(3) (1972): 568–598.

Afriat, S. N. 1972a. "A non-parametric approach to production." Conference on Applications of Duality Theory, Ottawa, 8–9 September 1972.

Afriat, S. N. 1972b. "The theory of international comparisons of real income and prices." In *International Comparisons of Prices and Output,* edited by D. J. Daly (Studies in Income and Wealth no. 37; proceedings of the conference at York University, Toronto, 1970). New York: National Bureau of Economic Research, 13–84.

Afriat, S. N. 1973. "On a system of inequalities in demand analysis: An extension of the classical Method." *International Economic Review* 14(2): 460–472.

Afriat, S. N. 1974a. "Sum-symmetric matrices." *Linear Algebra and its Applications* 8:129–140.

Afriat, S. N. 1974b. *Production Duality and the von Heusann Theory of Growth and Interest.* Meisenheim am Glan: Verlag Anton Hain.

Afriat, S. N. 1974c. "Review of 'The Effect of Education on Efficiency in Consumption by Robert T. Michael.'" *Monthly Labour Review* 97(1): 86–87.

Afriat, S. N. 1976. *Combinatorial Theory of Demand.* London: Input-Output Publishing Co.

Afriat, S. N. 1977a. *The Price Index.* Cambridge: Cambridge University Press.

Afriat, S. N. 1979. "The power algorithm for generalized Laspeyres and Paasche indices." Athens meeting of the Econometric Society, September 1979.

Afriat, S. N. 1980a. "Matrix powers: Classical and variations." Matrix Theory Conference, Auburn, Alabama, 19–22 March 1980.

Afriat, S. N. 1980b. "Production functions and efficiency measurement." Conference on Current Issues in Productivity, Columbia University, New York, 16–18 April 1980.

Afriat, S. N. 1980c. *Demand Functions and the Slutsky Matrix.* Princeton Studies in Mathematical Economics no. 7. Princeton University Press.

Afriat, S. N. 1981. "On the constructibility of consistent price indices between several periods simultaneously." In *Essays in Theory and Measurement of Demand: In Honour of Sir Richard Stone,* edited by Angus Deaton. Cambridge University Press, 133–161.

Afriat, S. N. 1982a. "The power algorithm for minimum paths, and price indices." Eleventh International Symposium on Mathematical Programming, University of Bonn, 23–27 August 1982.

Afriat, S. N. 1982b. "Models of inefficiency." Conference on Current Issues in Productivity, Cornell University, Ithaca, NY, 30 November–2 December 1982.

Afriat, S. N. 1985. *Logic of Choice and Economic Theory.* Oxford: Clarendon Press.

Aigner, D. J., and S. F. Chu. 1968. "On estimating the industry production function." *American Economic Review,* 58(4): 826–839.

Aigner, D. J., and P. Schmidt, eds. 1980. "Specification and estimation of frontier production functions, profit and cost functions." Supplementary issue, *Journal of Econometrics* 13:1–138.

Banker, R. D., A. Charnes, W. W. Cooper, and A. P. Schinnar. 1981. "A bi-extremal principle for frontier estimation and efficiency evaluations." *Management Science* 27(12): 1370–1382.

Banker, R. D., R. F. Conrad, and R. F. Strauss. 1981. "An application of data envelopment analysis to the empirical investigation of a hospital production function." Working Paper, Carnegie-Mellon University, School of Urban and Public Affairs, Pittsburg.

Berge, C. 1963. *Topological Spaces.* New York: Macmillan.

Berge, C., and A. Ghouila-Houri. 1965. *Programming, Games and Transportation Networks.* London: Methuen; New York: Wiley.

Berge, C. 1982. "Invariant multiplicative efficiency and piecewise Cobb-Douglas envelopments." Research Report CCS 441, Center for Cybernetic Studies, University of Texas, Austin. Presented at the Conference on Current Issues in Productivity, Cornell University, Ithaca NY, 30 November–2 December 1982.

Charnes, A., W. W. Cooper, and E. Rhodes. 1978. "Measuring the efficiency of decision making units." *European Journal of Operational Research* 2(6): 429–444.

Charnes, A., and A. P. Schinnar. 1976. "A theorem on homogeneous functions and extended Cobb-Douglas forms." *Proceedings of the National Academy of Sciences* (USA), 73(10): 3747–3748.

Charnes, A., L. Seiford, and J. Stutz. 1981. "A multiplicative model for efficiency analysis." *Research Report* CCS 416, Center for Cybernetic Studies, University of Texas, Austin. Published in *Socio-Economic Planning Sciences* 16 (1982): 223–224.

Dantzig, G. 1963. *Linear Programming and its Extensions.* Princeton: Princeton University Press.

Dantzig, G., B. Curtis Eaves, and U. G. Rothblum. 1983. "A decomposition and scaling inequality for line-sum-symmetric nonnegative matrices." Technical Report SOL 83-21, Department of Operations Research, Stanford University.

Eaves, B. Curtis, U. G. Rothblum, and H. Schneider. 1983. "Line-sum-symmetric scalings of square nonnegative matrices." Technical Report, Department of Operations Research, Stanford University.

Eggleston, H. G. 1963. *Convexity* (2nd edition). Cambridge: Cambridge University Press.

Eichhorn, W. 1972. *Functional Equations in Economics.* Applied Mathematics and Computation Series, no. 11. Reading, MA.: Addison-Wesley.

Fan, Ky. 1956. "On systems of linear inequalities." In Kuhn and Tucker (1956), 99–156.

Färe, R., S. Grosskopf, and C. A. K. Lovell. 1985. *The Measurement of Efficiency of Production.* Boston: Kluwer-Nijhoff.

Farrell, M. J. 1957. "The measurement of productive efficiency." *Journal of the Royal Statistical Society,* ser. A, 120(3): 253–281.

Farrell, M. J. 1959. "The convexity assumption in the theory of competitive markets." *Journal of Political Economy* 67, 377–391.

Farrell, M. J., and M. Fieldhouse. 1962. "Estimating efficient production functions under increasing returns to scale." *Journal of the Royal Statistical Society,* ser. A, 125(2): 252–267.

Fenchel, W. 1949. On conjugate convex functions. *Canadian Journal of Mathematics,* 1, 73–77.

Fenchel, W. 1953. Convex cones, sets and functions. Notes by D. W. Blackett of lectures delivered in the Department of Mathematics, Princeton University.

Fiedler, M., and V. Ptak. 1967. "Diagonally dominant matrices. *Czechoslovak Mathematical Journal* 17:420–433.

Gale, D. 1956. "The closed linear model of production." In Kuhn and Tucker (1956), 285–303.

Gale, D. 1960b. *The Theory of Linear Economic Models.* New York: McGraw-Hill.

Geiss, Charles. 1969. Private communication. Department of Economics, University of North Carolina at Chapel Hill.

Geiss, Charles. 1971a. "Computations of critical efficiencies and the extension [Afriat 1969b and 1971] of Farrell's method in production analysis." Department of Economics, University of North Carolina at Chapel Hill. Mimeo.

Geiss, Charles. 1971b. "Program descriptions and operations guide: A set of programs designed to furnish efficiency estimation of production functions using the method described in 'Efficiency Estimation of Production Functions' [Afriat 1971]." Department of Economics, University of North Carolina at Chapel Hill. Mimeo.

Goldman, A. J., and A. W. Tucker. 1956. "Polyhedral convex cones." In Kuhn and Tucker (1956).

Gorman, W. M. 1976. "Tricks with utility functions." In *Essays in Economic Analysis,* edited by M. J. Artis and A. R. Nobay. Cambridge: Cambridge University Press.

Hanoch, G., and M. Rothschild. 1972. "Testing the assumptions of production theory." *Journal of Political Economy* 80:256–275.

Jazairi, N. T., and Louis Lefeber. 1984. "Productivity measurement." In *Encyclopedia of Statistical Sciences, 6.*, edited by Samuel Kotz and Norman L. Johnson. New York: Wiley.

Koopmans, T. C., ed. 1951a. *Activity Analysis of Production and Allocation.* Cowles Commission Monograph no. 13. New York: Wiley.

Koopmans, T. C., ed. 1951b. "Analysis of production as an efficient combination of activities." In Koopmans (1951a), 33–97.

Kuhn, H. W., and A. W. Tucker. 1956. *Linear Inequalities and Related Systems.* Annals of Mathematics Studies no. 38. Princeton: Princeton University Press.

Lorch, E. R. 1951. "Differentiable inequalities and the theory of convex bodies." *Transactions of the American Mathematical Society* 71(2): 243–266.

Meeusen, Wim, and Julien van den Broeck. 1977. "Efficiency estimation from Cobb-Douglas production functions with composed error." *International Economic Review* 18(2): 435–444.

Richmond, J. (1974). "Estimating Efficiency of Production," *International Economic Review,* 15:2 June pp. 515–521.

Rubin, H. 1967. Private communication. Purdue University, Lafayette, Indiana.

Shephard, R. W. 1953. *Cost and Production Functions.* Princeton: Princeton University Press.

Simon, H. 1954. "A behavioral theory of rational choice." *Quarterly Journal of Economics* 69:99–118.

Tucker, A. W. 1950. "Dual systems of homogeneous linear relations." In Kuhn and Tucker (1950), 3–18.

Varian, Hal. 1981. "Non-parametric methods in demand analysis." *Economic Letters* 9:23–29.

Varian, Hal. 1982. "The non-parametric approach to demand analysis." *Econometrica,* 50(4): 945–973.

Varian, Hal. 1984. "The non-parametric approach to production analysis." *Econometrica* 52(3): 579–598.

Walters, A. A. 1963. "Production and cost functions: An econometric survey." *Econometrica* 31:1–66.

Author Index

Subject Index

GPSR Compliance

The European Union's (EU) General Product Safety Regulation (GPSR) is a set of rules that requires consumer products to be safe and our obligations to ensure this.

If you have any concerns about our products, you can contact us on ProductSafety@springernature.com

In case Publisher is established outside the EU, the EU authorized representative is:

Springer Nature Customer Service Center GmbH
Europaplatz 3
69115 Heidelberg, Germany

Batch number: 10823775

Printed by Printforce, the Netherlands